LISZT

Books by David Whitwell

Philosophic Foundations of Education
Foundations of Music Education
Music Education of the Future
The Sousa Oral History Project
The Art of Musical *Conducting*
The Longy Club: 1900–1917
A Concise History of the Wind Band
Wagner on Bands
Berlioz on Bands
Chopin: A Self-Portrait
Mendelssohn: A Self-Portrait
Schumann: A Self-Portrait
La Téléphonie and the Universal Musical Language
Extraordinary Women
Aesthetics of Music in Ancient Civilizations
Aesthetics of Music in the Middle Ages
Aesthetics of Music in the Early Renaissance

The History and Literature of the Wind Band and Wind Ensemble Series

Volume 1 The Wind Band and Wind Ensemble Before 1500
Volume 2 The Renaissance Wind Band and Wind Ensemble
Volume 3 The Baroque Wind Band and Wind Ensemble
Volume 4 The Wind Band and Wind Ensemble of the Classical Period (1750–1800)
Volume 5 The Nineteenth-Century Wind Band and Wind Ensemble
Volume 6 A Catalog of Multi-Part Repertoire for Wind Instruments or for Undesignated Instrumentation before 1600
Volume 7 Baroque Wind Band and Wind Ensemble Repertoire
Volume 8 Classical Period Wind Band and Wind Ensemble Repertoire
Volume 9 Nineteenth-Century Wind Band and Wind Ensemble Repertoire
Volume 10 A Supplementary Catalog of Wind Band and Wind Ensemble Repertoire
Volume 11 A Catalog of Wind Repertoire before the Twentieth Century for One to Five Players
Volume 12 A Second Supplementary Catalog of Early Wind Band and Wind Ensemble Repertoire
Volume 13 Name Index, Volumes 1–12, The History and Literature of the Wind Band and Wind Ensemble

www.whitwellbooks.com

LISZT: A SELF-PORTRAIT IN HIS OWN WORDS

David Whitwell

Liszt: A Self-Portrait In His Own Words
Second Edition
Dr. David Whitwell

WHITWELL PUBLISHING
815-A BRAZOS ST. #491
AUSTIN, TX 78701
WWW.WHITWELLPUBLISHING.COM

Second edition 2012

Composed in Bembo Book.
Published in the United States of America.
All images used in this book are in the public domain except where otherwise noted.

ISBN-13: 978-1-936512-57-7
ISBN-10: 1936512572

FOREWORD

This volume is not intended to be the traditional kind of biography, which all too often relegates the reader to the role of one on the side-line who can only observe the procession of dates, people, and facts which define the life of the subject. The purpose of the present volume is quite different. Here we will pass by the usual parade of events and happenings of Liszt's life (excepting the brief chronological sketch below) and concentrate instead on his own thoughts, as expressed in his own words.

The purpose has been to bring together Liszt's thoughts, drawn from many years and a variety of sources, and to present his thoughts chronologically by subject, to permit the reader insights into Liszt's thinking on a subject and the development of these thoughts as they surface during his lifetime.

Apart from selecting subjects which would be of interest to the modern reader, the actual selection of the material herein has been limited to only those comments by Liszt which seem to offer revelation on the man and his music. For example, not every reference to a particular composition has been included, but rather only those which might offer the reader an insight into how Liszt himself viewed that composition.

With the hope of allowing the reader the most direct possible relationship with this master composer, I have resisted the strong and constant urge to add connecting or amplifying text and have left Liszt's own thoughts to speak for themselves. My own experience in reading this material has been that I have felt a much closer relationship with Liszt the man, something I somehow never quite achieved from traditional accounts of this master and his music. It is my hope that perhaps the reader as well might enjoy this experience.

David Whitwell
Austin, Texas

ACKNOWLEDGEMENT

We wish to acknowledge our gratitude to the graphic artist, Daniel Ferla, for his important help in making possible this new edition of a work first published in 1986.

A BRIEF CHRONOLOGY OF THE LIFE OF FRANZ LISZT

Perhaps the span of Liszt's life is best reflected not in the actual dates which frame his life, 1811–1886, but in his having known in person both Beethoven and Debussy!

The young Liszt received his first influence in both music and religious studies with his father, Adam, a court official in the service of Prince Nikolaus Esterhazy. When the family moved to Vienna in 1821 Liszt was able to study with Salieri and Czerny and gave, with great success, a public recital. After the family moved to Paris in 1823 he continued his studies with Reicha and Paer.

It was in Paris, in 1824, that he gave the first of countless sensational private concerts before Parisian society. It was this period when aesthetic concerts were moving from the palace to the public and the career of Liszt came too early to enjoy the money and leisure of today's greatest artists through public demand. These salon recitals, in particular, were entertainment occasions for the ladies and Liszt was expected to entertain them with anecdotes and stories of the music. It is easy to see why he unfortunately burned-out so early, playing in public only rarely during the final 35 years of his life.

Nevertheless the period 1834–1847 saw the height of both his professional career as a pianist and collector of mistresses, among them the Countess Marie d'Agoult, who bore him children. In 1847 Liszt met and fell in love with Princess Carolyne Sayn-Wittgenstein, sister to the Tsar of Russia. It was she who persuaded him to draw his artistic career to a close and to devote his remaining years to composition. At this time he also began the life of a court Kapellmeister in Weimar.

The couple waited for years in vain for either the Tsar or the Pope to grant a divorce to the Princess. By the time her husband died in 1864, this long relationship had finally exhausted itself, the Princess having turned to writing and Liszt to the church, taking minor orders in Rome in 1865.

His final years included extensive teaching in Rome, Weimar, and Budapest. No piano teacher before or since has had such a strong influence. To this day one will hear a pianist say 'I am a granddaughter of Liszt,' meaning they studied with a student of Liszt. My mother studied with a student of Liszt and for the following 70 years she performed his compositions from memory, assuring her listeners that this was exactly how Liszt said to interpret the music.

Contents

Foreword v

Acknowledgment v

A Brief Chronology of the Life of Franz Liszt vii

Part I: Liszt: A Self-Portrait

Chapter One: Liszt on his Personality and Character Traits 3

Chapter Two: Liszt on his Professional Life 21

- As Pianist 21
- As Conductor 32
- As Teacher 39

Chapter Three: Insight into Liszt's General Outlook on Life 43

- Ideals 53
- Mankind 56
- Women 59
- The Jewish People 65
- Friends 68
- Faith 69
- Nature 77
- Habit 79
- Pain 80
- Desire 82

Chapter Four: Liszt on his Daily Life 85

Chapter Five: Liszt on his Physical and Mental Health 101

Part II: Liszt's View of the World of Music

Chapter Six: Liszt's General Outlook on Music and Art 115

Aesthetics 121

The New Art 136

On Music Literature 142

Chapter Seven: Liszt on Performance 149

On Pianoforte Performance 154

On Virtuosity 158

Chapter Eight: Liszt's Views on Criticisms and the Public 165

On Criticism 165

The Public 169

Chapter Nine: Liszt's Observations on Various Countries 173

England 173

Germany 174

Hungary 176

Italy 182

Paris 183

Poland 184

Vienna 184

Chapter Ten: Mendelssohn's Views on the Personalities of his Day 187

Bach 187

Balakireff 187

Beethoven 188

Berlioz 190

Brahms 195

Bülow 195

Chopin 199

Cui 202

Czerny 202

Franck ... 203
Glinka ... 204
Goethe ... 205
Gounod ... 205
Grieg ... 206
Handel ... 206
Haydn ... 207
Heine ... 207
Henselt ... 207
Hiller ... 208
Hummel ... 208
Joachim ... 209
Cosima Liszt ... 209
Litolff ... 210
Ludwig II ... 211
Mendelssohn ... 211
Meyerbeer ... 211
Michelangelo ... 212
Mozart ... 213
Nietzsche ... 214
Paganini ... 215
Remenyi ... 215
Rimsky-Korsakof ... 215
Rossini ... 215
Rubinstein ... 216
Saint-Saëns ... 217
George Sand ... 218
Sarasate ... 219
Schubert ... 220
Clara Schumann ... 221
Robert Schumann ... 221
Sgambati ... 224

Smetana 225
Spohr 225
Tausig 226
Tolstoy 227
Wagner 227
Weber 239

Part III: Listz's Reflections on his Own Music

Chapter Eleven: Listz on his own Musical Studies 243
Chapter Twelve: Listz on his Creative Process 245
Chapter Thirteen: Listz on his Own Compositions 255
Chapter Fourteen: Liszt's Views on the Acceptance of his Music 269
Bibliography 289
About the Author 291

Part I

Liszt: A Self-Portrait

Chapter One

Liszt on his Personality and Character Traits

1830

There has been only one event here in the last six months, and that event is myself.[1]

1. Letter to George Sand, Geneva, Spring, 1830.

1834

A man false and vulgar as you think me would not have said 'I have no love but what you give me.' *I don't take back an iota* of my past life, however shameful or bitter it may have been! I accept everything completely, and if I were a hundred times more criminal, I would still accept everything, because I want the woman I love to be *happy* to forgive me. It is only from her that I would *accept* pardon.[2]

2. Letter to Marie d' Agoult, 1834.

1837

[Speaking of his youth]: There came over me a bitter disgust against art. Vilified and degraded to the level of a more or less profitable handicraft, a source of amusement for distinguished society. I felt I would sooner be anything in the world than a musician in the pay of the exalted, patronized and salaried by them like a conjuror, or the learned dog Munito.[3]

3. *'Lettre d'un bachelier ès musique,' Gazette Musicals,* January, 1837.

Will my life be forever tainted with this idle uselessness which weighs upon me? Will the hour of devotion and of *manly action* never come? Am I condemned without respite to this trade of a Merry Andrew and to amuse in drawing-rooms?[4]

4. Letter to Abbé de Lamennais, Como, December 18, 1837.

1839

I shall come to you a little older, a little more matured, and, permit me to say, *more finished an artist*, than I was when you saw me last year, for since that time I have worked enormously in Italy.

What joy, what an immense happiness it will be to be once more in my own country, to feel myself surrounded by such noble and vigorous sympathies, which, thank God, I have done nothing to forfeit in my distant and wandering life. The love of my country, of my chivalrous and grand country, has ever lived most deeply in my heart.[5]

5. Letter to Count Leo Festetics, November 24, 1839.

1840

If I cared a lot about an aristocratic origin, I could easily claim it. The authentic documents exist and are in the hands of the Fiscal of Ofen. I'll look into it (out of curiosity) one of these days.

Tenderness being the least habitual of my defects, it is natural that men who please you … appear to be lakes of tenderness. Since in me energy often takes the form of harshness and violence, others necessarily seem to you frail reeds agitated by the breeze.[6]

6. Letter to Marie d' Agoult, 1840.

Allow me to protest against an inexact assertion in your last issue: 'Messieurs Liszt and Cramer have asked for the Legion of Honor,' etc. As to myself, if it be true that my name has figured in the list of candidates, this can only have occurred entirely without my knowledge. It has always seemed to me that distinctions of this sort could only be *accepted*, but never 'asked for.'[7]

7. Letter to the Editor of the *Gazette Musicale*, London, May 14; 1840.

I have some thoughts of spending the following winter in Constantinople. I am tired of the West; I want to breathe perfumes, to bask in the sun, to exchange the smoke of coal for the sweet smoke of the narghileh. In short, I am pining for the East![8]

8. Letter to Franz von Schober, Stonehenge, August 29, 1840.

I am hungering and thirsting to go back to Hungary recollection of it has taken deep root in my soul.[9]

9. Letter to Franz von Schober, Manchester, December 5, 1840.

1844

God reward you for your love to such a jaded, worn-out creature as I am![10]

10. Letter to Franz von Schober, Berlin, March 4, 1844.

1845

Forgive me for growing old and arriving at the point when noble recollections grow in proportion as the narrowing meannesses of daily life find their true level.[11]

11. Letter to George Sand, Lyons, May 21, 1845.

1846

Through what absence of mind, let me ask you, could you have written to me, 'I do not speak to you of our affairs because I *remember* that your sympathies are not with us?' Frankly, if you were to tell me that I have never played any but false notes on the piano, and that my calling was that of a retail grocer, this opinion would offer, to my thinking, a greater degree of probability. Evidently, in my double character of citizen and musician, I am not even to exonerate myself from the fault you [ascribe] to me. Suffer me then not to dwell longer upon it, and deign for the future to spare me the pain which all suspicion of this kind would cause me.[12]

12. Letter to an unknown lady, 1846.

13. Letter to Herr Baron von Dornis, Weimar, March 6, 1848.

14. Letter to Marie zu Sayn-Wittgenstein, Weimar, April, 1851.

1848

I cannot help taking this opportunity of remarking that, in view of the far too many busts, medallions, statuettes, caricatures, medals, and portraits of all kinds existing of my humble self, I long ago resolved not to give occasion to any further multiplication of them.[13]

1851

The thought that I deserve to be scolded drives me wild.[14]

1852

The idea of fishing for compliments [has] never entered my head, since this kind of fishing is no more to my liking than that with line and net.[15]

15. Letter to Marie zu Sayn-Wittgenstein, Ballenstedt, June 23, 1852.

1854

You may rest assured that no stupid self-conceit is sticking in me, and that I mean faithfully and earnestly towards our Art, which in the end must be formed of our hearts' blood.[16]

16. Letter to Louis Köhler, Weimar, March 2, 1854.

You know that I am overdone with correspondence, and, unless it is absolutely necessary for me to write, I abstain from it, so as not to interrupt my work of composition, which is my first *raison d'être*.[17]

17. Letter to Gaeatano Belloni, September 9, 1854.

'Fine talk without deeds' is very distasteful to me.[18]

18. Letter to Franz Brendel, December 1, 1854.

I have no other pride than to serve, as far as in me lies, the *good cause* of Art, and whenever I find intelligent men conscientiously making efforts for the same end I rejoice and am comforted by the good example they give me.[19]

19. Letter to William Mason, Weimar, December 14, 1854.

1855

You know well that I am a poor, much-bothered mortal, and can but seldom dispose of my time according to my wishes.[20]

20. Letter to Rosalie Spohr, January 4, 1855.

Marr has given in his resignation as artistic Director [of the Weimar Court Theater], and one cannot get clear about the entire theater management for some weeks to come. I keep myself very passive in the matter, and don't fish in troubled waters. This much is certain—that if Weimar wants to do anything regular, it cannot do without my ideas and influence.[21]

21. Letter to Franz Brendel, Weimar, June, 1855.

I would gladly satisfy your wish [for an autograph of Wagner] sooner, but that the letters which Wagner writes to me are a perfectly inalienable benefit to me, and you will not take it amiss if I am more than avaricious with them.[22]

22. Letter to August Kiel, Weimar, September 8, 1855.

1856

My natural appearance is that of a *very serious* man, and one sincerely *modest*.[23]

23. Letter to Marie zu Sayn-Wittgenstein, Vienna, January 31, 1856.

I have only too many opportunities of experiencing what you so justly say of the troubles and inconveniences which arise to us from intercourse with heterogeneous persons, although I may boast of possessing a thicker and more impenetrable skin, and a much larger portion of patience, than you.[24]

24. Letter to Wagner, July, 1856.

You would be making a great mistake if you put any mistrust in my conduct, and I can assure you with a perfectly good conscience that to me there is nothing more agreeable and more to be desired than to rely entirely on one's friends.[25]

25. Letter to Joachim Raff, Weimar, August 7, 1856.

Make allowances for my letters, for I don't know how to express myself.[26]

26. Letter to Marie zu Sayn-Wittgenstein, Budapest, September 9, 1856.

1857

As I have for years been conscious of the artistic task that lies before me, neither consistent perseverance nor quiet reflection shall be wanting for the fulfillment of it. May God's blessing, without which nothing can prosper and bear fruit, rest on my work!

Do I not then stand up in the whole world of Art as an honest fellow, who, faithful to his conviction, despising all base means and hypocritical stratagems, strives valiantly and honorably after a high aim?[27]

27. Letter to Eduard Liszt, Weimar, March 26, 1857.

I've taken a firm resolution never to rush into business dealings, and never to give up something without bringing it to the best conclusion I can. If it's a good thing to mull over your words seven times before talking, one oughtn't to hesitate pondering even more when it's a matter of signing something with the pen. Without relying on anyone at all … I have occasionally made the error of becoming involved in untimely dealings: out of boredom, weakness, ineptitude and inexperience in business; and these have more than once played me the trick of forcing me to confess myself a first-class fool.

My motives being usually honest, I don't indulge sufficiently in that drop of suspicion that is so rigorously necessary for peace of mind, as well as for the dignity of existence: that ingredient from which I theoretically at least, am not exempt. The fact is, that on the one hand I esteem myself too highly, and on the other I give myself too cheaply to others. There is something there that has to do with pride, inadvertence, and a premature laziness; and I ought to be on triple guard against them.[28]

28. Letter to Marie zu Sayn-Wittgenstein, Aachen, July 28, 1857.

1858

Fischer (the organist) wrote to me lately, to ask me for a testimonial to his musical ability … Please to make my friendly excuses to him for not fulfilling his wish—possibly, in view of the enmity which I have to bear on all sides, such a document would do him more harm than good; apart from the fact that I very unwillingly set about drawing up such testimonials.[29]

29. Letter to Felix Draseke, Weimar, January 10, 1858.

My son, Daniel always maintains much reserve and a fair amount of embarrassment towards me. On the whole it's better that way, and I shall do nothing to change it.[30]

30. Letter to Marie zu Sayn-Wittgenstein, Prague, April 20, 1858

Trips of pleasure or recreation are not my affair any longer, and I could not consent to one.[31]

31. Letter to Wagner, August 6, 1858

I could follow no other influences, no other counsels, than those of a *scrupulous conscience*.[32]

32. Letter to Prince Constantin von Hohenzollern-Hechingen, Weimar, August 18, 1858.

1859

Really I often require the patience beseeming a *confrater* of the Franciscan order to bear so many intolerable things.[33]

33. Letter to Wagner, January 1, 1859.

1860

I think I understand and can manage the *art of program-making* in a masterly manner.[34]

34. Letter to Franz Brendel, Spring, 1860.

I don't know whether you'll be able to decipher this scrawl. In proportion as my ideas become clearer, it seems to me that my handwriting becomes more atrociously illegible.[35]

35. Letter to Marie zu Sayn-Wittgenstein, Weimar, May 27, 1860.

1861

I especially beg of you, dear friend, not to make any protest against the song of Hiller. The plainly fair and just thing, which has nothing in common with the 'elevated right' which is bestowed exclusively on Kapellmeister Rietz and his associates, consists simply in not shutting the door to publicity in anybody's face, or maliciously and silly casting stones and mud at him. Regardless of the fact that we must not expect that they on their side will deal thus with us, we must consistently and faithfully carry out and fulfill this *simple justice and fairness*, and thus show the gentlemen how people of a nobler mind and more proper cultivation behave.[36]

36. Letter to Franz Brendel, January, 1861.

1862

I have no longer any taste for moving about from one place to another, and, unless something very unforeseen happens, I shall not stir from here so soon. Now, although I have become very indifferent as to the fate of what I write, *work* none the less continues to be the first need of my nature. I write therefore simply to write—without any other pretensions or care.[37]

37. Letter to Jessie Laussot, Rome, May 3, 1862.

In the first place, however, comes the question whether I can take any personal part in the meeting of the *Tonkünstler-Versammlung* the year 1863? And unfortunately this question I am forced to answer decidedly in the *negative*. Owing to its being my custom not to enlighten others by giving an account of my own affairs, I avoid, even in this case entering further into particulars.

At my age (51 years!) it is advisable to remain at home; what there is to seek, is to be found within oneself, not without; and, let me add, I am as much wanting in inclination to wander about as I am in the necessary means for doing so.[38]

38. Letter to Franz Brendel, November 8, 1862.

Yet as long as we are upon earth we must attend to our daily task. And mine shall not lie unproductive. However trifling it may seem to others, to me it is indispensable. My soul's tears must, as it were, have lacrymatoria made for them; I must set fires alight for those of my dear ones that are alive, and keep my dear dead in *spiritual and corporeal* urns. This is the aim and object of the *Art task* to me.

Meanwhile I remain quietly in Rome, honestly striving to do my duty as a Christian and an artist.[39]

39. Letter to Eduard Liszt, Rome, November 19, 1862.

1863

I was especially pleased with the axiom: 'The artistic temperament, when genuine, corrects itself in consequence of the change of contrasts.' May it prove so in my case;—this much is certain,—that in the tiresome business of self-correction few have to labor as I have, as the process of my mental development, if not checked, is at all events rendered peculiarly difficult by a variety of coincidences and contingencies. A clever man, some twenty years ago, made the not inapplicable remark to me: "You have in reality three individuals to deal with in yourself, and they all run one against the other; the sociable-individual, the virtuoso and the thoughtfully-creative composer. If you manage one of them properly, you may congratulate yourself.'—*Vedremo!*[40]

40. Letter to Franz Brendel, Monte Mario, September 7, 1863.

The melancholy familiarity with death that I have perforce acquired during these latter years does not in the least weaken the grief which we feel when our dear ones leave this earth.[41]

41. Letter to Jessie Laussot, Rome, October 15, 1863.

1864

Pohl seems to have put on wrong spectacles if he reads in my letter that I have no greater wish than to return to unique Germany! People may think about it what they please; the *positive* truth is that I do not bother myself about fools of any species, whether German, French, English, Russian or Italian, but am peacefully industrious in my seclusion here.

Besides, thank God, I am too honest and truth-loving to fall a victim to vanity.[42]

42. Letter to Franz Brendel, January 22, 1864.

I am resolved not to tire people with my presence, as also to withdraw myself from the idle fatigue that people cause me. Thank God I have something to work at without disturbing myself at my work further than is necessary for the good conscience I hope always to keep. For this Rome is peculiarly adapted to me, and I shall not go away for the smallest thing without *well knowing* what it is for.[43]

43. Letter to Eduard Liszt, Rome, June 22, 1864.

1865

Only at certain moments I fancy that the judicious maxim of Champfort is somewhat applicable to me: 'Celebrity is the punishment of talent and the chastisement of merit.'[44]

44. Letter to Jessie Laussot, Rome, March 6, 1865.

1866

My address is simply: To Commandeur Abbé Liszt—Rome.[45]

45. Letter to Franz Brendel, Rome, October 2, 1866.

1868

During the winter my innumerable social duties rendered it absolutely impossible for me to write any longer compositions. This enforced idleness vexes me extremely—and I intend to assume an air of rudeness to rid myself of a great many people. It is more especially intrusive correspondents who are a vexatious waste of time to me.[46]

46. Letter to Franz Brendel, Rome, June 17, 1868.

[Regarding the *Biographie Pascallet*, 1843] This notice is both the most exact, the best edited, and the kindest of all that have appeared about me in *French*.[47]

47. Letter to E. Repos, Rome, July 1, 1868.

To satisfy rational and righteous people is the better part of my life … I pledge myself always to be *true* in speech and action, however many annoyances and misinterpretations may be hurled at me in return. In confidence I will tell you what is the rule of my whole existence; it consists of the daily prayer: '*O veritas Deus, fac me unum tecum in perpetua caritate!*'[48]

48. Letter to Siegmund Lebert, Rome, September 10, 1868.

1869

Do not look for [flattery] from me; I never knew much about it, and I can still less try my hand at it now in my old age.[49]

49. Letter to Heinrich Schulz-Beuthen, Weimar, June 18, 1869.

At my age the *role of the young composer* is no longer suitable—and there would not be any other for me in Paris, as I cannot continue indefinitely that of an old disabled pianist.[50]

50. Letter to Camille Saint-Saëns, Rome, July 19, 1869.

To fulfill my duties as a Christian, and to spend my time suitably by continuing to write my music, is my whole life: nothing else concerns me in the slightest.[51]

51. Letter to Marie zu Sayn-Wittgenstein, Villa d'Este, October 26, 1869.

I wish, and urgently entreat and command, that my burial may take place without show, and be as simple and economical as possible. I protest against a burial such as Rossini's was, and even against any sort of invitation for friends and acquaintances to assemble … Let there be no pomp, no music, no procession in my honor, no superfluous illuminations, or any kind of oration … The inscription on my tomb might be: '*Et habitabunt recti cum vulto suo*.'[52]

52. Letter to Princess Caroline Sayn-Wittgenstein, November 27, 1869.

Many people have very kindly invited me to go to Paris; I have excused myself from doing so for reasons of expediency which you know. Henceforth it is not *myself* that I have to bring forward, but simply to continue to write in perfect tranquility and with a free mind. To do this obliges me to seclude myself, to avoid the *salons*, the half-opened pianos and the society drudgery imposed by the large towns, where I very easily feel myself out of place.[53]

53. Letter to Franz Servais, Villa d'Este, December 20, 1869.

1871

I am as much a stranger to sentiments of rancor as of envy.[54]

54. Letter to Olga von Meyendorff, April 9, 1871.

I am usually given to seeing things neither in rose nor in black, but in gray—half in mourning: and even so I have to make a certain effort of will not to see things more somberly still.[55]

55. Letter to Olga von Meyendorff, Rome, October 23, 1871.

Summary and violent judgments are repugnant to my nature. Do you recall the verse in the Gospel [Matthew, 5 22]: 'But I say unto you, That whosoever is angry with his brother without a cause shall be in danger of the judgment: and whosoever shall say to his brother, Raca, shall be in danger of the council: but whosoever shall say, Thou fool, shall be in danger of hell fire.' I try not to violate this precept and even tend to hold excessively mild opinions with regard to the conduct of others … being aware how much indulgence and compassion would be needed in order to absolve mine![56]

56. Letter to Olga von Meyendorff, Rome, November 2, 1871.

Your comment on Pascal's 'two kinds of men' seems to me very true and I pride myself somewhat on belonging to the third kind, the most numerous according to you, the 'sinners who feel that they are not sinners.' Besides, one must not argue with Pascal about whether his thoughts are more, or less, true, but climb to the luminous gloom of his torments concerning the Infinite. Consequently, I stick to my mythological comparison of the Phoenix, all the more so since the Hydra is an ugly; monster which was dispatched by Lord Hercules. If you still find me too enigmatic in this I shall not contradict you further. Very humbly, thank you for striking this word from your letters.[57]

57. Letter to Olga von Meyendorff, Budapest, December 28, 1871.

1872

Not knowing what to say was Brid'oison's mode of thinking. I'm just about at that stage myself, and on the verge of completely losing the use of words which correspond to my mode of thinking and feeling.[58]

58. Letter to Olga von Meyendorff, Weimar, June 4, 1872.

Your pamphlet [*Die grossen Pianoforte-Virtuosen unsrer Zeit*] draws down upon itself a capital reproach; it is that you make me out too grand and too fine. I am far from deserving it, and I confess it without any false modesty; but since you have been pleased thus to overwhelm me I can but bow in silence,—and press your hand.

The greater part of the things which are easily said is indifferent to me, and those what I wish to say resist ordinary language.[59]

59. Letter to Wilhelm von Lenz, Weimar, September 20, 1872.

At the age of 61, my celebrations consist of memories only.[60]

60. Letter to Olga von Meyendorff, Bayreuth, October 20, 1872.

I have always had the misfortune of hearing those I love best tell me that I did not love them much.[61]

61. Letter to Olga von Meyendorff, Vienna, October 28, 1872.

The Grand Duke has replied with a most gracious and witty letter in which he reproaches me for not telling him about myself. That is a fault I have no desire to correct, being of the opinion that 'myself,' if not always 'hateful,' as Pascal used to say, is usually superfluous. Hence I would like to flatter myself that I am becoming even more of an impersonal individual. However, I still have far to go in this respect.[62]

62. Letter to Olga von Meyendorff, Budapest, November 13, 1872.

1873

I have never owned more than a few feet of land, in Bonn, in a street which, after the Beethoven Fest in 1845, was to be named after me. I refrained from having the house built, and my cousin Eduard did me the service of selling the ground at not too great a loss. I am totally incompetent in such matters.[63]

63. Letter to Olga von Meyendorff, Budapest, January 22, 1873.

Of course I do not mean to *bargain* with Zumbusch (that is a thing I do only in case of dire necessity—and even then am a bad hand at it).[64]

64. Letter to Eduard Liszt, Budapest, February 10, 1873.

I wholeheartedly detest meanness, platitudes, selfish and vulgar scheming. Consequently, all that is opposed to these comforts me.[65]

65. Letter to Olga von Meyendorff, Budapest, February 11, 1873.

Although I do not go in for any luxuries, money vanishes quickly and readily in my hands.[66]

66. Letter to Eduard Liszt, Weimar, August 19, 1873.

1874

At my age one must try to behave reasonably, and to avoid excess.[67]

67. Letter to Countess Marie Donhoff, January, 1874.

I feel qualified neither for theology nor politics, nor for business in general—and remain a very humble musician.[68]

68. Letter to Olga von Meyendorff, Budapest, February 21, 1874.

You know that letter writing is a punishment for me, often a very harsh one. My pen knows not how to flow, and easily becomes petrified. I absolutely must have the stimulus of *viva voce* talk for my modest wits to have running room.[69]

69. Letter to Olga von Meyendorff, Villa d'Este, June 24, 1874.

I have a high regard for rewards, honors, decorations, while feeling that those who deserve them must well and cheerfully be able to do without them. They are not a goal in themselves but an accompaniment *quasi ad libitum*.[70]

70. Letter to Olga von Meyendorff, Villa d'Este, July 8, 1874.

Please ask me all the questions you wish without any embarrassment or oratorical hedging whatsoever. My answers will be straight and true. I have nothing to hide from anyone and sometimes commit the error of making this too clear.[71]

71. Letter to Olga von Meyendorff, July 27, [18741].

An anonymous man of letters has me confessing in public in my own name to one of my crimes and to my 'immeasurable pride'! … As for my immeasurable pride, it reaches the point of believing that people have often been mistaken with regard to me, and of not feeling in the slightest obliged to subscribe to opinions and judgments which seem to me false.[72]

72. Letter to Olga von Meyendorff, Rome, October 5, 1874.

I cannot flatter myself that I am skillful at Court, nor that I am able to judge from a distance little things which can only be properly seen close to.[73]

73. Letter to Olga von Meyendorff, Villa d'Este, December 2, 1874.

1875

Superfluous words are unbecoming to me; let us onward and act.[74]

74. Letter to Franz Witt, August or September, 1875.

1876

A Weimar publisher asks me to contribute to a *Tanz Album* to be published in honor of Princess Marie. I don't care much for *Albums*, or for dancing either.[75]

75. Letter to Olga von Meyendorff, Villa d'Este, January 16, 1876.

I shall always endeavor to come up to the expectations of my friends.[76]

76. Letter to Kornel von Abrányi, Villa d'Este, January 20, 1876.

People are singing the praises of *Le Finance de Mlle Saint-Maur* by Cherbuliez, but being totally devoid of romantic feeling, I avoid reading anything which calls for it.[77]

77. Letter to Olga von Meyendorff, Budapest, March 15, 1876.

To harbor a grudge seems to me mean and unworthy. Not to do as others have done, or might do, suits me better; and without bragging too much, I maintain complete personal objectivity toward my friends or my enemies. *To serve well* is the main thing in this world—while awaiting a better one.[78]

78. Letter to Olga von Meyendorff, Hanover, May 4, 1876.

The precept of Horace and Boileau, 'Make haste slowly,' does not please me much; however, I have to follow it in practice, including my travels.[79]

79. Letter to Olga von Meyendorff, Nurenberg, October 9, 1876.

My lack of wit does not go to the point of lacking heart, where required. If I express myself poorly, it's my fault, my very great fault.[80]

80. Letter to Olga von Meyendorff, Budapest, November 3, 1876.

You know that I like fine French style and literary manners.[81]

81. Letter to Olga von Meyendorff, Budapest, November 16, 1876.

If I sometimes utter a harsh word, please believe that its *real* meaning applies only to me, not to others.[82]

82. Letter to Olga von Meyendorff, Budapest, December 4, 1876.

1877

Let us strike the word 'displeasure' entirely from the vocabulary of our intimate conversation. I have too many reasons for being displeased with myself to find room for others …

Writing is becoming more and more onerous and sometimes odious for me. Banalities repel me no less than affectations. It is indeed difficult for me to make my way between them with my pen.[83]

83. Letter to Olga von Meyendorff, Budapest, January 28, 1877.

Please send the money for the journey. I must not have any other debts except moral ones.[84]

84. Letter to Eduard Liszt, Weimar, July 3, 1877.

I have become quiescent to the point of impassivity.[85]

85. Letter to Olga von Meyendorff, Marienbad, August 17, 1877.

I will always maintain a most peaceful attitude towards my honored colleagues, and, wherever they please, allow their influence and opinion to have free play.[86]

86. Letter to Breitkopf and Härtel, Villa d'Este, September 26, 1877.

Let me tell you once again that I am extremely tired of living; but as I believe that God's Fifth Commandement, 'Thou shalt not kill,' also applies to suicide, I go on existing with deepest repentance and contrition for having formerly ostentatiously violated the Ninth Commandment, not without effort or humility.[87]

87. Letter to Olga von Meyendorff, Budapest, November 28, 1877.

1878

I am absorbed here in the most difficult of tasks—to put up with myself. Happily I receive plenty of help; noble friendships and dear and beautiful memories light up the path which I still have to follow before I reach the grave.[88]

88. Letter to Jessie Laussot, Budapest, January 29, 1878.

I am following Berlioz' bad example and don't much listen to music for pleasure.[89]

89. Letter to Olga von Meyendorff, Rome, September 12, 1878.

1879

I read fifty or so pages of the *Cahiers* by Sainte-Beuve—an exquisite little book which I recommend to you. In it I am charged with 'affectation' (a reproach launched against me when I started frequenting the high society of the Paris salons and of which I hardly thought it possible to be accused), but Sainte-Beuve adds a corrective which M. Blaze de Bury and his consorts would have taken great care not to admit. I venture to confess that people err in imputing to me any egoistic urge. My faults and mistakes spring elsewhere.[90]

90. Letter to Olga von Meyendorff, Budapest, January 21, 1879.

1880

Last Friday I entered my seventieth year. It might be time to end things well—all the more since I have never wished to live long. In my early youth I often went to sleep hoping not to awake again here below.[91]

91. Letter to Olga von Meyendorff, Villa d'Este, October 30, 1880.

It never enters my head to make exaggerated pretensions with regard to my residential requirements. Decency without display continues to be the right thing for me.[92]

92. Letter to Amalie von Fabry, Villa d'Este, November 1, 1880.

At my age, unless one is a minister, one has to limit and economize one's travels.[93]

93. Letter to Marie zu Sayn-Wittgenstein, Villa d'Este, November 7, 1880.

To know and to achieve belong to the human condition—starting with *savoir vivre*, something we, even the most learned among us, spend our lives in learning to do badly.[94]

94. Letter to Olga von Meyendorff, Villa d'Este, December 1, 1880.

1881

My ignorance keeps me from the heights of ecclesiastical and worldly politics: I would not even know how to venture an opinion thereon.[95]

95. Letter to Marie zu Sayn-Wittgenstein, Budapest, February 2, 1881.

In suggesting to Bösendorfer to invite Madame Hanslick, I was displaying my customary quality: impartiality. People have made great use of this in respect to me, and to my detriment.[96]

96. Letter to Marie zu Sayn-Wittgenstein, Budapest, March 30, 1881.

Correctness remains [my] motto.[97]

97. Letter to Kornel von Abranyi, Weimar, May 22, 1881.

There may be something original in reproaching me for being 'solemn.' Being innocent of this, I ignore the reproach while admitting that various kinds of *sans-facon* behavior, even if fashionable, displease me just as dirty linen does and even more, for with it goes a contempt for others which is highly unseemly and cheap in the bad sense.[98]

98. Letter to Olga von Meyendorff, Undated.

Antipathy to letter-writing is becoming a malady with me.[99]

99. Letter to Ludwig Bösendorfer, Rome, December 8, 1881.

1882

I shall practice great sobriety in the matter of visits. Wagner does not pay any, and I shall imitate him on this point to the best of my ability.[100]

100. Letter to Adelheid von Schorn, Venice, November 20, 1882.

Here, in Palazzo Vendramin, a peaceful and most united family life goes on without monotony. But I cannot speak of the things which touch me most, except clumsily. So it is better to keep from doing so.[101]

101. Letter to Adeıheim von Schorn, Venice, December 9, 1882.

1883

If you were here, dear friend, you would perhaps find means to put into some sort of order the hundreds of letters that rain upon me from everywhere. These bothers and burdens of the amiability with which I am credited are becoming insupportable, and I really long, some fine day, to cry from the house-tops that I beg the public to consider me as one of the most disagreeable, whimsical and disobliging of men.[102]

102. Letter to Adelheid von Schorn, Budapest, February 14, 1883.

The price seems to me exorbitant. Perhaps one should have recourse to bargaining, which is something almost improper, but sometimes of practical value.[103]

103. Letter to Olga von Meyendorff, Weimar, April 9, 1883.

For thirty years past I have entirely abstained from adding to collections of autographs and of writing my name in any albums whatever.[104]

104. Letter to Baroness Wrangel, Weimar, May 20, 1883.

1884

Le Figaro publishes a comical fragment of Heine' s *Memoiren* featuring an account of his grandparents' wigs. For many years now my mood has not at all been inclined toward the humorous style, and I willingly leave to others the pleasure of finding it amusing. [105]

105. Letter to Olga von Meyendorff, Budapest, March 12, 1884.

Without in the least taking part in politics, yet I take that interest in them which it behoves every not uneducated man to do.[106]

106. Letter to Kornel von Abrányi, Weimar, July 1, 1884.

To return to Paris and show myself off there as a young composer or to continue the business of an old pianist in the *salons* does not attract me in the least.[107]

107. Letter to Louise de Mercy-Argenteau, October 24, 1884.

1886

When I happen to be discourteous, this is much against my will.[108]

108. Letter to Olga von Meyendorff, Budapest, February 24, 1886.

Munkacsy and I have one thing in common, which is that work makes us surly and sleepy.[109]

109. Letter to Olga von Meyendorff, Colpach Castle, Luxemburg, July 12, 1886.

Chapter Two

Liszt on his Professional Life

As a Pianist

1832

I practice four to five hours of exercises (3rds, 6ths, 8ths, tremolos, repetition of notes, cadences, etc.).[1]

1. Letter to Pierre Wolff, Paris, May 2, 1832.

1836

[On his piano career]: It is my only fortune, by only title, my unique possession that I don't want anyone whatever to touch.[2]

2. Letter to Marie d'Agoult, Spring, 1836.

1837

Am I condemned without respite to this trade of a Merry Andrew and to amuse in drawing-rooms?[3]

3. Letter to Abbe de Lamennais, Como, December 18, 1837.

1838

You see my piano is for me what his frigate is to a sailor or his horse to an Arab - more indeed: it is my very self, my mother tongue, my life. Within its seven octaves it encloses the whole range of an orchestra, and a man's ten fingers have the power to reproduce the harmonies which are created by hundreds of performers.[4]

4. 'Lettre d'un bachelier ès musique à Adolphe Pictet,' *Gazette Musicale* (February 11, 1838).

The post is leaving. Two lines only. Enormous success. Applause. Called back fifteen or eighteen times. Hall packed. Everyone astonished. Thalberg hardly exists for the Viennese. I am deeply moved by it all. I have never had anything like this success. You would have enjoyed it … Without exaggeration no one since Paganini has had such a success. I am the man of the hour.[5]

5. Letter to Marie d'Agoult, Vienna, April, 1838.

1839

What a contrast to the tiresome *musical soliloquies* (I do not know what other name to give to this invention of mine) with which I contrived to gratify the Romans, and which I am quite capable of importing to Paris, so unbounded does my impudence become! Imagine that, wearied with warfare, not being able to compose a program which would have common sense, I have ventured to give a series of concerts all by myself, affecting the Louis XIV style, and saying cavalierly to the public, 'The concert is—me.' For the curiosity of the thing I copy one of the programs of the soliloquies for you:

1. Overture to William Tell
2. Reminiscences of the Puritani
3. Etudes and fragments [by myself]
4. Improvisation on given themes.

And that was all; neither more nor less, except lively conversation during the intervals, and enthusiasm if there was room for it.[6]

6. Letter to Princess Christine Belgiojoso, Albano, June 4, 1839.

I mean to play in public your *Carnaval,* and some of the *Davidsbündlertänze* and [some] of the *Kinderscene*. The Kreisleriana, and the *Fantaisie* are more difficult of digestion for the public. I shall reserve them till later.[7]

7. Letter to Robert Schumann, Albano, June 5, 1839.

1840

I mentioned a splendid day. The word is no exaggeration. I won't write about it to anybody, and even to you I will write badly because these things can't be described. On January 4, I played at the Hungarian Theater the Andante from *Lucia*, the Galop, and the applause not ceasing, the *Rakoczy March* (a sort of aristocratic 'Marseillaise'). Just as I was going backstage, in comes Count Leo Festetics, Baron Banfy, Count Teleky (all magnates), Eckstein, Augusz and a sixth whose name I forget, all in full Hungarian costumes, Festetics holding a magnificent saber set with turquoises, rubies, etc. (worth 80 to 100 louis), in his hand. He addresses me with a little allocution in Hungarian before the public, which applauds with frenzy, and buckles on the sword in the name of the Nation. I ask through Augusz for permission to speak to the public in French. I pronounce in a grave and firm voice the discourse I will send you printed tomorrow. It is frequently interrupted with applause …

You can't have an idea of the serious, grave and profound sensation of this scene, which anywhere else would have been ridiculous and which could easily have become so even here … It was magnificent. It was unique. But that wasn't all. The performance over, we get into carriages. And behold an immense crowd blocking up the square and 200 young people carrying lighted torches, led by military music …

The shouting never stopped. It was a triumphal march such as La Fayette and one or two men of the revolution have experienced.[8]

8. Letter to Marie d'Agoult, Budapest, January, 1840.

A propos of concerts, I gave six (in nine days!) at Prague, three at Dresden, and the same number at Leipzig (in twelve days)—so I am perfectly tired out, and feel great need of rest.[9]

9. Letter to Franz von Schober, Metz, April 3, 1840.

For a fortnight past I have again put my neck into the English yoke. Every day which God gives—a concert, with a journey, previously, of thirty to fifty miles. And so it must continue at least till the end of January.[10]

10. Letter to Franz von Schober, Manchester, December 5 1840.

1841

Paris, I don't hide it from you, has been a real satisfaction to my self-love. My two concerts *alone*, and especially the third, at the Conservatoire, for the Beethoven Monument, are concerts out of the ordinary run, such as *I only* can give in Europe at the present moment. The accounts in the papers can only have given you a very incomplete idea. Without self-conceit or any illusion, I think I may say that never has so striking an effect, so complete and so irresistible, been produced by an instrumentalist in Paris.[11]

11. Letter to Simon Lowy, London, May 20, 1841.

1845

My Vienna journey will pretty much mark the end of my *virtuoso* career.[12]

12. Letter to Franz von Schober, Gibraltar, March 3, 1845.

1850

The arrival of your piano is one of the most pleasant events in my peacefully studious life at Weimar. Although, to tell the truth, I don't intend to do much *finger-work* in the course of this year, yet it is no less indispensable for me to have from time to time a perfect instrument to play on. It is an old custom that I should regret to change.[13]

13. Letter to Breitkopf and Härtel, Weimar, January 14, 1850.

1854

I shall have done for the present with the piano, in order to devote myself exclusively to orchestral compositions, and to attempt more in that domain which has for a long time become for me an inner necessity.[14]

14. Letter to Louis Köhler, Weimar, April or May, 1854.

If I remember rightly, I employed a good deal of *Tempo rubato* in the times when I was giving my concerts (a business that I would not begin again for anything in the world).[15]

15. Letter to William Mason, Weimar, December 14, 1854.

1855

While thoroughly agreeing with the performance of the different items as a whole, I have nevertheless one request to make—namely, that you would be good enough to excuse me from the performance of the Mozart Pianoforte Concerto which has been so kindly designed for me. Apart from the fact that for more than eight years I have not appeared anywhere in public as a pianist, and that many considerations lead me to adhere firmly to my negative resolve in this respect, the fact that the direction of the Festival will require my entire attention may prove … my sufficient excuse.[16]

16. Letter to Ritter von Seiler, Weimar, December 26, 1855.

1857

Do not be alarmed, dear sir, and do not be in the least afraid that I am going to struggle, in the usual style of our unchivalrous Don Quixote of musical criticism, with the windmill of virtuosity. You could not fairly expect this of me—either, for I have never concealed that, since the grapes of virtuosity could not be made sour for me, I should take no pleasure whatever in finding them sour in somebody else's mouth.[17]

17. Letter to Herr von Turanyi, Weimar, January 3, 1857.

The frequent ill-success of my performances of Schumann's compositions, both in private circles and in public, discouraged me from including and keeping them in the programs of my concerts which followed so rapidly on one another—programs which, partly from want of time and partly from carelessness and satiety of the 'Glanz-Periode' of my pianoforte playing, I seldom, except in the rarest cases, planned myself, but gave them now into this one's hands, and now that one, to choose what they liked. That was a mistake, as I discovered later and deeply regretted, when I had learned to understand that for the artist who wishes to be worthy of the name of artist the danger of not pleasing the public is a far less one than that allowing oneself to be decided by it humors –and to this danger every executive artist is especially exposed, if he does not take courage resolutely and on principle to stand earnestly and consistently by his conviction, and to produce those works which he knows to be the best, whether people like them or not.

It is of no consequence, then, in how far my faintheartedness in regard to Schumann's compositions might possibly be excused by the all-ruling taste of the day, but I did without thinking of it thereby set a bad example, for which I can hardly make amends again. The stream of custom and the slavery of the artist, who is directed to the encouragement and applause of the multitude for the maintenance and improvement of his existence and his renown, is such a pull-back, that, even to the better-minded and more courageous ones, among whom I am proud to reckon myself, it is intensely difficult to preserve their better ego in the face of all the covetous, distracted, and despite their large number backward-in-paying *We*.

There is in Art a pernicious offence, of which most of us are guilty through carelessness and fickleness; I might call it the *Pilate offence*.[18]

18. Letter to J. W. von Wasielewski, Weimar, January 9, 1857.

1858

I shall go to Dresden, where I have promised Rietschel to pay my *old* debt to Weber, and to make one exception by playing several of Weber's pianoforte compositions at a concert for the benefit of the Weber monument … If I had a little more money I should. Have preferred to pay the balance which is still due on the subscription for the Weber monument in hard cash, instead of playing to the people a few hackneyed pieces. Weber must forgive a poor devil like me that I can do nothing better for him.[19]

19. Letter to Wagner, Salzburg, October 9, 1858.

1860

Several papers are saying, that good report has it, my marriage blessing will be performed by His Eminence the Bishop of Fulda. The *Frankfurt Journal* is careful to dress me up for the occasion with the title of *celebrated pianist*. It really seems to me that my name is sufficiently clear and distinct by itself, so that it might be spared the irksome encumbrance of a superannuated title.[20]

20. Letter to Marie zu Sayn-Wittgenstein, Weimar, May 27, 1860.

1863

There is only one point on which I would venture even to an act of rebellion—it is that of the pedals, a *bass* [base] passion of which I cannot correct myself, no matter how annoying the reproaches it may draw upon me![21]

21. Letter to Breitkopf and Härtel, Rome, August 28, 1863.

1869

As to your Method, you won't expect me to make a deep study of that. I am much too old for such a thing, and it is only in self-defense that I still work sometimes at the piano, in view of the incessant botherations and indiscretions of a heap of people who imagine that nothing would be more flattering to me than to amuse them![22]

22. Letter to William Mason, Rome, May 26, 1869.

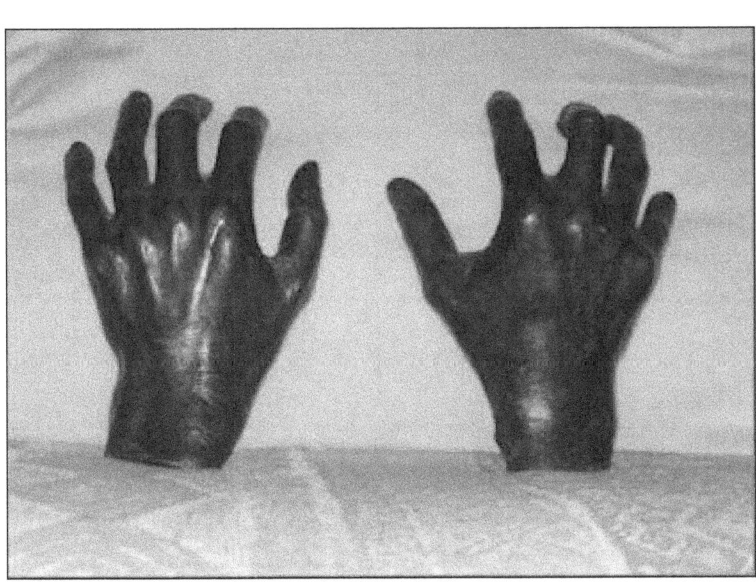

1872

About mid-March there well be a charity concert sponsored by fine ladies and Princess Frederique Auersperg, who entered the Order of St. Dominic seven or eight years ago. Your very humble servant will perform there with a Beethoven sonata, some Chopin nocturnes, etc.[23]

23. Letter to Olga von Meyendorff, Budapest, February 28, 1872.

Give Bösendorfer my friendly greetings, and at the same time tell him how I praise the excellent piano upon which I have been practicing a little here.[24]

24. Letter to Eduard von Liszt, Horpacs, November 6, 1872.

I shall take no part in the Concerts planned by Sister Mary, Princess Raymondine Auersperg, who had the kindness to write me from Trieste inviting me to display my small talent as a pianist there for the benefit of her Dominican school. I answered her yesterday that I felt quite paralyzed and disconcerted by concerts.[25]

25. Letter to Marie zu Sayn-Wittgenstein, Horpacs, November 8, 1872.

1873

[Regarding a benefit concert] I replied that an interval of 25 years separated me from my last public appearance as a pianist, and that I considered it advisable for me to remain within the interval.[26]

26. Letter to Eduard Liszt, Budapest, February 10, 1873.

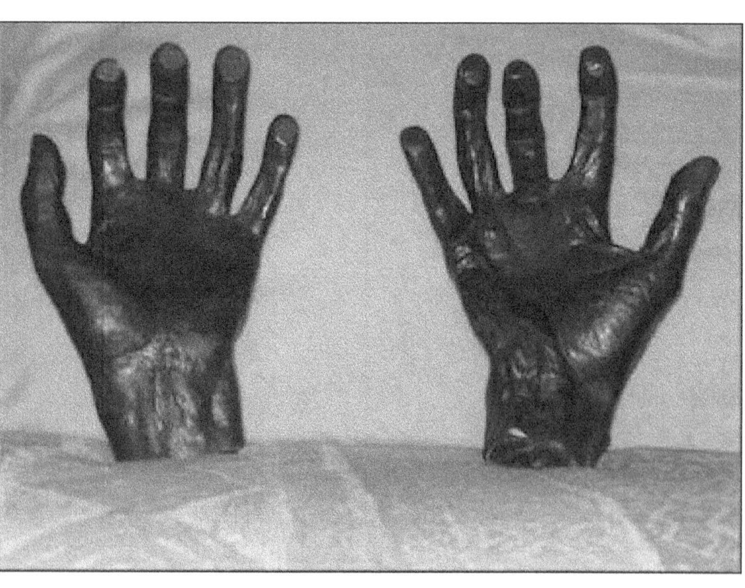

In a fortnight's time I shall have a similar [performance] before me as pianoforte player, at a charity concert which Countess Anna Zichy is patronizing.[27]

27. Letter to Eduard Liszt, Budapest, March 3, 1873.

1874

M. Sach persists in the erroneous opinion that the fiftieth anniversary of my little deeds and doings as a pianist falls on April 13, 1874. He was so kind as to send me on that date a telegram of 'sympathetic remembrance,' with which the Grand Duchess and her august family deign to associate themselves. I replied yesterday with a letter of thanks, in which I made the comment that a biographical slip concerning me is a matter of complete indifference, but that in fact my name already appeared on concert posters (of which several were kept and recently republished) in the winter and spring in Vienna and in Budapest *in 1823*; later on in the fall of the same year in Munich and in Stuttgart when I was on my way to Paris and London where I performed my tricks as an infant prodigy in 1824. The Jubilee Committee in Budapest wisely kept to the date *1823*, the year of my concerts in Vienna and Budapest, although I had played in public at Oedenburg one year before as an eleven year old boy, but in fact it is from the time of the subsidy which six Hungarian grandees granted to my father in 1822 or 1823 for six years, in order to provide for my musical education, that my strange musical career dates.[28]

28. Letter to Olga von Meyendorff, Budapest, April 15, 1874.

Your friendly communication rests upon a harmless mistake. You do not seem to know that for 26 years past I have altogether ceased to be regarded as a pianist; hence I have for a long time not given any concerts, and only very occasionally played the piano in public, for some very special reason, to aid some charity or to further some artistic object, and then only in Rome, Hungary, and in Vienna –nowhere else. And on these rare and very exceptional occasions no one has ever thought of offering me any remuneration in money.[29]

29. Letter to A. F. Eggers, of the Liverpool Muscial Festival, Villa d'Este, June 21, 1874.

1876

Although I scruple to weary the extraordinary good-will which the public of Budapest has evinced towards me, I nevertheless make so bold as to offer the assistance of my two hands for the concert shortly to be given in aid of the sufferers by the floods. In the year 1838, when I returned for the first time to Vienna, I gave my *first* concert there in aid of the sufferers by the inundation at Budapest. It will be a comfort to me if I can now *close* my protracted career as virtuoso by the fulfillment of a similar duty.[30]

30. Letter to August von Trefort, Budapest, March 1, 1876.

After the concert for the flood victims, I hope never to play the piano again in public.[31]

31. Letter to Olga von Meyendorff, Budapest, March 15, 1876.

Please keep my surprise [arrival] a secret. In mid-March it would be hard for me to avoid the boring chore of a Concert for the Vienna Beethoven Monument; I shall probably perform the E-Flat *Concerto* (the same one I played to the satisfaction of the Bonn critics in 1845) on the 18th of March, 1877. After this required pleonasm, I shall go to Rome.[32]

32. Letter to Marie zu Sayn-Wittgenstein, Budapest, November 20, 1876.

I should not think of performing any other work at this concert than one absolutely written by Beethoven, and consequently my share in the concert program will consist of the Eb major *Concerto*.[33]

33. Letter to the Committee of the Beethoven Monument in Vienna, December 10, 1876.

1877

On my arrival here this morning, I was fairly tired. My stay in Vienna won't afford me much rest, for the Friday concert for the Beethoven monument is combined with an extraordinary and very profitable dress rehearsal, in order to satisfy the many people who cannot get tickets for the concert. The rehearsal too is already sold out, people assure me.. I cannot account for such a crowd.[34]

34. Letter to Olga von Meyendorff, Vienna, March 12, 1877.

This time, the Vienna public was *extremely* responsive, to the point of causing my modesty (which few people are aware of but which, I am so bold as to admit, is nonetheless sincere) extraordinary embarrassment.[35]

35. Letter to Olga von Meyendorff, Amberg, March 24, 1877.

I hope that in the next world I'll be spared from playing the *Fantasie du Diable aux Anges*; and contrary to Vauvenargues' thought ('Servitude debases man to the point of making him love it'), I have always protested from the depths of my heart against the servitude of success.[36]

36. Letter to Olga von Meyendorff, Budapest, December 9, 1877.

1879

Since the year 1847 I only played *in public* twice in Rome, often in Budapest later on, twice in Vienna, once in Pressburg and Odenburg as a child of my country. Nowhere else. May my poor pianoforte performing at last come to an end! It has long been a torment to me. Therefore—Amen![37]

37. Letter to Marie Lipius, Budapest, March 2, 1879.

Everyone in Hungary feels duty-bound to come to the aid of the many thousands of victims of the terrible floods at Szeged. I too must contribute with my ten old fingers to a benefit concert.[38]

38. Letter to Olga von Meyendorff, Budapest, March 21, 1879.

1881

Princess Czartoryska will speak to you about her *Ruthenian* concert. I will gladly provide the accompaniment for it. lt must be without street-corner billboards, for I bore my cross of pianistic publicity at the Beethoven concert.[39]

39. Letter to Marie zu Sayn-Wittgenstein, Budapest, February 2, 1881.

For my own part I would much prefer it if they finally left me with a little peace. Tiring the public is the hardest and most ungrateful of all fatigues. It goes without saying that my name, as pianist, can no longer be displayed on any kind of a poster.[40]

40. Letter to Marie zu Sayn-Wittgenstein, March, 1881.

1883

Unfortunately my age of 72 years invalidates me as a pianist. I could no longer risk in public my ten fingers—which have been out of practice for years—without incurring just censure. There is no doubt on this point; and I am perfectly resolved to abstain from any exhibition of my old age at the piano in any country.[41]

41. Letter to Arthur Meyer, Budapest, January 28, 1883.

They seem determined in London to push me to the Piano. I cannot consent to this in public, as my seventy-five-year-old fingers are no longer suited to it, and Bülow, Saint-Saëns, Rubinstein, and you, dear Bache, play my compositions much better than what is left of my humble self.

Perhaps it would be opportune … to let the public know, by a short announcement, that Liszt only ventures to appear as a grateful visitor, and neither in London nor anywhere else as a man with an interest in his fingers.[42]

42. Letter to Walter Bache, Budapest, February 11, 1886.

As Conductor

1850

If you will do me a service, dear friend, send me, if possible by return mail, some metronomical indications for the introduction and several other important pieces, the duet between Lohengrin and Elsa in the third act amongst others. I believe I am not mistaken as to your wishes and intentions, but should still prefer to have conviction *in figures*, as to this matter.[43]

43. Letter to Richard Wagner, Summer, 1850.

1852

The orchestra and opera of Weimar were greatly in need of reform and of stirring up. The remarkable and extraordinary works to which our theater owes it new renown—*Tannhäuser, Lohengrin, Benenuto Cellini*—required numerous rehearsals, which I could not give into the hands of any body else.[44]

44. Letter to Carl Czerny, Weimar, April 19, 1852.

1853

In various accounts that I have read of the Festival at Karlsruhe, there is one point on which people seem pretty much agreed -namely, the *insufficiency* of my conducting. Without here examining what degree of *foregone* judgment there may be in this opinion, without even seeking to know how much it has been influenced by the simple fact of the choice of myself as conductor, apart from the towns of Karlsruhe, Darmstadt, and Mannheim, it certainly would not be for me to raise pretensions quite contrary to the assertion which it is sought to establish if this assertion were based on facts or on justice. But this is precisely what I cannot help contesting in a very positive manner.

As a *fact* one cannot deny that the *ensemble* of the Karlsruhe program was very remarkably performed, that the proportion and sonority of the instruments, combined with a view to the *locale* chosen, were satisfactory and even excellent. This is rather naively acknowledged in the remark that it is really surprising that things should have gone so well '*in spite of*' the insufficiency of my conducting. I am far from wishing to deck myself in the peacock's feathers of the Karlsruhe, Mannheim, and Darmstadt orchestras, and am assuredly more disposed than anyone to render full justice to the talents—some of them very distinguished—of the members of these three orchestras; but, to come to the point, whatever may be said to the contrary, it is acknowledged, even by the testimony of my adversaries, that the execution was at times astonishing, and altogether better *than there had been reason to expect*, considering that I was conductor.

This *fact* placed beyond discussion, it remains to be seen whether I am so completely a stranger there as they try to make out, and what reasons there can be for thus crying down a conductor when the execution was satisfactory, especially if, as is just, one bears in mind the novelty of the works on the program for almost the entire audience. For, as everyone knew at Karlsruhe, the Ninth Symphony, as well as the works of Wagner, Berlioz, Schumann, etc., were not well known by anyone but myself, seeing that they had never been given before in these parts.

Now as regards the question of *right*—to know whether in good conscience and with knowledge of the matter one can justly accuse me of being an insufficient conductor, inexperienced, uncertain, etc.: without endeavoring to exculpate myself (for which I do not think there is any need amongst those who understand me), may I be permitted to make an observation bearing on the basis of the question?

The works for which I openly confess my admiration and predilection are for the most part amongst those which conductors more or less renowned (especially the so-called qualified [tüchtigen] Kapellmeistern) have honored but little, or not at all, with their personal sympathies, so much so that it has rarely happened that they have performed them. These works, reckoning from those which are commonly described nowadays as belonging to Beethoven's *last style* (and which were, not long ago, with lack of reverence, explained by Beethoven's deafness and mental derangement!)—these works, to my thinking, exact from executants and orchestras a *progress* which is being accomplished at this moment but which is far from being realized in all places in accentuation, in rhythm, in the manner of phrasing and declaiming certain passages, and of distributing light and shade—in a word, *progress* in the style of the execution itself. They establish, between the musicians of the desks and the *musician chief* who directs them, a link of a nature other than that which is cemented by an imperturbable beating of the time. In many cases even the rough, literal maintenance of the time and of each continuous bar—1, 2, 3, 4 / 1, 2, 3, 4—clashes with the sense and expression. There, as elsewhere, *the letter kills the spirit*, a thing to which I will never subscribe, however specious in their hypocritical impartiality may be the attacks to which I am exposed.

For the works of Beethoven, Berlioz, Wagner, etc., I see less than elsewhere what advantage there could be in a conductor trying to go through his work like a sort of *windmill*, and to get into a great perspiration in order to give warmth to the others. Especially where it is a question of understanding and feeling, of impressing oneself with intelligence, of kindling hearts with a sort of communion of the beautiful, the grand, and the true in Art and Poetry, the *sufficiency* and the old routine of usual conductors no longer *suffice*, and are even contrary to the dignity and the sublime liberty of the art. Thus, with all due deference to my complaisant critics, I shall hold myself on every occasion ulterior to my 'insufficiency' on principle and by conviction, for I will never accommodate myself to the role of a [dictator] of time, for which my twenty-five years of experience, study, and sincere passion for Art would not at all fit me.

Whatever esteem therefore I may profess for many of my colleagues, and however gladly I may recognize the good services they have rendered and continue to render to Art, I do not think myself on that account obliged to follow their example in every particular—neither in the choice of works to be performed, nor in the manner of conceiving and conducting them. I think I have already said to you that the real task of a conductor, according to my opinion, consists in making himself *ostensibly quasi*-useless. We are pilots, and not mechanics. Well, even if this idea should meet with still further opposition in detail, I could not change it, as I consider it just. For the Weimar orchestra its application has brought about excellent results, which have been commended by some of my very critics of today. I will therefore continue, without discouragement or false modesty, to serve Art in the best way that I understand it—which, I hope, will be the best.[45]

45. Letter to Richard Pohl, Weimar, November 5, 1853.

1855

The Mass will not take up an excessively long time, either in performance or studying. But it is indispensable that I should conduct the general rehearsal as well as the performance myself; for the work cannot be ranked among those in which ordinary singing, playing, and arrangement will suffice. It is a matter of some not usual trifles in the way of accent, devotion, inspiration, etc.[46]

46. Letter to Edmund Singer, August 1, 1855.

1856

The manner in which you have given an account in the *Presse* of the two concerts corresponds entirely with the opinion which I had of you—and you have proved yourself on this occasion [Mozart Jubilee concerts, conducted by Liszt], according to your custom, an eminent critic and a perfect gentleman.[47]

47. Letter to Eduard Hanslick, January 31, 1856.

Opinion, public and press, are quite unanimously favorable toward [your Franz] - notwithstanding the feeling against him for his refusal to play the piano (something no one cares to understand, and about which 'admirable' and unadmirable friends bore him from morn to eve) notwithstanding also the skeptical attitude, at the very least, concerning his capacity as an orchestral conductor, which he met upon his arrival here. This attitude displayed rather disagreeable nuances right up to the last minute in several of the personnel with whom it was a question of conducting; and it caused scarcely restrainable agitation to our friend Löwy.[48]

48. Letter to Marie zu Sayn-Wittgenstein, Vienna, January 31, 1856.

1857

The result of the choice of myself as conductor of the Musical Festival at Aix-la-Chapelle this year is a welcome sign to me of the gradual recognition which an open and honestly expressed, consistent, and thoroughly disinterested conviction may meet with in different places ...

I think there is no need for me to accentuate the fact that a musical conductor cannot blindly subscribe to just every program that is put before him.[49]

49. Letter to Herr von Turanyi, Weimar, January 3, 1857.

About the 15th of May I shall be going to Aix-la-Chapelle, to conduct the Musical Festival there at Whitsuntide. That will be another good opportunity for many papers to abuse me, and to let off their bile![50]

50. Letter to Eduard Liszt, Weimar, April 27, 1857.

Things look promising and are going well here—and Suermondt assures me that my adversaries of a week ago admit themselves to be completely beaten and in the process of conversion.[51]

51. Letter to Marie zu Sayn-Wittgenstein, Aix-la-Chapelle, May 30, 1857.

H. wrote to you about the Aix Musical Festival, which, upon the whole, was satisfactory, both in arrangement and execution, although our friend Hiller may demonstrate in the *Köln Gazette* that I have no talent either as a conductor or a composer.[52]

52. Letter to Wagner, Weimar, June 9, 1857.

1859

I will willingly do something to help—as, for instance, to undertake the conducting of the *Prometheus*. I would rather not let myself in for much more than that, because conducting in general becomes more burdensome to me every year,and I don't in the least desire to offer further active resistance to the ill-repute with which I am credited as a conductor. Indeed I owe my friend Dingelstedt many thanks for having (without perhaps exactly desiring to do so) given me the chance of freeing myself from the operatic time-beating here, and I am firmly resolved not to wield the baton elsewhere except in the most unavoidable cases![53]

53. Letter to Franz Brendel, Weimar, September 2, 1859.

I require my whole time for my further works, which must go on incessantly—consequently I have resolved to keep at a distance all the *delights* of conductorship, and to give the baton a rest equally with the piano.[54]

54. Letter to Felix Draseke, Weimar, October 20, 1859.

1860

I am quietly waiting for the spring, when I shall in all probability move on further of course not to renew my occupation of conducting, as it is said I shall do in Munich, Berlin, or elsewhere—an occupation I have gladly given up;—but in order to be able to pursue my work further than I am able to do in Weimar, which to me is a more important matter.[55]

55. Letter to Friedrich Hebbel, Weimar, February 5, 1860.

With regard to the performance I have at once mentioned decidedly that *nothing* will induce me to make an exception and conduct it.[56]

56. Letter to Franz Brendel, Weimar, November 16, 1860.

1862

In spite of the unsatisfactory performance of the *Dante Symphony* in Dresden (partly, moreover, the fault of the bad, incorrectly written orchestral parts, and my careless conducting), and without regard to the rapture of the *spiritual* substance (a matter which the general public tolerates only when demanded by the higher authority of *tradition*, and then immediately gapes at it upside down!) ...[57]

57. Letter to Franz Brendel, Rome, August 29, 1862.

1867

Herbeck would be an excellent one to arrange and conduct these concerts, provided he were not too much afraid of the obligations due to criticism. My personal position will not permit of my taking any part in them as a conductor; nevertheless I should not care to be altogether idle on the occasion, and hence should like, first of all, to have a careful discussion with Herbeck about various points that must absolutely be given *thus* and in no other way.[58]

58. Letter to Eduard Liszt, Munich, October 16, 1867.

1868

Present my most gracious thanks to the Committee of the 'Musikfreunde,' with the request that they will in future regard me as quite *inadmissible* as a conductor.[59]

59. Letter to Johann von Herbeck, Rome, December 29, 1868.

1871

I have been urged to conduct the *Weihnachts Oratorium*; but I would sooner call off the performance than yield on this point.[60]

60. Letter to Olga von Meyendorff, Budapest, December 1, 1871.

1879

Bösendorfer called on me yesterday and told me of the intention of the Vienna Friends of Music to perform the *Gran Mass* at the end of March. If Bösendorfer's intimations are correct I am not disinclined to conduct this performance, although for many years I have refused all such invitations. I should be rejoiced if at last the *Gran Mass* had a fair hearing in Vienna.[61]

61. Letter to Eduard Liszt, Budapest, January 22, 1879.

1880

Should any work of mine have been admitted to your -program, I would fain request Peter Benoit to conduct it, since for the last fifteen years I have declared myself unfit for this work in all countries.[62]

62. Letter to the Committee of the Antwerp Musical Society, Villa d'Este, November 16, 1880.

1883

At the Musical Festival which I had the honor of conducting some twenty-five years ago at Aix-la-Chapelle, Hiller, the friend of my young days in Paris, took up quite a critical attitude against the conductor and his compositions.

I took no particular notice of his behavior, but I heard that it displeased many people, who made no secret of it to him. I was also told that at one of the rehearsals Hiller did not exactly leave of his own accord.[63]

63. Letter to Otto Lessmann, Weimar, October 14, 1883.

As Teacher

1829

I am so full of lessons that each day, from half-past eight in the morning till ten at night, I have scarcely breathing time. I don't write you a longer letter, for there is a pupil who has been waiting for me for an hour.[64]

64. Letter to M. de Mancy, December 23, 1829.

1831

I have my pupils go into the selections in depth, so that often one lesson is spent studying two pages.

Give all that you feel and do not encumber your touch ... Be patient with yourself. You ruin everything if you wish to hasten; calmly take each step in turn to be certain of reaching the top; be patient; nature itself works slowly. Follow its example. Your efforts, led wisely, will be honored with success, but if you want to acquire everything too quickly, you would lose time and fail.[65]

65. Comments of Liszt noted in the lesson diary of Mme. Auguste Boissier, 1831–1832, in Elyse Mach, *The Liszt Studies* (New York: Associated Music Publishers, 1973), xiff.

1842

It is in vain for me to attempt to express to you the deep and heartfelt emotion you have aroused in me by your rare mark of honor. The honorable name of *Teacher* of Music (and I refer to music in its grand, complete, and ancient-signification), by which you esteemed gentlemen, dignify me, I am well aware that I have undertaken the duty of unceasing *learning* and untiring labor.[66]

66. Letter to the Faculty of Philosophy, University of Königsberg, Mittau, March 18, 1842.

1856

Don't forget to let me have your *Method*. Although I have grown too old and too lazy to improve my piano playing, yet I will get some good out of it for my pupils, amongst whom are two or three really brave, earnest fellows.[67]

67. Letter to Louis Köhler, Weimar, May 24, 1856.

Your X is a perfect madman, and I should certainly not advise you to have anything to do with a man like him. He asked me to attend a vocal practice of his pupils, when the poor people had to shout nothing, but four or five notes do, de, da! X has entirely surrendered himself to his monomania of method, which to him has become a kind of dram-drinking.[68]

68. Letter to Wagner, Munich, December 25, 1856.

1872

Bülow's edition of Beethoven outweighs in the matter of instruction a dozen Conservatories.[69]

69. Letter to Otto Lessmann, Eisenach, September 26, 1872.

1874

It would be a poor luxury to add a third music school to the two schools already existing (meagerly) at Budapest. If one cannot emulate with honor the similar establishments of Vienna, Leipzig, etc.—what is the good of troubling any further about it? Now, to give a vigorous impulse to Art among us, we must first unite and fuse into one spirit a set of professors of well-known capability,—a very arduous and ungrateful task, the accomplishment of which demands much intelligence, and a sufficient amount of cleverness and of money.[70]

70. Letter to Edmund von Mihalovich, Villa d'Este, December 8, 1874.

1876

On March 2 I shall start my course of piano lessons with eight or ten pupils of both sexes.[71]

71. Letter to Olga von Meyendorff, Budapest, February 20, 1876.

I shall remain here quietly until mid-March, teaching a dozen pianists of both sexes at the new Academy of Music. Part of my instruction consists of telling them that several hundred of their profession are already 'in excess' in this world of 'concerts' and harmony trimmed with dissonance.[72]

72. Letter to Marie zu Sayn-Wittgenstein, Budapest, November 20, 1876.

1877

Four times weekly I have a class for pianists and *pianistes*, native and foreign. Half a dozen of these distinguish themselves and will be able to grow into capable public artists. Unfortunately there are far too many concerts and concert-players. As Dingelstedt quite truly said, 'The theater is a necessary evil, the concert a superfluous one.' I am trying to impress this sentence on my disciples of the Hungarian Academy of Music.[73]

73. Letter to Eduard Liszt, Budapest, January 2, 1877.

Mme Schumann having in the past been so kind as to play this transcription [*Prelude and Fugue* in A minor] in public, it has been accepted as tolerable, even in the conservatories of the pure conservatories where my name is excluded, and is considered an insult to sound doctrine.[74]

74. Letter to Olga von Meyendorff, Hanover, May 20, 1877.

The work best praises the Master: in like manner do the pupils, when preparing themselves for pre-eminence, praise their teacher.[75]

75. Letter to Kornel von Abrányi, Weimar, July 28, 1877.

My chief occupation here is teaching the piano to about fifteen people, of whom seven or eight already show remarkable talent; let me name M. de Rossel who comes from Kharkov, as did Joseph Rubinstein five years ago; M. Roth, a pupil of Reinecke and several times a prize winner at Leipzig; two Hungarians, Juhary and Agghazy. This whole young generation will be far more deserving than the two preceding ones to which I belong, while at the same time facing more obstacles than these on the road to fame and – to box office receipts. So I do not fail to repeat clearly to young pianists that most of them are superfluous, and that only male and female singers for opera are in demand and hence well paid.[76]

76. Letter to Olga von Meyendorff, Budapest, December 9, 1877.

1878

My three pianists whom you saw at Weimar, MM. Roth, Pohlig, Brunner, are hard at work here. I give them my brief instructions in the *Sala Dante*. In my rooms in the Via de' Greci I wish neither to see nor hear any piano.[77]

77. Letter to Olga von Meyendorff, Rome, October 23, 1878.

1879

Your *Paraphrases* charm me: nothing can be more ingenious than these 24 Variations and the 16 little pieces. In short, here we have an admirable compendium of the science of harmony, of counterpoint, of rhythms, of figuration, and 'The Theory of Form!' I shall gladly suggest to the teachers of composition at all the Conservatoires in Europe and America to adopt your *Paraphrases* as a practical guide in their teaching.[78]

78. Letter to Borodin, Cui, Liadoff, and Rimsky-Korsakoff, Weimar, June 15, 1879.

1880

My pianists (of both sexes) come here three times a week for their treatment. There are ten or twelve, of whom a third are making good progress.[79]

79. Letter to Olga von Meyendorff, Budapest, January 22, 1880.

1885

With regret, and a firm conviction, I repeat to you in writing that Kheodor Kullak's forgetfulness ought to be made good by his heirs. Otherwise it would be severely denounced as unfaithfulness to his position as an artist. A fortune of several millions gained by music teaching ought not to remain buried without any regard to music students. Unless the heirs prefer to found a Kullak Scholarship, I consider that they are in duty bound to endow the four existing musical scholarships—those in the names of Mozart, Mendelssohn, Meyerbeer, Beethoven—with 30,000 marks each.[80]

80. Letter to the Editor of the *Allgemeine Musik-Zeitung,* Weimar, September 5, 1885

1886

I spend a couple of hours a day with my students.[81]

81. Letter to Olga von Meyendorff, Budapest, February 24, 1886.

Chapter Three

Insights into Liszt's General Outlook on Life

1832

Earthly life is but a malady of the soul, an excitement which is kept up by the passions. The natural state of the soul is rest![1]

1. Letter to Pierre Wölff, Paris, May 2, 1832.

1851

It is the fate of human joys—to swim constantly in a sea of misery and suffering …

Behold how good intentions facilitate follies.[2]

2. Letter to Marie zu Sayn-Wittgenstein, Weimar, February 8, 1851.

1852

The fame or success that crowns talent or genius is partly owing to fortunate circumstances. Lasting triumphs are, in truth, seldom unfair. Since justice, however, is possibly the rarest quality of the human mind, it happens that some artists achieve success within, others outside the confines of, their true worth. It is well known that in the ebb and flow of the tides, a tenth wave comes that is stronger than the others; so it is in the world—there are men, swept along by this tenth wave of fortune, who go higher and farther than others who may be their equals or even their superiors.

……

In the bustling, preoccupied world of great cities, where no one has leisure to guess the riddle of another's destiny, surely very few think it worth while to explore beneath the surface of personal traits.

……

A natural curiosity centers around the lives of men who have dedicated great talents to the glorification of noble feelings in works of art where they shine like resplendent meteors before the amazed and delighted throng. The crowd willingly associates the admiring, sympathetic impressions thus awakened with their names, which it would promptly accept as a symbol of nobleness and greatness. It is tempting to believe that those who can so eloquently express and voice these sentiments must know no others. But this kindly prejudice and favorable presumption need to be justified by those to whom they apply and to be supported by their lives. When in his work the poet's heart is caught reacting, with such exquisite delicacy, to sweet inspiration, divining in a flash of intuition what is veiled by pride or timid modesty or vexing bitterness, caught painting the love of youthful dreams and of later desperation—when his genius is observed mastering such grand situations, rising calmly above all the vicissitudes of human destiny, finding in the entanglement of its unsolvable knots the threads that triumphantly and proudly free it, soaring above all manner of grandeur and disaster, climbing toward the summits that others no longer reach—when he is known to hold the secret of the most subtle shades of tenderness and the most imposing forms of stark courage—how evade the question: Is this marvelous insight the miracle of a deep belief in these feelings or is it a clever abstraction of thought and a play of the mind?

How can the query be avoided: In what way have these men, so in love with the beautiful, made their lives different from those of ordinary beings? How was that poetic splendor maintained as it struggled with the realities and material interests of life? To what extent were those ineffable emotions of love actually independent of the usually poisonous mildews and acerbities? To what extent were they protected from that frivolity and inconstancy that lead to their neglect? Other queries: Were they always just who felt such righteous indignation? Those who exalted integrity, did they never traffic with their conscience? Were those who sang of honor never timorous? Were those who vaunted bravery never compromised by their weakness?

There are many eager to know the relationships between honor, loyalty, and fineness, and the gains and advantages only won at their expense, which are admitted by those entrusted with the noble task of sustaining our faith and affection for great and lofty feelings by giving them life in art when they had no refuge elsewhere. For many, a denial of these relationships would be impossible or foolish. Thus when some unfortunate examples lend their words a lamentable support, how promptly do they call the poet's loveliest conceptions vain deceits! what wisdom they flaunt in preaching doctrines, knowingly premeditated, of a honeyed and ruthless hypocrisy, of a continual and hidden contradiction between words and actions! With what cruel joy do they cite these examples to weak and disturbed souls whose youthful aspirations (or dwindling forces and convictions) still endeavor to elude these mournful compacts! What fatal depression seizes these latter before the harsh alternatives and beguiling interventions encountered at every turn on the road of life! They are persuaded that hearts most passionately enamored of sublimity, most skilled in delicate susceptibilities, most affected by the beauties of simplicity have, nevertheless, by their acts, denied the objects of their worship and their song! What agonizing doubts must grasp and consume them as they face these flagrant contradictions! And what mockery is showered upon their sufferings by those who repeat: *Poetry is that which might have been*—and who rejoice to blaspheme it by this guilty negation! For Poetry is no mere shadow of our Imagination, cast and magnified beyond measure on that soaring plane of the Impossible; for 'Poetry and Reality' are not two incompatible elements destined to brush each other and never join together: so the opinion of Goethe, who said of a contemporary poet that 'having lived to create poems, he had made a poem of his life.' Goethe himself was too much a poet not to realize that Poetry exists only because it finds its eternal Reality in the finest instincts of a human heart.

......

Evil is contagious, but good is fertile![3]

3. Franz Liszt, *Chopin*, 1852.

1853

Work is the only salvation on this earth. Sing and write, therefore, and get rid of your brain abscess by that means. Perhaps your sleep will become a little more reposeful in the same manner.[4]

4. Letter to Richard Wagner, October 31, 1853.

1854

I have learned to understand people, although the real kernel of their phrases has not been, and cannot be, clearly expressed. I have seen too much of this to be deceived.[5]

5. Letter to Richard Wagner, June 8, 1854.

Philosophic formulas are sometimes the envelope, the outside shell, as it were, of knowledge; but it may also happen that they only show empty ideas, and contain no other substance than their own harsh terminology. To demonstrate the rose by the ferule may seem a very scientific proceeding to vulgar pedants; for my part it is not to my taste[6]

6. Letter to Franz Brendel, Weimar, August 12, 1854.

1855

Like loving gifts of a nature infinitely exalted above his own, like traces within himself of elements that lie without him, man carries in his mind the concepts *eternity* and *nonexistence*. Kant first observed the enigmatic contradiction with which the mind, capable of grasping neither the one nor the other, accepts them both. These concepts constitute the two opposite poles of the axis about which man revolves, the idea of existence without beginning or end, and that of nonexistence. Ceaselessly he circles about these two points of reference, inclining now toward the one, now toward the other, shrinking back from the thought of annihilation, horrified by the thought of the immutable. Man's whole environment is but end and beginning, life after death and death before life. Nevertheless he is seized instinctively and inexplicably with an aversion to the weaknesses of all beginnings, to the painful character of every end, while a no less instinctive and inexplicable impulse urges him to destroy in order to re-create. Experiencing disgust once he has reached the saturation point and provoked to desire by his eagerness for novelty, he feels himself impelled in perpetual alternation by an innate and sovereign longing for a satisfaction to which he cannot give a name, but which every change seems to promise him. From the struggle between these two exertions arise conflict and sorrow, our common, inevitable lot.[7]

7. "Berlioz and his ‚Harold' Symphony, *Neue Zeitschrift für Musik* [1855] XLIII

1857

There are so many *demi*,-people, and *demi*-clever people (who are at least as dangerous to Art as the *demi-monde* is to morals, according to Alexandre Dumas), who say such *utter* stupidities about me in the papers and elsewhere, that I really should not like to die yet, if only not to disturb their beautiful business.[8]

8. Letter to Wilhelm von Lenz, Weimar, March 24, 1857.

At dinner we talked about a lot of things, and of Kaulbach among others; nothing was said worth the trouble of remembering, which is usually the case in society.[9]

9. Letter to Marie zu Sayn-Wittgenstein, Aix-la-Chapelle, July 26, 1857.

1858

The rest of the world reminds me of Bedlam broken loose; and God help me to know as little about it as possible.[10]

10. Letter to Marie zu Sayn-Wittgenstein, Prague, April 20, 1858.

1859

Alas I we are miserable creatures, and the few who have penetrated the deepest secrets of life are the most miserable of all. That snarling old cur, Schopenhauer, is quite right in saying that we are ridiculous in addressing each other as *Monsieur* or citizen. *Compagnon de misere et de souffrance*, or fellow-sufferers, and worse we are, *tutti quanti,* and nothing we can do can make any essential change in this. The worst is that we know it quite well, and yet never like to believe it.[11]

11. Letter to Wagner, Weimar, August 22, 1859.

I don't care to go on any further with these mortuary details—It is not for death to absorb life—but rather for us to *conquer death!*[12]

12. Letter to Marie zu Sayn-Wittgenstein, Weimar, December 26, 1859.

1871

A witty woman defined forgiveness as 'a form of contempt': I am far from treating it thus, and feel that it must be free of all presumptuousness and arrogance, thus retaining only Christian humility and gentleness.[13]

13. Letter to Olga von Meyendorff, April 9, 1871.

During the journey from Eisenach to Wilhelmsthal, I read some forty pages of the *Commentaire sur l'Evangile* by Gratry, which you had recommended to me. There are some beautiful and gentle things in it, nobly expressed. I found, scored with your fingernail: 'gentleness is the fullness of strength'—a luminous aphorism, which should not be pressed too far in order not to spoil it. Prosaically speaking, true strength is accompanied by gentleness, just as true justice leans toward mercy. Truly great men are those who combine contrary qualities within themselves. You will find this thought vigorously expressed in Pascal: 'I do not admire a man who has only great qualities if he does not at the same time have contrary qualities,' etc. (I am not quoting the exact words, but the idea.) Indeed, we know by experience that gentleness without strength degenerates into weakness, justice without mercy into harshness and cruelty, and every gift, every quality, every virtue without charity becomes sterile!

Moreover, Father Gratry seems to me greatly to exaggerate the possibility of the immediate effect of Christianity on the peoples of Europe, and I do not really believe as he does that at the burning words of a 'small number of men, the crowd, a heroic and simple mass, would follow the call as it did for the crusades.' In my humble view the great results of our time are achieved principally through work and organization. This is slower and strewn with more difficulties than the enthusiastic approach which has unfortunately shown itself to be powerless in many circumstances, starting with the crusades themselves![14]

14. Letter to Olga von Meyendorff, August 13, 1871.

1872

It would be very bad taste, to say the least, to repudiate my superlative attachment to Napoleon III. As for Henry V, I have, not seen him since 1826 or 1827, when I had to honor of performing my little tricks as a little pianist at the house of the Duchess de Berry and of Mme de La Bouillerie.[15]

15. Letter to Olga von Meyendorff, Budapest, March 8, 1872.

The complete fiasco of my political ramblings makes me feel quite sheepish; I promise you that I shall not again expose myself to a repetition.[16]

16. Letter to Olga von Meyendorff, Budapest, March 20, 1872.

Some one well said to me: 'Words seem to me to intercept feeling rather than to express it; and actions, alas! seem to me sometimes like a thick veil thrown over our soul: looks even seem to be trammeled by phantom barriers, and souls which seek one another across the sufferings of life only find one another—such is my belief - in prayer and in music.'[17]

17. Letter to Wilhelm von Lenz, Weimar, September 20, 1872.

Napoleon III is dead! A great soul, an all-embracing intelligence, experienced in the wisdom of life, a gentle and noble character - with a disastrous fate! He was a bound and gagged Caesar, but still closely related to the Divine Caesar who was the ideal embodiment of earthly power. He has set noble examples, and accomplished or undertaken great deeds: amnesties which were more complete under him than under other governments; the protection of the Church in Rome and in other countries; the rejuvenation of Paris and other great cities in France; the Crimean war and the Italian war; the great Paris Exhibition, and the rise of local exhibitions; the earnest attention paid to the lot and the interests of the country people, and of the working classes; the generosity and encouragement to scholars and artists,—all these things are historical facts, and are things in which the Emperor took the initiative, and which he carried out in spite of all the difficulties that stood in his way. It can be affirmed without adulation that throughout life the Emperor unswervingly practiced those great virtues which are in reality one and the same thing and are known by the names of benevolence, goodness, generosity, nobility of mind, love of splendor and munificence.[18]

18. Letter to Eduard Liszt, Horpacs, November 6, 1872.

1873

The best advice usually suffers from being quite useless. It comes either too late or too early, and any pretext serves not to follow it …

One should ignore comments by members of the household. It is better to suffer than to demean oneself.[19]

19. Letter to Olga von Meyendorff, Rome, October 9, 1873.

1874

I recite every morning and evening: 'Forgive us our trespasses as we forgive those who trespass against us.' This prayer renders unnecessary much argumentation and redundancy.[20]

20. Letter to Olga von Meyendorff, Horpacs, January 31, 1874.

'Do good, and let others talk' certainly applies to our time, when a frightening epidemic of useless, evil words—spoken, printed and repeated—rages about us.[21]

21. Letter to Marie zu Sayn-Wittgenstein, Budapest, February 27, 1874.

There are moral sufferings which call for more radical treatment than physical illness. To swerve off course at the key point means losing all.[22]

22. Letter to Olga von Meyendorff, Budapest, April 15, 1874.

To complain is miserable; to arouse pity, ridiculous.[23]

23. Letter to Olga von Meyendorff, Budapest, April 27, 1874.

I must not answer the key point in your last letter, for were I to do so it would probably be in a most unreasonable manner; so let us continue to talk about minor matters; all together they make up roughly two-thirds of life; to neglect them is a fault which does harm.[24]

24. Letter to Olga von Meyendorff, Budapest, May 6, 1874.

As in the case of the military, marriage should be forbidden to artists and men of letters so long as their income cannot provide regular sustenance for their wives and children.[25]

25. Letter to Olga von Meyendorff, Rome, October 17, 1874.

It is better to do nothing than to do stupidities.[26]

26. Letter to Albert Apponyi, Villa d'Este, December 6, 1874.

1875

They say about eloquence, that it is as much a part of the listener as it is of the speaker. The same, and even more, holds true for music.[27]

27. Letter to Marie zu Sayn-Wittgenstein, Rome, February 1, 1875

There is nothing more appropriate than to mingle with that high society to which you belong. Its faults and failings are not basically different from those of other levels of society. They come from human nature, which is everywhere much the same and imperfect. A little girl from a bourgeois family could have been just as astonished as was the daughter of Louis XVI at the fact that her maid had, like her, five fingers on her hand.[28]

28. Letter to Olga von Meyendorff, Rome, October 17, 1875.

To heal certain sores, it is better to be silent than to babble.[29]

29. Letter to Marie zu Sayn-Wittgenstein, Villa d'Este, November 9, 1875.

1876

All his life this poor FL has constantly been scolded, lectured, counseled, reprimanded, denounced. Sick persons have, on many occasions, proved to him that he was neglecting his health, though he was well; and people who were ruining themselves have triumphantly demonstrated to him that he understood nothing about his business interests, even though he has never owed a penny to anyone. He has, willy-nilly, had to learn that most of the time the best arguments are superfluous, and that of all faults, that of being right is the least excusable.[30]

30. Letter to Olga von Meyendorff, Budapest, March 1, 1876.

No one is bound by the impossible.[31]

31. Letter to Camille Saint-Saëns, Hanover, October 2, 1876.

1877

I like mutes when it's a matter of giving advice: they do not impair accuracy of pitch, and, save for exceptional cases, it is better to be restrained rather than noisy.[32]

32. Letter to Olga von Meyendorff, Budapest, February 12, 1877.

I don't know who said: 'Were it not for me, I would be in very good health.' Were it not for the moi, which Pascal denounced as hateful, and which to me seems to be chiefly a nuisance to each of us, one would also be fairly happy in this world of ours.[33]

33. Letter to Olga von Meyendorff, Budapest, February 23, 1877.

The most enviable prerogative of sovereigns is that of exercising the right of grace, not only toward the guilty but also to honor good people endowed with superior talent.[34]

34. Letter to Olga von Meyendorff, Budapest, December 16, 1877.

1878

Some truths just can't be expressed in dulcet tones. 'Be angry, but sin not,' says St. Paul.[35]

35. Letter to Olga von Meyendorff, Budapest, January 19, l878.

Those who live ought to prepare themselves for dying, and accustom themselves to seeing others die,—young and old.[36]

36. Letter to Marie zu Sayn-Wittgenstein, Budapest, March 12, 1878.

Self-centeredness is a wrong attitude; while it keeps very fine company, it does not suit fine natures.[37]

37. Letter to Olga von Meyendorff, Villa d'Este, September 22, 1878.

1879

The world here below is much like a hospital in which the doctors themselves are sick.[38]

38. Letter to Olga von Meyendorff, Rome, November 30, 1879.

1880

One must know how to wither on the vine without thereby losing one's faculties.[39]

39. Letter to Olga von Meyendorff, Budapest, February 1, 1880.

Among the best lines arising out of Moliere's wonderful genius, is: 'A plague on misers and those who are stingy!'[40]

40. Letter to Marie zu Sayn-Wittgenstein, Weimar, May 12, 1880.

Chance always plays a great part in any success.[41]

41. Letter to Marie zu Sayn-Wittgenstein, Weimar, July 30, 1880.

To go slow is the essence of the wisdom of rulers.[42]

42. Letter to Olga von Meyendorff, Villa d'Este, October 12, 1880.

1881

Small towns have but small successes to offer.[43]

43. Letter to Francois Gevaert, Weimar, September 19, 1881.

Not that I incline toward the wisdom of stoical non-involvement. I admire its [the writings of Marcus Aurelius] heroic aspect but do not feel up to practicing it sincerely. Pain is not to me the same thing as pleasure, or even peaceful absence of suffering. Everything passes, as we well know, but until this happens one is either at ease or ill at ease. As for a certain contempt of things and men, I only understand this within very narrow limits, beginning with one's self; but the gentle and wise Marcus Aurelius seems to me to have uttered a truly imperial stupidity in counseling us to divide up each thing in our thoughts so as to become imbued with the emptiness of everything. To reduce music to single sounds, to isolate the features of a beloved person, is this to philosophize? Away with this method; let us look for the whole, the harmony. It is there we will find beauty and truth.[44]

44. Letter to Olga von Meyendorff, Rome, November 29, 1881.

1882

Please tell me in your next letter what penalty Schopenhauer intends to substitute for the abominable social crime of the death penalty. It is obvious that we are all more or less guilty, deranged, or crazy, but it does not follow that we ought to be guillotined, hanged, or, as an act of mercy, shot.[45]

45. Letter to Olga von Meyendorff, Florence, January 29, 1882.

Shorn of moral law and its practice, life is but a sad delusion.[46]

46. Letter to Olga von Meyendorff, Budapest, March 11, 1882.

1883

Heroism exists here below and in a great many ways even in the lower strata of society. Not to recognize this amounts to impertinent stupidity.[47]

47. Letter to Olga von Meyendorff, Venice, January 7, 1883.

Ever since the days of my youth I have considered dying much simpler than living. Even if often there is fearful and protracted suffering before death, yet is death none the less the deliverance from our involuntary yoke of existence.[48]

48. Letter to Lina Ramann, Budapest, February 22, 1883.

1884

Marriages, births, troubles, pleasures, vanities, a thousand things, and halves and quarters of things, errors and miseries are the lot of human life so long as it does not steep itself in abnegation and in the infinity of divine love.[49]

49. Letter to Olga von Meyendorff, Budapest, February 5, 1884.

Ideals

1851

'Remain true to yourself!' Remain true to all you feel to be highest, noblest, most right and most pure in your heart! Don't ever try to be or to become *something* (unless there were opportune and immediate occasion for it), but work diligently and with perseverance to be and to become more and more *some one*.[50]

50. Letter to Eduard Liszt, Weimar, undated, c. 1851.

1852

My aspirations are directed towards acquiring a durable position in the History of Art.[51]

51. A statement Liszt recalled, in a letter to Henriette Liszt, Weimar, May 11, 1882, as having made at this time.

1857

In business always look for the most *precise*, the most *detailed* and the most noble elements.[52]

52. Letter to Marie zu Sayn-Wittgenstein, Aachen, July 28, 1857.

You may safely expect various disagreeables which are inseparable from musical work. The great thing is to remain cheerful, and to do something worth doing. The cuckoo take the rest![53]

53. Letter to Carl Haslinger, Weimar, December 5, 1857.

1859

It is only with high-minded, brave, and trusty comrades that we move forward, no matter though the number remain small. In matters of intelligence the majority always follows the minority, when the latter is sufficiently strong to hold its own.[54]

54. Letter to Louis Kohler, Weimar, September 3, 1859.

1860

Certainly it is always the *gentlemanly* thing entirely to ignore certain things and people.[55]

55. Letter to Franz Brendel, Weimar, January 25, 1860.

1864

He who endures little will not endure long![56]

56. Letter to Eduard Liszt, Rome, June 22, 1864.

1867

I give you my best wishes that you may happily pursue this noble career of an artist, with work, perseverance, resignation, modesty, and the imperturbable faith in the *Ideal*.[57]

57. Letter to William Mason, Rome, July 8, 1867.

1868

The world is so formed that the practice of the Good and the search for the Better is not made agreeable to anyone; not in the things of Art, which appear the most inoffensive, any more than in other things. In order to deserve well one must learn to endure well. The best specific for the prejudice, malice, imbroglios and injustice of others is not to trouble oneself about them. It seems that such and such people find their pleasure where we should not in the least look for it: so be it, reserving to ourselves to find ours in nobler sources. Besides, how could we dare to lament over difficulties that run counter to our good pleasure? Have not the worthiest and most illustrious servants of Art had to suffer far more than we? This consolation has its melancholy side, I know; nevertheless it confirms the active conscience in the right road.[58]

58. Letter to Jessie Laussot, Rome, January 13, 1868.

Courage is the vital nerve of our best qualities; they fade away when it is wanting, and unless one is courageous one is not even sufficiently prudent. To examine, reflect calculate and weigh are assuredly necessary operations. But after that one must determine and act without troubling too much about which way the wind blows and what clouds are passing.[59]

59. Letter to Richard Fohl, Rome, November 11, 1868.

1873

Failures will not do you any great harm, provided that you know how to keep that attachment to work, and that perseverance in noble ideas, which are the chief heirloom of the artist.[60]

60. Letter to Franz Servais, Weimar, August 19, 1873.

One need only live simply and in a Christian manner; never to be either a dupe or a rogue.[61]

61. Letter to Olga von Meyendorff, December 13, 1873.

1875

Berlioz used to take offense when people assumed that he listened to Beethoven's sublime last quartets 'for his own pleasure.' Nor is it for the sake of pleasure that one goes on living. However, Frederick the Great seems to have found the clue to the riddle when he said: 'One must find one's pleasure in doing one's duty.' One can philosophize and quibble about this; for, if duty is easy to define in the case of tradesmen, innkeepers, and the man in the street, it sometimes becomes hard to define within ourselves, since it also implies rights. Now this equilibrium between rights and duties remains the philosopher's stone of the human species, which only the catechism leads to heavenly salvation, and to relative rest, in this earthly life.[62]

62. Letter to Olga von Meyendorff, Wilhelmsthal, July 27, 1875.

As in the case of great thoughts, true nobility springs from the heart.[63]

63. Letter to Olga von Meyendorff, Rome, October 17, 1875.

Even more than cleanliness, kindness is a duty.[64]

64. Letter to Olga von Meyendorff, Villa d'Este, October 24, 1875.

1878

It is a good thing to attach oneself to good causes, whether favored by the gods or not.[65]

65. Letter to Jessie Laussot, Budapest, February 3, 1878.

1880

Thank you for having sent me your comments on the feverish and relentless boredom of the salons. Caro quotes most pertinently Pascal's thought which says in brief that you don't escape from yourself by vainly seeking the company of others. Indeed, what is to become of one on this earth if one ceases praying and loving with the least possible egoism? Otherwise, to brief illusions are added disillusions; and these last, and are not dispelled by social talents.[66]

66. Letter to Olga von Meyendorff, November 2, 1880.

1881

I go on writing—not without fatigue—from inner necessity and old habit. We are not forbidden to aspire towards higher things: it is the attainment of our end which remains the note of interrogation.[67]

67. Letter to Camille Salnt-Saëns, Rome, December 12, 1881.

Mankind

1835

You know how men are lacking in noble and generous sentiments, and how they make the most of their own ignoble ends and interests, to which their words and actions yet give the lie.[68]

68. Letter to Abbe de Lamennais, January 14, 1835.

1838

I know that a great many of the people who approach me with a smile on their lips, and protestations of friendship on their tongues, have nothing better to do than to pull me to pieces as best they can as soon as they are outside my door. It is, moreover, the fate of all the world. I resign myself to it willingly, as I do to all the absurd and odious necessities of this lower world. There is, besides, just this much good in these sad experiences of various relations with men—which is, that one learns to relish and appreciate better the devotion of the few friends whom chance has thrown in your path.[69]

69. Letter to Simon Löwy, Milan, September 22, 1838.

1840

[Regarding a student] He is lacking in a certain *point of honor,* without which a man is not a man as I understand the word.[70]

70. Letter to Franz von Schober, Metz, April 3, 1840.

1859

Among the artists of all nations we must remember that it is those who are the least sure of posterity who are the most sure of themselves and of the moment …

Do we not meet in every society, however civilized and prosaic it may be, or however occupied it may seem with positive duties and mercantile profits—exceptional individuals, strongly inclined to resist all regulation of their ardent and subversive desires? The difference is that, there, such groups occur but rarely; because, by its silently deteriorating influence, the atmosphere of civilization chills and weakens those children who threaten to become ungovernable, if they are not at an early age brought under conventional rule. For all that, such instances occur; and, under the form of eccentricity, are far more frequent than is generally supposed.

We regard such persons as defectives, incapable as they are of performing their share of servile regulated work in the great social factory; but they, on the contrary, glory in their inaptitude, calling the malady from which they suffer 'sacred,' and one from which they would consent on no conditions to be relieved. Poetic pathology has by no means left this sad anomaly without admirable descriptions; they exist in every style, under various titles, by various authors, dating from every period and in divers tongues.

We possess some beautiful examples of this - some in fresco, some in water-color - written by princes of the poetic art. We shall not quote any, because each reader will certainly find it more agreeable to recall to mind the immortal and well-known specimens he treasures from the literature of any language with which he is familiar. Moreover the identity of sentiment, the resemblance of impressions, the conformity of emotions, of sighs and languors, of joys and heart-breakings do not constitute identity.[71]

71. Letter to *The Gipsy in Music,* 1859.

1860

You speak of your *uselessness*. In all truth, there are, I believe, those physicists who claim that we can see quite well enough without the sun, and that after a fashion this lovely star is merely *useless*. Your own state is similar.[72]

72. Letter to Marie zu Sayn-Wittgenstein, Weimar, January 14, 1860.

1863

As we grow old we deliberate more and are less readily satisfied.[73]

73. Letter to Franz Brendel, Monte Mario, September 7, 1863.

There is truly a great dearth of men in this world! When they are put to the test they prove themselves useless. My ten years' service in Weimar gave me abundant proof of this![74]

74. Letter to Franz Brendel, October 10, 1863.

1875

Certain conversational phrases used even in very high circles strike me as the equivalent of repeated sneezes, which one should rather apologize for than indulge in.[75]

75. Letter to Olga von Meyendorff, Rome, October 17, 1875.

1879

Thank you for the article by Caro on 'pessimism.' I always feel drawn to this kind of literature though I am rarely quite of the same mind as the learned philosophers when it is a matter of certain ideas which touch my intimate beliefs. Thus King Solomon himself doesn't impress me much with his pompous Vanitas Vanitatum! Confidentially speaking (for my ignorance forbids me to argue philosophy or politics with others), to consider everything as being in vain seems to me the worst of vanities. From a Christian point of view every action, every word and thought has its own value, according to whether these draw us nearer to, or farther away from Heaven. There is a basic coarseness in this thesis which I find repugnant. M. Renan and others dress it up in seductive verbiage but don't really believe in it. To plow one's own field, cultivar son jardin (as Voltaire used to recommend), and to discharge one's duties toward one's neighbor, starting with servants and ending with princes, these are not vain matters nor is Dante's Divina Commedia, or Beethoven's Ninth Symphony. Mankind's common sense will ever protest against crushing nihilistic arguments. Renan will go on writing good French. The Sisters of St. Vincent de Paul will nurse the sick, Catholic missionaries will preach the Gospel to all the nations, save when they suffer martyrdom. Scientists will make new discoveries, soldiers will shed their blood for the sake of honor, artists will produce works of beauty, etc. All this is not vanity, with all due deference to King Solomon and to his glib imitators. There is, and there will ever constantly be something new under the sun; and in the end the Father of heavenly mercy will reward the long and persevering labor of mankind. This is our hope![76]

76. Letter to Olga von Meyendorff, Budapest, January 31, 1879.

In ingratitude there is, alas, only too much rivalry; the matter grows contemptible, and contemptible people like to find amusement in it. My nature absolutely forbids me such despicable behavior.[77]

77. Letter to Ludwig Bösendorfer, Budapest, February 19, 1879.

1884

For many people doubtful profits and manoeuvres contrary to their dignity exercise an irresistible attraction. The idea of honor seems to them too troublesome.[78]

78. Letter to Camille Saint-Saens, Weimar, May 18, 1884.

Women

1832

It was in a paroxysm of madness that I wrote you; a strain of work, wakefulness, and those violent desires (for which you know me) had set my poor head aflame; I went from right to left, then from left to right (like a sentinel in the winter, freezing), singing, declaiming, gesticulating, crying out; in a word, I was delirious. Today the spiritual and the animal are a little more evenly balanced; for the volcano of the heart is not extinguished, but is working silently.—Until when?[79]

79. Letter to Pierre Wolff, May 8, 1832.

1840

Love is not justice. Love is not duty; it isn't pleasure either, and yet it contains mysteriously all these things. There are a thousand ways to feel it, to practice it, but for those whose souls thirst for the absolute and the infinite, it is one, with neither beginning nor end.[80]

80. Letter to Marie d'Agoult, London, 1840.

1842

It seems to me I have forgotten how to live. I can attach myself to nothing; I would throw up the whole thing if you could be happy living with me again. But whether from perversity, hardness of heart, blindness of the spirit and the heart at once, I could no longer believe I was enough in your life, and as an alternative I preferred this life of vagabondage to a sickly stagnation which would have killed me without making you live. I am not deceiving myself. My life for the last three years has been nothing but a series of excitements leading to disgust and remorse. I must spend, and spend again, life, strength, money and time, without joy in the present or hope in the future.[81]

81. Letter to Marie d'Agoult, December 8, 1842.

1844

I have told no lies to my intimate friends. I have said flatly that you disapprove and condemn my orgiastic life, that you have therefore told me that it would be better not to meet again, and therefore that we will see each other no more …

However moved I may be at the softening of your anger, I can nevertheless not at all condemn my past. That past, Madame, was full each day of a serious and passionate devotion to yourself. The impulses and mistakes to be found there were neither lasting nor serious. The hand you promise to hold out to me some day when all is forgotten, I would be happy to seize and hold forever, but I can't, no, I never could tell myself that it ought to have been withheld for a single instant.[82]

82. Letter to Marie d'Agoult, 1844.

1852

Polish women have always inspired fervent homage, for they all have a poetic comprehension of an ideal that they reflect in their remarks, like an image ever present in a mirror that they fancy can be caught. Despising the weak and too facile pleasure of merely pleasing, they would have the pleasure of admiring those who love them. Romantic sustenance of their desires, it sometimes holds them in long hesitation between the world and the cloister where, at some moment of her life, nearly everyone of them has earnestly and bitterly thought of seeking refuge.[83]

83. Letter to Franz Liszt, *Chopin*, 1852.

1854

A. Ritter is going to marry Mdlle. Wagner, who has played in comedy at the Breslau theater, and who, by her husband's orders, will not continue playing when she has her home to keep. Let us hope so at least![84]

84. Letter to Bernhard Cossmann, Weimar, September 8, 1854.

1856

An elegant, young woman, a Social Lioness, and an Artist, whom I see rather often and who will also pass through Weimar this summer, is the Hungarian Princess Nako. She plays gipsy songs in a ravishing way, sketches and paints with a kind of genius and maintains at her expense a troupe of gipsy musicians whom she has shown to Meyerbeer.[85]

85. Letter to Marie zu Sayn-Wittgenstein, Vienna, January 31, 1856.

1859

Mother love is like an endless ladder of fantasy and feeling, -moving to the point of being irritating—and one might put at both ends of the scale, in order to make the allegory more complete, the oldest magician and the most youthful fairy.[86]

86. Letter to Marie zu Sayn-Wittgenstein, Weimar, December 26, 1859.

1860

I thank my mother with reverence and tender love for her continual proofs of goodness and love. In my youth people called me a good son; it was certainly no special merit on my part, for how would it have been possible not to be a good son with so faithfully self-sacrificing a mother?[87]

87. Letter to Princess Caroline Sayn-Wittgenstein, Weimar, September 14, 1860.

1872

There are numberless things which lie outside of and beyond the 'war of the sexes' in love, and as far as I am concerned I do not accept the thesis that 'to love is to be either the anvil or the hammer.' Why the choice between these two very hard instruments? To love is to ascend into heaven.[88]

88. Letter to Olga von Meyendorff, Schillingsfurst, October 10, 1872.

1873

Your imagination runs away with you when you attribute to me incongruous 'desires' such as, among others, that Miss F. should play at court. Frankly this kind of remark and its correlatives coming from you make me impatient, for you must know, since Rome, that I practice abstention from desires.... I also know Tasso's graceful line, 'I wish for much, hope for little, and ask for nothing.' Young ladies in bouts of melancholy like to apply it to themselves, but for my part I retain only the last two words ...

As for local events, which are scarcely diverting, I inform you that Mlle Hortense Vogt (of Weimar) has been staying in Budapest for about two weeks. She had taken care to send me ardent telegrams ahead of time from Nice which I no more answered than her letters, which I never read any longer and only open by mistake when the address is in another hand—a subterfuge to which Mlle Hortense often has recourse, but without success.[89]

89. Letter to Olga von Meyendorff, Budapest, February 4, 1873.

1874

Mademoiselle Hortense Vogt appeared, very much unheralded. I took her immediately to the sacristy to entrust her to the care of the ecclesiastic, while excusing myself for not being able, in such circumstances of major absurdity, to attend mass. The said demoiselle won't give up the idea that she has the vocation of bringing about my matrimonial happiness in spite of myself! I forget who it was who defined happiness as: 'A blow which has more or less healed.' Alas! Mine must forego these correctives.[90]

90. Letter to Olga von Meyendorff, Horpacs, January 31, 1874.

Your comments on Mlle Vogt are, as usual, most judicious. It could indeed be that behind her formal role, carried to the point of scandal, of being my imaginary and hostile wife, she may be discharging other and less exalted functions. Fortunately I am entirely blameless in this whole too laughable and odious affair. I shall avoid calling in the police as long as possible; but in Budapest it will probably be necessary to have recourse to do this ... I learned yesterday in a letter from Budapest that having been evicted at my request from the Hotel Frohner, she brazenly camped at the Hotel Hungaria;

that she called on the Catholic priest and on the Protestant pastor, and that she parades everywhere as my wife, whose wedding, in a church or before the mayor, has unfortunately been hitherto delayed by intrigues of the blackest hue.[91]

91. Letter to Olga von Meyendorff, Horpacs, February 8, 1874.

Something more sacred has merged with my deep love for and inexpressible gratitude to [Princess Carolyne von Sayn-Wittgenstein]. She has revived my conscience and kept alive the few good qualities with which I have been endowed.[92]

92. Letter to Olga von Meyendorff, Budapest, April 10, 1874.

Although you have several times told me that, basically, no one had a decisive influence over me, you seem now to allow that the Princess [Carolyne von Sayn-Wittgenstein] exerts a kind of ' pressure. *That is not so and shall not be so*. Of course I have often sought her council and advice, all the more so since she has nobly helped me in circumstances which it was hard to settle satisfactorily; however, I have never either understood or indulged in smug or surly subjection where love is concerned, and except for the dogmas of the Church, I retain my *complete independence*.

In fact, it was my opinion which triumphed in the major decisions of the Princess for twenty-seven years. This was so in the matter of her stay in Weimar and in Rome with all that flowed therefrom. People almost blamed her for my having entered the Vatican, of which she had no suspicion, and which I simply announced to her, one month before, as settled. On this and other matters the falsest views on the Princess have gone the rounds; I could not prevent, and only rarely contradicted them to the extent that it seemed appropriate to me to do so, knowing the superlative degree of deafness of those who do not wish to hear! So I have not been able to 'defend her against her enemies' who are too powerful. Don't speak of the 'same old story,' if the wound you inflicted on me by such a reproach has not healed. Woe to me if a shadow of cowardice should darken my life![93]

93. Letter to Olga von Meyendorff, Budapest, April 27, 1874.

Your emotions and enjoyment of *Tristan und Isolde* are not very pleasing to me. You pen superb indictments against me in a fine style, but of these there have been too many examples both before and after Cicero. The guilty party is never sufficiently accused; in dealing severely with him one is still being too indulgent, for beneath his visible crimes there are certainly others hidden which deserve harsher punishments.

In this noble zeal, Princess, Daniel Stern anticipated you by more than a quarter of a century. Her novel of indictment, Nelida, condemns me to loss of civil rights for possessing only 'sham' lofty sentiments and even genius. Consequently, I should be relegated to the company of the menials of Princes, and 'dine' with the scullions and broomsweeps who, contrary to the holy Christian law, are quite wrongly despised, in the servants' hall of Monseigneur the Grand Duke of Saxony.

Shall I complain of such a fate, decreed by noble ladies who are over-prodigal in sacrifices? Not at all. I have, thanks to this, tested the truth of the well-known maxim: 'Judging by its effect, love is closer to hate than to kindly and helpful friendship.'[94]

94. Letter to Olga von Meyendorff, Villa d'Este, June 22, 1874.

1877

Peterle will do well to acquire skill in the pleasures of dancing and of courtesy toward ladies and girls, without pushing attentiveness beyond that of a *gallant homme*, not going too far. To observe a delicate and affable measure in relations between the two sexes befits true aristocracy to which all well-born hearts belong.[95]

95. Letter to Olga von Meyendorff, Budapest, December 31, 1877.

1879

Italy's martial hero [Garibaldi] boldly declares, 'Man created God, and not God man.' Now we know everything, don't we? It only remains to know who will claim the copyright for having invented women. There are those who claim that the devil had something to do with it.[96]

96. Letter to Olga von Meyendorff, Bayreuth, August 28, 1879.

1880

[My mother] loved me, and in order to please her I did not enter a seminary (in 1830), for her sincere and naive piety did not consider my vocation for the priesthood to be necessary. Thus because of her I remained a layman and have lived only too secularly. She liked to say: 'Whatever people may say against my son doesn't offend me in the slightest, for I know what he is.'[97]

97. Letter to Olga von Meyendorff, Villa d'Este, October 30, 1880.

1882

It seems to me inadmissible for any man to exploit a woman in love for purposes of business and of his own reputation.[98]

98. Letter to Olga von Meyendorff, Rome, January 20, 1882.

1883

I think I told you Balzac's theory that no man with fewer than seven women in his life has achieved the perfect state of a complete being. It remains to be known how many men ladies require in order to become complete too?[99]

99. Letter to Olga von Meyendorff, Venice, January 7, 1883.

The Jewish People
Artistic Standpoint of the Jew

1859

The Jews have also cultivated art, and have naturally concluded by invading it. But, after reviewing all their sentiments for about twenty centuries and taking severe care not to allow anything to come to the surface (thus rendering still more acute their adroitness in cozenage and fraud) they have only been able to exercise and practice art as they have astrology—that is to say, as the result of study only. This means that they neither believed in it themselves, nor did they trouble to understand what those thought who really did believe in it.

In the result they have never known how it is that art actually *creates* by force of inspiration. They have never realized that to pronounce the word 'art' is precisely the same thing as if the word uttered were 'creation.' …

The Israelites have never produced anything really new; for the reason that what they have sung has never been their own sentiment. They have been in the habit of sealing up every movement of their heart, with a religious silence as far as they were concerned, but a silence intended contemptuously as towards others; and, never having been able to cast this off, how would it have been even possible for them to confide those feelings to art? Before they could do that, it would have been necessary for them to unlearn feigning to the Christians; an idea which would never so much as occur to them. The views which they had so long entertained about their inherent nobleness, elevation and general superiority, as compared with others, would have prevented them. In short, their religion of silence would never have permitted them to express the aspirations of their souls, to chant the sufferings of their hearts, or to detail the throbbings of their passions, loves or hatreds, in the language of the ideal.

It follows that they have produced neither an architecture, a school of painting, or of music; neither songs nor poems which could be considered *national*, and which would therefore have revealed to us the sort of feeling possessed by these men of an iron faith –men with such prodigious hopes, who gild their darksome days with a light invisible to other eyes.

Shall we be told that Mendelssohn has composed the oratorio of *Elijah*, or that Halevy has produced the opera of *La Juive*? Or that Bendemann has painted 'The Jews weeping on the banks of the Euphrates,' and that another has given us a theatrical representation of Solomon in all his glory? If so, we need only ask—what is there herein essentially Jewish? Neither the sentiment nor the form. That oratorio, that opera, that painting, and that play would all have been thought out and felt in precisely the same way by Christians.

The Reason of Jewish Artistic Isolation

The onward movement of musical art has been much favored by Jewish participation in it; being thereby enriched with superior talents and names of great celebrity. It is even doubtful whether, without their having taken this share in its 'business,' music would have arrived at the flourishing condition in which it now is. There would therefore be neither good faith nor dignity in declining to recognize what we owe them in this respect.

Considered in bulk, however, their success was not always merited. The press has much overstated the achievements of certain composers; and completely gone beyond those of many virtuosi.

……

Exactly as, at the theater and in painting, the Jew's art in music is cut and trimmed to the Christian pattern. He does not even try to free himself from our methods; showing no wish to avoid copying our masters, or any desire to speak other sentiments or vibrate any other chords than ours.

The Jewish Case Stated

There will come a moment, however, when all those Christian nations amongst whom the Jew at present has his dwelling will have to recognize that the question of expelling him or allowing him to remain is one really of life or death. It is a choice between health or perpetual sickness—between social peace or perpetual debility and constant disturbance ... Evidently, the European nations have an urgent common interest in giving back Palestine to those to whom it belongs. Humanly speaking this is as much an act of reason as of equity. Palestine for the Israelites, Italy for the Italians, France for the French, and so forth. Moreover, as Italians have already recovered their country, it is only just that Jews should do the same; indeed, it is doubly so if their presence among the European nations causes numerous evils and grave perils. How can it concern us to inquire what is likely to happen afterwards?[100]

100. Letter to *The Gipsy in Music* [1859], 40ff, 46ff, 65ff.

1873

I will tell you of a delightful reply of Baron Rothschild (of Vienna) to Count Edmond Zichy. The latter asked the most illustrious Baron how it was that all Rothschild affairs prospered, while several of his were going less well: 'The reason is simple; you have become a Jew with age and experience; as for me, I was born a Jew.'[101]

101. Letter to Olga von Meyendorff, Budapest, January 22, 1873.

1885

It is not without regret that I address these lines to you; but, as there has been some report spread here about my pretended hostility to the Israelites, I ought to rectify the mistake of this false report.

As is well known in the musical world, many illustrious Israelites, Meyerbeer first and foremost, have given me their esteem and friendship, and the same in the literary world with Heine and others.

It seems to me that it would be superfluous to enumerate the many proofs I have given, during fifty years, of my active loyalty towards Israelites of talent and capacity, and I abstain in like manner from speaking of my voluntary contributions to the charitable institutions of Judaism in various countries.

If, by some mutilated quotations from my book on the *Gipsies* in Hungary, it has been sought to pick a quarrel with me, and to make what is called in French *une querelle d'Allemand*, I can in all good conscience affirm that I feel myself to be guiltless of any other misdeed than that of having feebly reproduced the argument of the kingdom of Jerusalem, set forth by Disraeli, George Eliot, and Cremieux, three Israelites of high degree.[102]

102. Letter to the Editor of the *Gazette de Hongrie*, February 6, 1883.

1885

War and peace between nations rest in [the hands of Jewish financiers]. They control the stock exchange and public opinion through the press—two sovereignties which the most majestic sovereigns cannot match. Too bad for the Christians, for letting themselves be thus dominated![103]

103. Letter to Olga von Meyendorff, Budapest, February 26, 1885.

Friends

1856

Kaulbach and I have become sincere friends. He is the right sort of fellow who will please you too, for the very reason that many people call him intolerable.[104]

104. Letter to Wagner, Munich, December 25, 1856.

1857

Friendship without heart and flame is something foreign to me.[105]

105. Letter to Eduard Liszt, Weimar, March 26, 1857.

1859

The many attacks on me which I have to bear enhance still more the value I place on the sympathy and concurrence of my friends.[106]

106. Letter to Max Seifriz, Weimar, February 22, 1859.

1872

If I used the word 'friendship,' this is because I know of no other which better conveys the sense of a certain noble soundness of outlook in matters of everyday life, and in making its practices agreeable and firm.[107]

107. Letter to Olga von Meyendorff, Budapest, January 31, 1872.

I don't indulge in finding fault with my friends even when I venture not to share their opinion.[108]

108. Letter to Olga von Meyendorff, Budapest, November 13 1872.

1873

What is the use of friendship or love if one is always looking for difficulties where there are none?[109]

109. Letter to Olga von Meyendorff, December 13, 1873.

1874

My friends are those who haunt the *Ideal*; there, dear friend, we *recognize* each other, and shall always do so.[110]

110. Letter to Edmund von Mihalovich, Villa d'Este, December 8, 1874.

1876

M. Doudan was fulfilling the role of a decent man when he wrote: "Let us not concede to anyone that our friends are inferior on any point whatever. Mean people abuse this. I'll always fire on those who want to attack a single tent of the camp in which I live.'[111]

111. Letter to Olga von Meyendorff, Budapest, November 16, 1876.

Faith

1844

During the ten days which I have just spent in Seville I have not allowed a single day to pass without going to pay my very humble court to the cathedral, that epic of granite, that architectural Symphony whose eternal harmonies vibrate in infinity!

As for me, I am constrained to stand with my nose in the air and mouth open. Nevertheless my prayer sometimes climbs up like useless ivy, lovingly embracing those knotted shafts which defy all the storms of the genius of Christianity. [112]

112. Letter to an unknown lady, Seville, December, 1844.

1851

This evening I am going to the Institute for the first time, to listen to *Nathan der Weise*, a loathsome play ... mephitically oozing the pantheistic stink through its bourgeois and philosophic triteness![113]

113. Letter to Marie zu Sayn-Wittgenstein, Weimar, April 9, 1851.

1853

Your letters are sad; your life is still sadder. You want to go into the wide world to live, to enjoy, to luxuriate. I should be only too glad if you could, but do you not feel that the sting and the wound you have in your own heart will leave you nowhere and can never be cured? Your greatness is your misery; both are inseparably connected, and must pain and torture you until you kneel down and let both be merged in *faith*!

'*Lass zu dem Glauben Dich neu bekehren, es gibt ein Gluck*', this is the only thing that is true and eternal. I cannot preach to you, nor explain it to you; but I will pray to God that He may powerfully illumine your heart through His faith and His love. You may scoff at this feeling as bitterly as you like. I cannot fail to see and desire in it the only salvation. Through Christ alone, through resigned suffering in God, salvation and rescue comes to us.[114]

114. Letter to Richard Wagner, Weimar, April 8, 1853.

1854

My heart is near to yours, sympathizing with your suffering, and trusting that 'the peace of the Lord,' that peace which the world can neither give nor take away, may sustain you.[115]

115. Letter to Eduard Liszt, on the death of his wife, October 10, 1854.

1856

The *Gran Mass* has sprung from the truly fervent faith of my heart such as I have felt it since my childhood.[116]

116. Letter to a Dr. Gille, Zürich, November 14, 1856.

1857

May God's blessing, without which nothing can prosper and bear fruit, rest on my work![117]

117. Letter to Eduard Liszt, Weimar, March 26, 1857.

One shouldn't give in, and should trust in God while persevering right up *to the last*. Let us pray God to test us in accordance with our strength, and don't give up hope.[118]

118. Letter to Marie zu Sayn-Wittgenstein, Aix-la-Chapelle, May 30, 1857.

1859

Alas! we are miserable creatures, and the few who have penetrated the deepest secrets of life are the most miserable of all. That snarling old cur, Schopenhauer, is quite right in saying that we are ridiculous in addressing each other as *Monsieur* or citizen. *Compagnon de misere et de souffrance*, or fellow-sufferers, and worse we are, tutti quanti, and nothing we can do can make any essential change in this. The worst is that we know it quite well, and yet never like to believe it.[119]

119. Letter to Wagner, Weimar, August 22, 1859.

1860

Yes, 'Jesus Christ on the Cross,' a yearning longing after the Cross and the raising of the Cross, this was ever my true inner calling; I have felt it in my innermost heart ever since my seventeenth year, in which I implored with humility and tears that I might be permitted to enter the Paris Seminary; at that time I hoped it would be granted to me to live the life of the saints and perhaps even to die a martyr's death. This, alas! has not happened—yet, in spite of the transgressions and errors which I have committed, and for which I feet sincere repentance and contrition, the holy light of the Cross has never been entirely withdrawn from me. At times, indeed, the refulgence of this divine light has overflowed my entire soul.—I thank God for this, and shall die with my soul fixed upon the Cross, our redemption, our highest bliss; and, in acknowledgment of my belief, I wish before my death to receive the holy sacraments of the Catholic, Apostolic, and Romish Church, and thereby to attain the forgiveness and remission of all my sins. Amen.[120]

120. Letter to Princess Caroline Sayn-Wittgenstein, Weimar, September 14, 1860.

1862

When the day comes for Death to approach, he shall not find me unprepared or faint-hearted. Our faith hopes for and awaits the deliverance to which it leads us.[121]

121. Letter to Eduard Liszt, Rome, November 19, 1862.

1863

I must tell you of an extraordinary, nay, incomparable honor I received last Saturday evening, the 11th of July. His Holiness Pope Pius IX visited the Church of the Madonna del Rosario, and hallowed my apartments with his presence. After having given His Holiness a small proof of my skill on the harmonium and on my work-a-day pianino, he addressed a few very significant words to me in the most gracious manner possible, admonishing me to strive after heavenly things in things earthly, and by means of my harmonies that reverberated and then passed away to prepare myself for those harmonies that would reverberate everlastingly.[122]

122. Letter to Franz Brendel, July 18, 1863.

1865

Your Highness will understand that it is a necessity of my heart to speak to you of a very happy juncture that assures me henceforth, in full degree, the stability of feeling and of conduct to which I aspired. It seems to me that I should be guilty of ingratitude and wanting in respect to the condescending friendship with which you are good enough to honor me, did I not let you know of the determination I have taken.

On Tuesday the 25th of April, the festival of St. Mark the Evangelist, I entered into the ecclesiastical state of receiving minor orders in the chapel of H. S. H. Monseigneur Hohenlohe at the Vatican. Convinced as I was that this act would strengthen me in the right road, I accomplished it without effort, in all simplicity and uprightness of intention. Moreover it agrees with the antecedents of my youth, as well as with the development that my work of musical composition has taken during these last four years, a work which I propose to pursue with fresh vigor, as I consider it the least defective form of my nature.

To speak familiarly; if 'the cloak does not make the monk' it also does not prevent him from being one; and, in certain cases, when the monk is already formed within, why not appropriate the outer garment of one?

But I am forgetting that I do not in the least intend to become a monk, in the severe sense of the word. For this I have no vocation, and it is enough for me to belong to the hierarchy of the Church to such a degree as the minor orders allow me to do. It is therefore not the frock, but the cassock that I have donned. And on this subject Your Highness will pardon me the small vanity of mentioning to you that they pay me the compliment of saying that I wear my cassock as though I had worn it all my life.

I am now living at the Vatican with Monseigneur Hohenlohe, whose apartment is on the same floor as the *Stanze* of Raphael. My lodging is not at all like a prison cell, and the kind hospitality that Monseigneur H. shows me exempts me from all painful constraints. So I shall leave it but rarely and for a short time only, as removals and especially journeys have become very burdensome to me for many reasons.[123]

123.Letter to Prince Constantine of Hohenzollern-Hechingen, The Vatican, May 11, 1865

1870

All else will come to you in good time, and in abundance. So let's not worry; and look instead, as it has been taught us to do, at the birds of the air and the lilies of the field, keeping complete faith in Our Father's goodness.[124]

124. Letter to Marie zu Sayn-Wittgenstein, Rome, February 18, 1870.

Even on the most troubled days, there is certain peace for those who have the signal felicity to be Christians. It is this continuous, ineffable, indestructible peace, the summation of all the goods here below, which is besought for you from the Celestial Father.[125]

125. Letter to Marie zu Sayn-Wittgenstein, Sexard, August 15, 1870.

1871

Mme de Helldorf had already told me that the aggressive insubordination of Father Hyacinthe had made a considerable impression on you. His eloquence and his successes have been stumbling blocks for him. The Catholic structure has no cement other than faith and absolute obedience. We no longer have enough of these left to us in Europe to be able to manage a schism. Consequently Father Hyacinthe will be reduced to that powerless isolation which is the most mortal sorrow of generous hearts.[126]

126. Letter to Olga von Meyendorff, Budapest, March 7, 1871.

In the same [unidentified] volume there is also a prayer which I often recite. It is by the abhorred St. Ignatius:

Soul of Jesus Christ sanctify me,
Body of Jesus Christ save me,
Blood of Jesus Christ exalt me, etc.[127]

127. Letter to Olga von Meyendorff, April 9, 1871.

1872

I just cannot indulge in holy ranting and raving, though I have unlimited respect for those who do so with consuming zeal. Veuillot's diatribe against Victor Hugo (very eloquent, be it noted) saddened me, and it already requires a certain effort for me to rise to the level of academic aloofness of Mgr Dupanloup, which, I am told, the *Revue des deux mondes* recently approved! My lukewarmness in this respect is such that it could not really heat up before the flames of the most fulminating preachers, whether lay or religious; but I beg you not to speak of this to anyone, for I almost reproach myself for this lukewarmness, and would be only too glad to rid myself of it, albeit rationally, the Catholic faith being above, but not contrary to, reason.[128]

128. Letter to Olga von Meyendorff, Budapest, January 31, 1872.

As for me, I have only reached the stage of a kind of sad resignation regarding men and events, sometimes tempered and as though illumined by faith in divine providence, and invincible hope in Christ's redemption![129]

129. Letter to Olga von Meyendorff, Budapest, February 28, 1872.

At Erfurt I bought an object of which I have often felt deprived at the Hofgärtnerei: a cross which now rests near my Roman books next to my bed.

I often repeat to myself the words of St. Paul: 'We must place our glory in the Cross of Jesus Christ,' and in Rome I used to repeat in St. Peter's Square this prayer: 'O crux, ave, spes unica … grant to the just increasing grace, and to sinners forgiveness of their faults.'[130]

130. Letter to Olga von Meyendorff, Weimar, June 4, 1872.

1873

It is understandable that writers who persist in presenting Christianity as a historical fact, more or less complex but natural and devoid of any miracles, would find that St. Paul is not free of the faults which are shocking in sectarians, and that 'his style is ponderous.' His role was not to sit 'weary on the side of the road, or to waste his time in noting the vanity of established opinions.' His faith in Our Lord Jesus Christ was not an 'opinion'; he preached of Jesus crucified, resurrected, risen into Heaven; he fought the good fight and awaited 'the crown of justice which Our Lord will confer in the full light of day on those who love his coming.'—Fine and great minds may understand nothing about all this; nevertheless millions of souls are illumined and fired by the words of St. Paul.[131]

131. Letter to Olga von Meyendorff, Schillingsfürst, August 7, 1873.

1874

Thank you for Veuillot's letter. I shall note this statement, which applies to situations other than his: 'On the roads which faith opens up for us accidents, misfortunes, and pain are neither pain, nor misfortunes, nor accidents. One's inner feelings alter the meaning of words and the nature of things.'[132]

132. Letter to Olga von Meyendorff, Horpacs, February 8, 1874.

Speaking of Jesuits, people are talking a great deal about Father Curci's latest pamphlet. I think it serves as introduction to a work of several volumes: *Commentaires sur l'Evangile*. I have not yet read it and don't even know its exact title; but people have assured me, *horresco referens!* (I shudder to say it!), that Father Curci has had no scruples in making short shrift of the Pope's temporal power. This, coming from a Reverend Father of the Company of Jesus is, to say the least, surprising, given the no less categorical than repeated statements by the Holy Father. I completely fail to understand what it's all about, and I also feel too ignorant to understand much of Nietzsche, who dazzles me with his fine style much more than he enlightens me. I agree that this is really my fault and in no way Nietzsche's; but how can I become converted to the man created by Schopenhauer (der Schopenhauer'sche Mensch! or to the man of Goethe and of Rousseau, whereas I adore our bon.Dieu, the creator, and call upon him as 'Our Father' who is in Heaven?—Ah! believe me, dear beloved soul, let us leave to others more learned than we the perilous paths of thought, and let us remain united in heart to our heavenly Father and to His Son Jesus Christ our Savior![133]

133. Letter to Olga von Meyendorff, Villa d'Este, November 11, 1874.

1877

Every year brings us nearer to the fulfillment of our hope in Jesus Christ the Savior![134]

134. Letter to Eduard Liszt, Budapest, January 2, 1877.

1878

The great maxim: 'In matters necessary, Unity; in matters doubtful, Freedom; in all matters, Charity,' remains for all time the rule of the Holy Apostolic See, founded on the rock of Peter. Let us not ask of it that it shift with opinions which change like the wind; these can only shatter themselves against its rock of immovable and infallible dogma. As for 'freedom in matters doubtful,' the Syllabus has reduced it almost to zero. Thus the noble dreams of liberal Catholics are evaporating. Our simple duty is obedience, without any reservation or commentary whatsoever.[135]

135. Letter to Olga von Meyendorff, Budapest, January 19, 1878.

1880

Supreme serenity still remains the Ideal of great Art. The shapes and transitory forms of Life are but stages towards this Ideal, which Christ's religion illuminates with His divine light.[136]

136. Letter to Marie zu Sayn-Wittgenstein, Weimar, July 30, 1880.

The fact is that the current trend in religious affairs in Belgium and France and the great festival of German unity in Köln cathedral don't seem to me to augur well for the restoration of papal temporal power in the near future. Fortunately, I am not involved in these great issues in which the cleverest people have so often failed. Simple faith, like that of the 'poor in spirit,' suffices for my prayers and musical work in which I persevere despite the fatigue of age.[137]

137. Letter to Marie zu Sayn-Wittgenstein, Weimar, July 30, 1880.

One need not be a disbeliever to feel that temporal power is more of a hindrance than an advantage to the Holy Apostolic See. Its relations with European diplomacy will always retain something equivocal, insoluble.[138]

138. Letter to Olga von Meyendorff, Villa d'Este, November 18, 1880.

Lassen's mother's death reminds me of this simple question, what sort of world is it which we enter with the hope of seeing our father and mother die?[139]

139. Letter to Olga von Meyendorff, Undated.

1882

I am astonished at your finding 'conclusive arguments' in Schopenhauer against immortality of the soul. To say that it is not possible to demonstrate *ex professo* the nature of life in the hereafter amounts to not saying anything at all, for our end as well as our beginning does not fall within the competence of man. But who would be qualified to determine on the basis of the blindness of the comprehension of the mortal race the supreme rights of God's mercy? It remains eternal! What do our lapses, our malignity, our faults and sorrows matter, which sometimes lead us to wish for the annihilation of our being, by God's grace created immortal? Ah! Let us not abjure our heavenly heritage; this would be infamous.[140]

140. Letter to Olga von Meyendorff, Budapest, February 14, 1882.

To hold those in error in scorn remains sound Christian advice on condition that we are not lacking in gentleness and humility of heart.[141]

141. Letter to Olga von Meyendorff, Budapest, March 11, 1882.

Nature

1852

In the practice of these encounters with Creation lie the attraction and nobility of rural life. Here is best caught the message it conceals in the infinite harmonies of shapes and sounds, of lights, of tumult and twitter, of terror and sensuousness—overwhelming combinations which, tested and confronted by a courage that no mystery or delay can weaken or weary, sometimes grants a glimpse of the key to analogies and conformities, to the relations of our meanings and feelings. They allow us to know simultaneously both the hidden ties that bind apparent dissimilarities, identical opposites, and equivalent antitheses, and the chasms which separate, by a narrow but unbridgeable space, that which is destined to draw close without merging, to resemble without mingling.[142]

142. Franz Liszt, *Chopin*, 1852,

1859

It may be that the light of one day neither resembles that of the preceding nor predicts that of the following, but the daylight faithfully reappears, and the seasons return with equal certainty. The stars which shine with such various degrees of brilliancy strictly return to the places designed for them in space. The varicolored water-fall has never yet appeared twice alike, but the stone over which it passes wears away. The blossom of each plant differs from stem to stem in grace, luxury and fullness, but each seed produces exactly that to which it was destined.

So also it is with vegetation and the earth which bears it; so with the return of the lion to his den and the warbler to its nest; so with the river ever running in its bed, or with the bird of passage returning to a warmer clime.

Nature never fails in this continuity of return, this permanence of reproduction, which thus presents the charm of habit. But the vastness of her movements exceeds the physical perception of man; who is soon overcome by terms so far removed in the infinities of time and space, should he undertake to devote himself exclusively to such a study. In the act of trying to identify himself with Nature's changes individually he loses, if not memory, at least remembrance. He becomes stupidly oblivious to the reflections which might have helped to enlighten his mind. He no longer knows how to combine his emotions one with another by the constancy of his will; he has no longer the power to resume their consideration as from the same time and point. His soul breathes itself out like the vapor of a liqueur which has been heated, or like a fluid from the hands, however tightly they may be clasped.[143]

143. Liszt, *The Gipsy in Music*, 1859.

1878

I attempted to put down on music paper. the conversation which I frequently told with these same cypresses [on the Villa d'Este estate]. Ah! how dry and unsatisfactory on the piano, and even in the orchestra,—Beethoven and Wagner excepted—sounds the woe and the sighing of almighty nature![144]

144. Letter to Ludwig Nohl, Budapest, March 20, 1848.

1885

The inability to speak which Mother Nature has imposed on fishes often makes me feel envious.[145]

145. Letter to Olga von Meyendorff, Budapest, March 3, 1885.

Habit

1859

Man is prevented from arriving at any full conception of uninterrupted happiness by his senses, his moral organization and the whole of the surroundings among which his lot is cast.

It is for this reason that all religious beliefs have placed their hope of lasting bliss in a future life; for it was impossible to reconcile the mental picture of it which the conditions ruling present human life. The only anticipation of it which here on earth it is given to man to know is habit; which, when sufficiently dear and cherished, yields him, for as long a time as his organs allow, emotions the permanent fullness of which would amount to felicity. Habit may therefore enable him to taste of happiness; which it even stimulates to such a degree that neither pleasure nor passion can rival the hold it takes upon the human soul as the sole conqueror of satiety.

In the absence of an exceptional issue from this difficulty man loses the power to cause his sentiments to converge upon one focus, and at the same time his chance of enjoying that succulent foretaste of lasting happiness which alone is given by habit. In separating completely from habit he becomes at once subject to a vague instability, which we can only liken to those tremulous agitations of the needle of the mariner's compass, which, in certain conditions, points in the course of a minute to everyone of the thirty-two winds of the dial, and is then described as 'mad' by the sailors.

The tie of habit is full of charm by its suppleness and elasticity; and no man can liberate himself from it or withdraw from the principle of gravitation, which tends to hold him within a determined orbit, without falling into a morbid state.

In inoculating himself with the need of continual change and tending perpetually towards the most divergent points of attraction, it is not alone the mere taste for habit which he loses; he acquires for everything remindful of it a repugnance which, by degrees, approaches horror. By dint of aspiring always to live in a state of febrile excitement his soul reaches a kind of intellectual somnambulism; in which it remains inaccessible to every social influence, and capable only of following instinctive impulse.[146]

146. Liszt, *The Gipsy in Music,* 1859.

Pain

1859

The implacable pride of an egoism which is unlimited because it possesses no knowledge of itself, united to a mad and unrestrained liberty, is, when reduced to its own isolated resources, very soon brought to realize its impotence—by contact with the precarious conditions of nature and human existence. At the cold hours of hunger, infirmity, ennui or lassitude, pride recoils and liberty assumes a morose immobility. The feelings of the soul at such times are like the great shadows thrown on ripe harvest fields by passing clouds; and, if an effort is made to collect them, there would certainly (though perhaps unconsciously) arise that great specter of *Pain* which haunts the waking hours of every human being.

Every human sentiment has been, at one time or another, overpraised or degraded beyond reason. The highest and purest of our inspirations have been, one after another, contested and laughed at. Every virtue has been discussed, and one passion has been excited in passing insult at another. Amid all these blessings and cursings (which no spiritual impulse of which we are capable has completely escaped) the one condition of the soul which has always imposed respect, arrested every sarcasm, and silenced all the outrage of a sacrilegious division, is pain. Even when it has been stifled with barbarism, or eliminated as an obstacle, the silent tribute of sympathy or admiration (according to its intensity or duration) has never been refused.

Pain sounds the depth of our aspirations and thus reveals their extent. Pain shows us especially the horror of discord, as it proceeds from an increased need of harmony. And by intensity of suffering we measure our craving for the ideal; for the more inconsolable the suffering may be, the more it rises above that vulgarity which is satisfied with an insipid well-being.

……

From whatever source it may come, whatever errors it may cause, pain, the great forsaken one, has only to show herself and instantly every other interest disappears. She takes first place at once in view of all; like an exiled queen, returning unexpectedly in all the vigorous majesty of her lugubrious sovereignty. She may have indulged in excesses; she may, like an insatiable and powerful Phryne, have descended to every material debauchery or spiritual insanity; but she has only to cast her veil or mask aside and present herself in the indelible character of her august origin, in order to resume all the rights due to her royal elevation.

……

She can as easily mount the throne as descend to the grave-digger's hut. Her pass-words enable her to enter and take her seat at the bedside of the fortunate. She glides into the philosopher's cabinet or into the artisan's workshop and even accompanies the messenger of mercy on her benevolent excursions. She tears at the breast of the offended man the day after he has taken his revenge; but at the repast of the just man oppressed she is erect and silent. She is invisible to profane regards; but, in the eyes of the angels, her eyes beam with the glories of pardon, and they escort her with the honor due to one of higher race than themselves.

……

As soon as Pain makes her appearance in art (whether furtive or solemn, simple or insinuating, or sudden and strenuous), her influence upon the heart changes character. She now becomes more calm and imposing, by investing her approach with trepidation, imagination and an unction quite irresistible. She is now delivered from the tinsel by which she was so often disfigured; and, shows herself as she is, calm or vehement, in a state of exasperation or passivity, but inevitably possessed of the communicative quality.

The expression of elevated sentiments, high aspirations and noble ambitions meets generally with very slow appreciation from the masses; but that of suffering always meets with an immediate and widespread approval. For, everyone who hears it carries, either under the rags of poverty or the jewels of opulence, some tender bruise, some open wound, or some badly healed cicatrice which reopens and bleeds freely at the magnetic contact of Pain, that sister of monstrous beauty the like of which everyone has begotten in his life—at least once.

Every work of art which possesses this fermenting element to a high degree will move, to the depths of their feeling, not only the best men but the best there is in each man. Such a work cannot fail to meet with an immediate response of approval; sometimes emanating from those whom one would have thought least susceptible, but who are to be met with in all ranks of society; sometimes from the powerful and disdainful on the one hand, as from the humblest and most disdained on the other; pain, by a strange irony, sometimes taking its most vulgar modulations to the first and unfolding it sublimest chords only to the last.[147]

147. Liszt, *The Gipsy in Music*, 1859.

1881

Suffering, pain, and sorrow are the lot of mankind. You have experienced this while constantly displaying the most noble kind of courage, that which consists in maintaining a firm character in the face of the afflictions of our *Vale of Tears* in which only the merciful eye of God gleams in the depths of our hearts, while consoling and strengthening them. Since we must all live and die, let us know how to do so in noble simplicity.[148]

148. Letter to Olga von Meyendorff, Budapest, February 1, 1881.

Desire

1859

Unquenchable desire is one of the greatest treasures of the human soul. It is the salutary leaven which alone gives zest to our existence: the ferment and aroma which preserve it from a state, the equivalent of bodily decay and corruption. For the mind, it is precisely the same intangible and imponderable element as that which, for the body, we call life; to which it owes movement, respiration, development, activity, sensibility—in fact, all the characteristic signs which are the contrary of *death*; inert, passive and dissolving.

Without an inspiration fired by incessant *desire* the human being would vegetate, a mere biped plant. He would remain a sociable animal truly; but he would be less industrious than the ant, less intelligent than the bee, and less disciplined than the beaver. He could have no idea of amelioration or progress; nor could he, while still on earth, imagine and hope for a better world on high.

Desire never satisfied, like a thirst never quenched, is the sure guarantee of every achievement to which man is predestined; and, as it were, a payment on account of his future inheritance. At each miscalculation, at each disillusion and deception, there may be tears forced from him. But each frustration of hope is like holy unction which consecrates and befits him for his task. That task is the attainment of the first of all royal ties—that of becoming sovereign of the earth; and, even beyond both earth and nature, towers that insatiable and unconquerable Desire which the beauties of the one can never content or the magnificences of the other ever extinguish.[149]

149. Liszt, *The Gipsy in Music*, 1859.

Chapter Four

Liszt on his Daily Life

1833

I saw our friend Hugo and Dumas again this week. Decidedly it's the only world, the only society I will frequent in future; the rest seems so empty to me, so boringly pointless.[1]

1. Letter to Marie d' Agoult, 1833.

1844

Weimar under the Grand Duke August was a new Athens; let us think today of constructing a new Weimar. Let us renew those traditions. Let us allow talent to function freely in its sphere and arrive little by little at the triple result that should constitute the whole politics, the whole government, the Alpha and Omega of all Weimar: a Court as charming, brilliant and attractive as possible; a theater and a literature that neither rots in the attic nor drowns in the cellar; and finally a university. Court, theater, university, that is the grand trilogy for a state like Weimar that can never have anything important in the way of commerce, an army or a navy. There it is, my principal theme that I will sound every note of in the distant hope that some good may come of it.[2]

2. Letter to Marie d'Agoult, 1844.

1847

I have worked pretty well these last two months, between two cigars in the morning, at several things which do not displease me; but I want to go back to Germany for some weeks in order to put myself in tune with the general tone.[3]

3. Letter to Carl Haslinger, Woronino, December 19, 1847.

1849

A thousand thanks for your exact and obliging packet of cigars. If you should have the opportunity of sending me some samples of a kind neither *too thin* nor *too light*, at about twenty to twenty-five thalers the thousand, I shall willingly give an order for some.[4]

4. Letter to Carl Reinecke, Weimar, May 30, 1849.

Please send a case of 250 cigars of a pretty good size from the Bremen Manufactory.[5]

5. Letter to Carl Reinecke, Weimar, September 7, 1849.

1851

I am bored with my daily meals at the *Erbsprinz*. On odd or even days (depending on rehearsals) I'll set up my little household at the Altenburg and give myself the pleasure of dining *solo*.[6]

6. Letter to Marie zu Sayn-Wittgenstein, Weimar, February 8, 1851.

I have just been told that the Jena Court of Appeals has completely absolved me, and I will neither have to pay a fine nor submit to prison for my supposed insults against the magistrates of the Grand Duchy.[7]

7. Letter to Marie zu Sayn-Wittgenstein, February 15, 1851.

For several days I haven't left the Altenburg, except at the hours of the frequent rehearsals and the operas (postponed), and the Concerts—but unfortunately I am scarcely left in peace, and there's a perpetual procession of blind singers, fleeced and fleecing tenors, disconcerting boors and bunglers, etc.[8]

8. Letter to Marie zu Sayn-Wittgenstein, Weimar, April 9, 1851.

Next week, thank God, there is to be neither Court nor Institute, due to Holy Week.[9]

9. Letter to Marie zu Sayn-Wittgenstein, Weimar, April 11, 1851.

The Grand Duke has recently signed a decree that will cause a certain upheaval in the Institute's orchestra, when it is published. Chelard is politely *unattached* and invited to make his request soon for a pension. Your very humble servant becomes *Kapellmeister* (Oh! Oh!) and has the whole crowd under his command.[10]

10. Letter to Marie zu Sayn-Wittgenstein, Weimar, the end of April, 1851.

1852

The rumor reported by several papers that I am about to leave Weimar and settle in Paris is quite unfounded. I stay here, and can do nothing but stay here. You will easily guess what has brought me to this maturely considered resolution. In the first instance I have faithfully to fulfill a serious duty. Together with this feeling of the most profound and constant love which occupies the faith of my whole soul, my external life must either rise or sink. May God protect my loyal intention.[11]

11. Letter to Richard Wagner, Late December, 1852.

1853

My poor days are going to slip away dull, monotonous, and languid—'The root of patience is bitter, but the fruits thereof are sweet,' as they say ...

At Mayence I bought two charming little volumes which are part of the Railroad Library (published in Paris)—'Joan of Arc,' by Michelet, and 'Saint Francis and the Franciscans' by F. Morin. The latter volume delights me. The dreams, the parables, the prayers, the teachings of the Saint all strike me as tender and impressive.[12]

12. Letter to Marie zu Sayn-Wittgenstein, Weimar, July 19, 1853.

1854

The course of my days is very monotonous—I get up at seven – work alone in my room until ten—Then my rehearsals begin and last until two—I come back to take up my scribbling again and we eat at five ...

I spoke to Abbe about my black servant—He makes a fetching contrast with the grand piano with its white tail (what wood it is I don't know), the main ornament in my room.[13]

13. Letter to Marie zu Sayn-Wittgenstein, Gotha, March 23, 1854.

My days go by very lonesomely here. I don't budge from my room, except at meal and rehearsal times.[14]

14. Letter to Marie zu Sayn-Wittgenstein, Gotha, March 31, 1854.

1855

Whether the great political event, the death of the Emperor, will have a softening influence on my personal fate, remains questionable ... Whatever it my turn out to be, I cannot waver or hesitate.[15]

15. Letter to Richard Wagner, March, 1855.

Best thanks for your munificence. The *weed* [cigars] is very welcome, and you will have to answer for it if it induces me to importune you with some more columns.

......

If you should by any chance have read that I am going to America (there are many people who would be glad to have me out of sight!), you can simply laugh, as I have done, at this old *canard*—but don't say anything to contradict it in your paper; such bad jokes are not worth noticing, and are only good as finding food for inquisitive Philistines.[16]

16. Letter to Franz Brendel, Weimar, June, 1855.

Our theatrical affairs are in a critical condition. The Intendant, Herr von Beaulieu, is going to leave, and the artistic director, Marr, is also said to have sent in his resignation. I do not trouble myself about these matters, and look forward with perfect peace of mind to the solution of these somewhat unimportant questions.[17]

17. Letter to Richard Wagner, Weimar, July 10, 1855.

Yesterday there was a driving rain *of Music* all day long; and from 8 in the morning until 11 in the evening I never left M. Hans, to whom I showed and played a pile of things.[18]

18. Letter to Marie zu Sayn-Wittgenstein, Weimar, July 21 1855.

It is to be presumed that neither the brilliant departure of which I was the hero a dozen years ago, nor the less flattering dismissal with which the infallible criticism of your capital has gratified me this time, will prevent me from returning from time to time, and without too long an interval, to Berlin.[19]

19. Letter to Frau Meyerbeer, Weimar, December 14, 1855.

1856

I am being quite economical and avoiding all unnecessary drinking.[20]

20. Letter to Marie zu Sayn-Wittgenstein, Budapest, September 9, 1856.

1857

Your wife must not refuse me the boon of getting me excellent coffee and a practicable coffee machine, for the abominable beverage which is served at the hotel as coffee is as disgusting to me as a *pièce de salon* by Kiicken, etc., and embitters my morning hours.[21]

21. Letter to Wagner, Weimar, July 10, 1857.

How sweet and good you are thus to take care of my intellectual nourishment by sending me Chateaubriand's *Memoirs*! You've catered to my tastes perfectly; for I don't know why, but through some chance or hidden coincidence, it is one of those books that forces me to read: a virtue not possessed by many volumes![22]

22. Letter to Marie zu Sayn-Wittgenstein, Aachen, July 28, 1857.

Yesterday I spent the day hearing Beethoven's *Mass* (a mediocre work by a first-rate genius) at the Cathedral—looking at a painting which depicted the Köln Dome as it will be when entirely finished—dining at the Suermondts'—reading through half of Bronsart's *Spring Fantasia* at the piano—posing for two hours for a new medallion by Mohr. I posed without the aid of a laurel wreath and of Mme Milde; since the. protests of Bülow and Bronsart were echoed by several members of the Committee, who decided that the only present to give me ought to be my own, personal likeness—and finally I dined on a chicken-wing and an apricot compote at the Suermondts' country house.[23]

23. Letter to Marie zu Sayn-Wittgenstein, Aachen, August 3, 1857.

1858

The musical evening (or rather night, since we sat down to eat at 10:15 and didn't begin to have any music until after midnight) ended with a four-handed march by Winterberger and myself.[24]

24. Letter to Marie zu Sayn-Wittgenstein, Prague, April 20, 1858.

Of my performances in Prague, Vienna, and Budapest, you have probably heard from others. Although I have no reason to complain, I am very glad that they are over, and that I may stop at home again; for I must candidly confess that the wear and tear connected with similar occasions is very unpleasant to me, and becomes almost unbearable if it lasts more than a few weeks.[25]

25. Letter to Wagner, May 7, 1858.

1859

The excessively stringent and restraining limits by which I have been hemmed in, have not allowed me to continue in a manner worthy of myself or of Your Highness the functions I have fulfilled in a slip-shod way up to the present … I am. quite aware how much the artist, or even art itself, may seem a useless luxury, and that in many ways I am no longer wanted at Weimar—that I find nothing but disdain on all sides and that everyone would like to make me shiver in a banal and bourgeois existence.[26]

26. Letter to the Grand Duke Carl Alexander, Weimar, February 14, 1859.

I should tell you that your little bust adorns my writing desk. You are of course without the company of any other celebrities—no Mozart, no Beethoven, no Goethe, or whatever their names may be. To this room, which is the heart of the house, none of them are admitted.[27]

27. Letter to Wagner, Weimar, August 22, 1859.

My position at Weimar is no longer tenable.[28]

28. Letter to the Grand Duke Carl Alexander, Weimar, February 14, 1859.

I don't want to talk to you at all about my grief. You know what sad days I had to spend in Berlin. A few hours before his death, Daniel [Liszt's son] said in his sleep, 'I am going ahead to prepare your places for you!'—So be it, and may God be blessed![29]

29. Letter to Marie zu Sayn-Wittgenstein, Weimar, December 24, 1859.

1860

The day before yesterday (for the first time since the death of Her Highness) there was a great Reception and Court Concert. Out of motives of 'discretion' and 'delicacy'—those are the terms that were used—Lassen was put in charge of the orchestra. Faineant was relegated to wearing his green uniform among the spectators and to chatting with everyone.—Their Highnesses were splendidly and royally bored—and the music suited their mood perfectly. I said to Mulinen upon leaving: 'Well, now you're even with Music'—which annoyed him to the point of rage.[30]

30. Letter to Marie zu Sayn-Wittgenstein, Weimar, January 14, 1860.

A pretty considerable amount of Hungarian *Paprika* and a little barrel of *Pfefferoni*. Please ask Kapellmeister Doppler where these things are to be procured genuine, and send them to me as soon as possible to Weimar.[31]

31. Letter to Eduard Liszt, Weimar, July 9, 1860.

To my daughter Cosima I bequeath the sketch of Stinle representing St. Francois de Paul, my patron saint; he is walking on the waves, his mantle spread beneath his feet, holding in one hand a red-hot coal, the other raised, either to allay the tempest or to bless the menaced boatmen, his look turned to heaven, where, in a glory, shines the redeeming word, 'Caritas.'—This sketch has always stood on my writing-table ...

I wish to buried simply, without pomp, and if possible at night.[32]

32. Letter to Princess Caroline Sayn-Wittgenstein, Weimar, September 14, 1860.

1861

On New year's Day we had a grand Court concert—on the top of which there was a banquet at the *Erbprinz*!, which lasted till four o'clock in the morning; on the other days perpetual dinners and suppers, at which I was also obliged to be present.[33]

33. Letter to Franz Brendel, January, 1861.

Between this and the beginning of August I shall fix on my next place of abode, which will, in any case, not for the present be a large town, because I want retirement and work above all. Briefly speaking, my situation is indicated by this dilemma: Either my marriage takes place, and that soon—or not. In the former case, Germany later on, and especially Weimar, may still be possible for me. Otherwise no![34]

34. Letter to Wagner, Weimar, July 7, 1861.

Although my acquaintance here is tolerably extensive and of an attractive kind (if not *exactly* musical!), I live on the whole more retired than was possible to me in Germany. The morning hours are devoted to my work, and often a couple of hours in the evening also.[35]

35. Letter to Franz Brendel, Rome, December 20, 1861.

1862

The services and ceremonies of the Sistine Chapel and of St. Peter's, to which I attached a special musical interest, have absorbed all my time during the last fortnight.[36]

36. Letter to Jessie Laussot, Rome, May 3, 1862.

1863

The last months brought so many interruptions in my work that I still feel quite vexed about it. Easter week I had determined should, at last, see me regularly at work again; but a variety of duties and engagements have prevented my accomplishing this. I must, therefore, to be true to myself and carry out my former intention, shut myself up entirely. To find myself in a net of social civilities is vexatious to me; my mental activity requires absolutely to be free, without which I cannot accomplish anything.[37]

37. Letter to Franz Brendel, Rome, April 14, 1863.

Father Theimer is kind enough to allow me to occupy his apartments in the almost uninhabited house of the Oratorian. The view is indescribably grand. I mean now, at last, to try and lead a *natural* kind of life. I hope I may succeed in approaching more closely to my monastico-artistic ideal.[38]

38. Letter to Franz Brendel, Rome, June 18, 1863.

The summer has passed quietly and I have not wandered abroad much; have, in fact,—been pretty constantly sitting at my work. My abode continues to suit me more and more, so I intend to spend the winter here … Unfortunately I cannot send you a picture of the grand, truly sublime view that can be enjoyed from every window. So you must imagine it to embrace all Rome, the wondrous *Campagna*, and all the past and present glories of the district.[39]

39. Letter to Franz Brendel, Monte Mario, September 7, 1863.

My stay in Rome is not an accidental one; it denotes, as it were, the third part—(probably the close) of my life, which is often troubled, but ever industrious and striving upwards. Hence I require ample time to bring various long works and myself to a *good ending*. This requisite I find in my retirement here, which will probably become even more emphatic; and my present monastic abode provides me not only with the most glorious view over all Rome, the Campagna and the mountains, but also what I had longed for; quiet from without and peacefulness.[40]

40. Letter to Dr. Gille, Rome, September 10, 1863.

In spite of my retirement and seclusion I am still very much disturbed by visitors, duties of politeness, musical protégés—and wearisome, mostly useless correspondence and obligations.[41]

41. Letter to Franz Brendel, November 11, 1863.

1869

I have been ensconced in the small tower of the Villa d'Este since the evening before last. Your most illustrious brother-in-law most graciously offered me this retreat. It is more than comfortable: above all during the winter, when the invasion of *civilized barbarians* makes my staying in Rome insufferable. Here I find myself again at my best; my apartment is very nicely arranged: two fireplaces, a new lamp hung from the ceiling of a little parlor which acts as a boudoir,—books and music in abundance.[42]

42. Letter to Marie zu Sayn-Wittgenstein, Villa d'Este, October 26, 1869.

1870

I came back here for the 8th of February, when my chief occupation was that of posing. A young French painter, M. Layrand, took into his head to do a masterpiece using my face: he has a most stubborn temperament, and forced me into sitting after sitting. Furthermore, Her Grace the Duchess Colonna Castiglione is being kind enough to make a little statuette of me; and Miss Ream, an American sculptress who has been commissioned to do the Lincoln monument for Washington, is undertaking to do a bust of me. Thus my likeness is fast becoming a kind of international symbol, and I am forced to act, at least in one way,—as a model.[43]

43. Letter to Marie zu Sayn-Wittgenstein, Rome, February 18, 1870.

1871

Notwithstanding the residue of sadness markedly accumulated within me by twelve years of agitation, of fights, of passion in Weimar, I feel less ill at ease there than elsewhere, thanks to the long-standing kindness of Their Highnesses, whom I shall ever try to serve gratefully and faithfully.[44]

44. Letter to Olga von Meyendorff, Budapest, February 7, 1871.

The copy of Pascal, which I thank you for remembering, has been mislaid somewhere, but we'll be able to share the pleasure of annotating another copy together at your Tuileries, where I also look forward to benefiting amply from your very obliging and much appreciated role of reader.[45]

45. Letter to Olga von Meyendorff, April 9, 1871.

From morning till night our time is taken up with those musical festivities in which, more than any others, I risk being given no respite. After the performances come public and private gatherings, speeches and resolutions, visits, meals, and entertainments.[46]

46. Letter to Olga von Meyendorff, Eichstatt, September 6, 1871.

A specter appeared here ready to commit a double murder—spare me the pain of a more detailed account. The specter vanished; my guardian angel protected me; and I am taking up again my usual way of life.[47]

47. Letter to Olga von Meyendorff, Budapest, December 1, 1871.

Today, I am devoting myself until about four o'clock to studying *ancient* history—very salutary at my old age.[48]

48. Letter to Olga von Meyendorff, Undated, c. 1871.

1872

My time here is spent or wasted with no diversions other than a little reading now and then. People are most kind to me; I try my best to show appreciation for this, but the balance of my existence is upset due to being unable to work a couple of hours a day at my music.[49]

49. Letter to Olga von Meyendorff, Budapest, February 28, 1872.

An American came to invite me, at all costs, to the Boston Festival, to take place in June, and for which a colossal hall is being built with a capacity of nearly 100,000 people. They'll probably install an orchestra there consisting of cannons.[50]

50. Letter to Olga von Meyendorff, Weimar, June 4, 1872.

Please ask Grosse to send me immediately to Bayreuth 200 Swiss Cigars of the same two kinds which he used always to get for me at Weimar.[51]

51. Letter to Olga von Meyendorff, Schillingsfürst, October 10, 1872.

1873

Now all I want in this world is to attend mass regularly and, on the important feast days of the year, to go to confession in order to draw near to the sacrament of Communion in Jesus Christ our Lord.

From Rome I continue to receive the most excellent advice; and moreover people are so kind as to add more. If I come to a bad end, it will certainly not be for want of sound advice![52]

52. Letter to Olga von Meyendorff, Budapest, January 22, 1873.

It was a good and friendly idea of yours to send me the photograph of Napoleon III on his deathbed. It has been framed and placed near my writing desk in the little room in which I sleep, eat, and work, and spend all my time, except for that which is taken up by more formal visits and by pianists to be auditioned, for there is no piano in this little room, which is very crowded with furniture and books.

In spite of the little time left over for reading, I read nearly every issue of *L'Univers* from cover to cover, as do conscientious provincial subscribers.[53]

53. Letter to Olga von Meyendorff, Budapest, February 24, 1873.

I don't have much success in distinguishing between the pure and the impure in politics in this world, and even go so far as to believe that we shall not know just what to think on the controversial point before Judgment Day unless one accepts prompt success as the decisive criterion of 'purity,' which, I must admit, I find most repugnant.[54]

54. Letter to Olga von Meyendorff, Vienna, April 3, 1873.

I had asked to be admitted to an audience of the Holy Father. He was so gracious as to receive me alone Monday evening and to converse with me for more than a quarter of an hour. The persuasive charm of his words touched me deeply.[55]

55. Letter to Olga von Meyendorff, Rome, October 18, 1873.

1874

The fact that certain polite customs are merely a convention does not prevent me from approving of them and even finding them sometimes very agreeable. So thank you, dearest one, for your New Year's wishes, which I fully reciprocate. If I refrained from anticipating yours, the fault for this lies with many others than myself. You know how harassed I am from all sides, and how absolutely impossible it is for me to set aside the minimum time I need.[56]

56. Letter to Olga von Meyendorff, January 2, 1874.

At this time I am hardly in a state to write with any coherence. Various minor tasks preoccupy and disturb me all the time. I need still another month before I can fully turn into my sad self again.[57]

57. Letter to Olga von Meyendorff, April 7, 1874.

Thank you for *L'Univers* which I continue to read *passionately*.[58]

58. Letter to Olga von Meyendorff, Budapest, April 15, 1874.

Fancy: not only have I read '93 of Victor Hugo, but I am driving myself silly by reading Flaubert' s *La Tentation de St. Antoine*—prodigiously colorful and erudite.[59]

59. Letter to Olga von Meyendorff, Budapest, April 27, 1874.

I will renew my subscription to *L'Univers* and to the *Allgemeine Zeitung* (Augsburger) (in which the *Bildunds-Philisterium* plays a prominent role; but there are some sly fellows on the editorial staff; and, of the German newspapers, it is the one I prefer to read—thereby imitating Beethoven!).[60]

60. Letter to Olga von Meyendorff, Budapest, May 6, 1874.

Having to write harasses me. And now, at the last moment the crushing blow has fallen on me of the Brunswick Musifest, where they are determined not to dispense with my uselessness even though I had already written very clearly in mid-March that I shall not be coming to Germany this year. This crusher coming on top of a number of other, more or less precious, stones is driving me out of my mind.[61]

61. Letter to Olga von Meyendorff, May 17, 1874.

I take the liberty again of inviting your Reverence to spend the next months with me here in the Villa d'Este, where you will find rest, quiet and coziness, mild air, glorious scenery, pleasant walks, good eating, good wine, books, music, pianos to make use of ad libitum, and a temperature mentally agreeable.[62]

62. Letter to Franz Haberl, Villa d'Este, Early Summer, 1874.

After arriving here Sunday evening I stayed alone in my rooms without stirring, except to go to the Franciscan church adjoining the Villa d'Este. I hope to continue this mode of life, which I greatly enjoy, during the summer and fall. Until now I have not even been down to the garden; the long terrace (with a superb view of the Roman Campagna) serves both as my dining room and a promenade.[63]

63. Letter to Olga von Meyendorff, Villa d'Este, June 13, 1874.

I pass my days very peaceably, and my evenings alone, in reading, writing or playing.[64]

64. Letter to Edmund von Mihalovich, Villa d'Este, July 30, 1874.

An ingenious invention of the celebrated Paris clockmaker, M. Haas: *the calendar-watch*! Have you seen one?[65]

65. Letter to Olga von Meyendorff, Villa d'Este, August 6, 1874.

1875

Will you please hand the enclosed note to Grosse, and ask him to get Burghardt to ship promptly to me the spirits I have listed.[66]

66. Letter to Olga von Meyendorff, Villa d'Este, November 9, 1875.

For the last couple of weeks I have been gloomily writing quantities of letters. I get nearly fifty a week, not counting shipments of manuscripts, pamphlets, books, dedications, and all kinds of music. The time required to peruse them, even casually, deprives me of the time needed to answer them.

Up till now it has been impossible for me to concentrate steadily on my musical work because of this too flattering and steady harassment by my correspondents in various countries. Some ask for concerts, for advice, for recommendations; others for money, for jobs, for decorations, etc.

I don't know what will become of me in such a purgatory.[67]

67. Letter to Olga von Meyendorff, Villa d'Este, November 20, 1875.

My *threefold* domicile, Budapest, Weimar and Villa d'Este, and all that is connected with it, makes my life very onerous.[68]

68. Letter to Eduard Liszt, Villa d'Este, November 26, 1875.

1876

I deserve at least a week's punishment on bread and water, with a xylophone accompaniment as sole entertainment, for my great blunder in having attributed to Lassen the diplomatic stroke of the change of title of Saint-Saën's *Danse Macabre*. I was extremely embarrassed to learn that the idea of this change came from such high places, and it only remains for me to crave your mercy for the offensive word 'nonsense,' intended *solely* for Lassen, and for no one above him.[69]

69. Letter to Olga von Meyendorff, Villa d'Este, January 12, 1876.

Thank you for the articles on the St. Joseph Psalter, and on the new works on linguistics—very interesting.[70]

70. Letter to Olga von Meyendorff, Budapest, March 1, 1876.

You did well to write to Cosima after her mother's death. As for me, the only thing to do is to keep quiet and to bury in silence the strange behavior of Mme d'Agoult toward her children.[71]

71. Letter to Olga von Meyendorff, Budapest, March 15, 1876.

During these three days I have done nothing but talk music with Mlle Ramann, who is very intelligent, hard-working, and of a rare and noble cast of character.[72]

72. Letter to Olga von Meyendorff, Nürenberg, October 9, 1876. An American artist who was commissioned to do the Lincoln statue in the US Capitol.

In Vienna I bought Wolzogen's pamphlet *Tragodie und Satyrspiel*. I like the title; but up till now I have only read some thirty pages without quite understanding how 'the impropriety of situations' in a drama brings out its basic morality.

In the *Concert of Europe*, the normal pitch is lacking, and the physicians who presume to cure the 'sick man,' Turkey, don't much agree on which treatment to apply. Some prescribe a series of amputations; the others, strangulation without more ado.[73]

73. Letter to Olga von Meyendorff, Szekszard, October 26, 1876.

In all Slavic countries, Russia has obvious and continuing advantages. It is up to her to know how to benefit from these, shamelessly or not. Her natural role in the Eastern question is that of *prima donna assoluta*, aside from certain husky tones and lack of responsiveness on the part of the orchestra in which Bismarck and d'Israeli are now playing first violin and trombone.[74]

74. Letter to Olga von Meyendorff, Budapest, November 3, 1876.

No doubt there is a threat of war; how could it be otherwise with the system of standing armies and the perfecting of engines of destruction?

In this old question of the East there is a huge difficulty and a great obstacle. The difficulty is how to be as thick as thieves when it comes to sharing the spoils. The obstacle is that the Christian powers are not so Christian that the Turks can take them at their word and trust them, under penalty of being crushed by them.[75]

75. Letter to Olga von Meyendorff, Budapest, December 2, 1876.

1877

Several passages in Legouve's academic speech in reply to that of the new immortal, M. Boissier, please me. First of all, with regard to Cicero: 'Ah, believe me, Sir, when one comes across such men in history, one must not depreciate their greatness because of their shortcomings, but rather absorb their shortcomings within their greatness,' etc. Then, on Juvenal: "Why demonstrate to us with your impeccable erudition and your implacable observation that this very Juvenal, so eloquently called by Victor Hugo *the ancient, free, soul of the defunct republics*, cared neither for the republic nor for freedom? Victor Hugo is nonetheless right!' Etc.[76]

76. Letter to Olga von Meyendorff, Budapest, January 3, 1877.

The Roman acts of kindness to Princess Wittgenstein are rather like those of St. Petersburg, with this difference, that in Rome it can no longer be a matter of governmental brutality, such as confiscation and loss of civil rights under false pretexts! Governments which still have recourse to these abominable measures should be scorned and spurned by European civilization.[77]

77. Letter to Olga von Meyendorff, Weimar, August 1, 1877.

I am told that one or two newspapers announce that I am going to Paris. I have no thought of doing so, and am moreover very weary of traveling. What I should prefer would be to remain, firmly fixed in one place, it matter not what, village or city, till my end, and to go on quietly as possible with my work.[78]

78. Letter to Eduard Liszt, Budapest, November 23, 1877.

1878

My life has for several years been regulated like a—somewhat broken-down—clock.[79]

79. Letter to Olga von Meyendorff, Bayreuth, April 9, 1878.

When [the Cardinal] is at the Villa d'Este we have dinner together at one o'clock and we meet again for an hour in the evening without other company. The rest of the time I stay in my room except for the morning hour at mass. I am served supper alone and I go to bed a little before ten.[80]

80. Letter to Olga von Meyendorff, Villa d'Este, September 22,1878.

Without knowing anything about politics I believe that the decline of the Austro-Hungarian monarchy would not be much of a contribution to the equilibrium of Europe.[81]

81. Letter to Olga von Meyendorff, Villa, d'Este, December 7, 1878.

1879

Let it be mentioned that since the end of 1847 I have not earned a farthing by pianoforte playing, teaching or conducting.[82]

82. Letter to Marie Lipius, Budapest, March 2, 1879.

I take my daily fare (with roast meat, good vegetables, and dessert, plus wine and coffee) everyday at about six o' clock with Cardinal Hohenlohe.[83]

83. Letter to Olga von Meyendorff, Villa d'Este, September 15,1879.

1880

People here honor me with an almost universal goodwill. This calls for my gratitude, which is never a burden.[84]

84. Letter to Olga von Meyendorff, Budapest, March 10, 1880.

In order to pursue my soliloquies I'm going to stroll to the cemetery.[85]

85. Letter to Olga von Meyendorff, November 2, 1880.

1881

My aversion to letter-writing has grown excessive. But who could answer more than two thousand letters a year without becoming an idiot?[86]

86. Letter to Edmund von Milhalovich, Bayreuth, October 8, 1881.

1882

With the exception of one incident, which stricter people than myself would call a regular fleecing on the part of the Custom House at Milan, whereby I parted with about 70 francs as a fine for having brought 50 cigars …

Wagner has lodged me splendidly in a spacious apartment of the Palazzo Vendramin, which formerly belonged to Madame la Duchesse de Berry. Wagner is the tenant for one year. The beautiful furniture still bears the impress of the old princely *regime*, and is perfectly preserved. The main inhabited part of the Palazzo Vendramin is in the best possible condition, so that Wagner did not have to go to any special expense, not even for stoves and other requisites, which are often neglected.[87]

87. Letter to Adelheid von Schorn, Venice, November 20, 1882.

I am housed in princely style at the Vendramin palace where family life is peaceful, complete, and not boring. Wagner goes out only for a stroll and dispenses with making or receiving calls. Cosima stays quietly at home, knowing that her husband prefers this. Thus, with a few exceptions, we are always by ourselves. For dinner (two o'clock) and supper (eight o'clock) we are nine at table. Some music, but not too much, before or after supper. Somewhat for my sake, the evening usually ends with two or three games of whist.[88]

88. Letter to Olga von Meyendorff, Venice, November 29, 1882.

1884

This time I was not able to have a thorough rest in Vienna. Such an extra [luxury] is hardly my lot anywhere. My life is one continued fatigue.

I hear for the first time through you of a cousin or niece, Mary Liszt, a concert giver. Concert givers have frequently misused our name by playing under it in provincial towns. A pianist in Constantinople, Herr Listmann, apologized to me for having knocked off the second syllable of his name. On this account he received a valuable present from the then Sultan Abdul Medgid.[89]

89. Letter to Henriette von Liszt, Budapest, February 8, 1884.

If Dorothea were willing to bring me forty or fifty cigars *Forti Napolitani*, not Cavours, she would do me a favor.[90]

90. Letter to Olga von Meyendorff, Budapest, April 11, 1884.

1885

To my regret the smallness of my income obliges me to leave no stone unturned to make money out of my transcriptions, for which I am now paid in Germany, Russia, France, at the rate of from twelve to 1500 marks apiece, for the copyright in all countries.[91]

91. Letter to Countess Mercy-Argenteau, Rome, November 21, 1885.

Chapter Five

Liszt on his Physical and Mental Health

1828

I have suddenly caught the measles, and have been obliged to say farewell to the concert.[1]

1. Letter to Carl Czerny, Paris, December 23, 1828.

1838

For nearly a week I have been confined to my bed with a very severe fever, which might easily have become more serious still…my hand trembles fearfully.[2]

2. Letter to Count Leo Festetics, November 24, 1839.

1844

I have been figuring as an invalid these last five weeks.—God be thanked and praised that I am already pretty fairly on my legs again, without rheumatism in the joints or gout![3]

3. Letter to Franz Kröll, Port Marly, June 11, 1844.

1848

I very obediently drank Goulon's medicine right down to the dregs –although homeopathic doses hardly sustain one more than certain prevention![4]

4. Letter to Marie zu Sayn-Wittgenstein, March, 1848.

1849

I have to betake myself in a few days' time to an almost unknown but very efficacious bath resort, and my doctor's orders are most strict that I must not make any break in my 'cure' during six weeks.[5]

5. Letter to Robert Schumann, Weimar, July 27, 1849.

I go to the baths of Eilsen, where I expect to spend all the month of October.[6]

6. Letter to Carl Reinecke, Weimar, September 7, 1849.

1850

Quite against my custom, I have just spent about ten days in bed fighting with a violent fever.[7]

7. Letter to Richard Wagner, Eilsen, November 26, 1850.

1851

I endeavor to work the utmost and the best that I can, though sometimes a sort of despairing fear comes over me at the thought of the task I should like to fulfill, for which at least ten years more of perfect health of body and mind will be necessary to me.[8]

8. Letter to Eduard Liszt, Weimar, undated, c. 1851.

1852

Of all the sad and disagreeable things which I have to suffer I shall not speak.[9]

9. Letter to Richard Wagner, Late December, 1852.

1853

I have been much depressed these last few days by many and various things. These are the day s of thunderstorms.[10]

10. Letter to Richard Wagner, June 8, 1853.

I returned last night from Leipzig with a bad cold.[11]

11. Letter to Richard Wagner, Weimar, December 13, 1853.

1854

On my own account I have not much reason to rejoice. My chief object and task is taking a very serious and painful turn. I had no right to expect much else in that direction, and was prepared, but these long entanglements which I have to submit to have caused me much trouble and have jeopardized my pecuniary position.[12]

12. Letter to Richard Wagner, Gotha, April 4, 1854.

For five days I have been in bed suffering from catarrh and intermittent fever, and shall probably have to be very careful till next week.[13]

13. Letter to Richard Wagner, Late April, 1854.

I have been obliged to keep to my bed, owing to a slight indisposition. My present indisposition is nothing but an overstrain and knock-up, which a couple of days rest and some homoeopathic powder will easily set right. I am still really very weak today.[14]

14. Letter to Franz Brendel, Weimar, April 26, 1854.

It is a wretched misery to have to spend one's time upon so many useless things and people, when one's head is quite full of other things!—Well, it must be so. God grant only patience and perseverance![15]

15. Letter to Louis Kohler, Weimar, June 8, 1854.

1855

Of my life, my hope, my endurance, I have nothing to say that is Cheerful.[16]

16. Letter to Richard Wagner, March, 1855.

If I had time, I would gladly go to Copenhagen again for a couple of weeks, to find a little solitude in the *Zoological Gardens* and to forget somewhat other *bestialities*. This satisfaction is not so easily attainable for me elsewhere.[17]

17. Letter to Edmund Singer, August 1, 1855.

1856

From Berlin I brought home so dreadful a cold that I had to go to bed for a few days.[18]

18. Letter to Wagner, Weimar, January 14, 1856.

Unfortunately, with regard to external matters, I cannot present you with many rosy things, although, as far as appearances go, I am counted amongst the happy. It is true I am happy, as happy as a child of this earth can be. I may confess this to you, because you know the infinite self-sacrifice and invincible love which have supported my whole existence for the last eight years. Why need I be disturbed by other troubles? All else is only the peace-offering for my exalted happiness.[19]

19. Letter to Wagner, July, 1856.

Your letter found me in bed, to which I am still confined by a somewhat protracted illness.[20]

20. Letter to Dr. Gille, Zürich, November 14, 1856.

1857

I am in bed once more, covered with the whole flora of my Zürich ills.[21]

21. Letter to Wagner, January 1, 1857.

Although I am still kept to my bed by a long-continued indisposition.[22]

22. Letter to Herr von Turányi, Weimar, January 3, 1857.

Your letter reached me, after some delay, in Zürich, where I had to keep my bed for several weeks—and today I write to you still from my bed, and sulking because the geographical change which I have made has not brought about any improvement in my pathological condition (which, by the way, is quite without danger).[23]

23. Letter to J. W. von Wasielewski, Weimar, January 9, 1857.

An illness, not in the least dangerous, but very inconvenient, since it obliges me to keep my bed rather often.[24]

24. Letter to Wladimir Stassoff, Weimar, March 17, 1857.

For the moment I am still pinned to my bed by a lot of boils which are flourishing on my legs, and which I consider as the doors of exodus for the illness which has been troubling me rather violently since the end of October.[25]

25. Letter to Wilhelm von Lenz, Weimar, March 24, 1857.

Owing to my long-continued illness, which obliges me for the most part to keep my bed ...[26]

26. Letter to Eduard Liszt, Weimar, April 27, 1857.

My feet and legs are feeling fine. There is no trace of an inflammation anymore.[27]

27. Letter to Marie zu Sayn-Wittgenstein, Aix-la-Chapelle, May 30, 1857.

I returned from Aix-la-Chapelle yesterday, and (bearing a little pain in both my feet, which requires some care) I feel so well that I can cheerfully go to my work and various occupations.[28]

28. Letter to Wagner, Weimar, June 9, 1857.

Though still obliged to keep my bed (which I have been able to leave so little during the whole winter) ...[29]

29. Letter to Countess Rosalie Sauerma, Weimar, June 22, 1857.

The condition of my *scaffolding* is improving.[30]

30. Letter to Marie zu Sayn-Wittgenstein, Aix-la-Chapelle, July 26, 1857.

1859

My health, fortunately gives me no trouble, and I have no lack of patience. The rest may come and will come.[31]

31. Letter to Wagner, Weimar, April 6, 1859.

I should have thanked you sooner had I not been kept to my bed for nearly a week in consequence of much emotion and fatigue.[32]

32. Letter to Ingeborg Stark, Weimar, November 2, 1859.

1860

I was in bed a whole week. There are moods and conditions in which we bear physical illness better than the uninterrupted sequence of everyday cares and tribulations.[33]

33. Letter to Wagner, Weimar, December 2, 1860.

1862

This last week I have had to spend in bed.[34]

34. Letter to Franz Brendel, November 8, 1862.

It is to be hoped that you would not be dissatisfied with the state of mind which my 50th year brought me; at all events I feel it to be in perfect harmony with the better, higher aspirations of my childhood, where heaven lies so near the soul of everyone of us and illuminates it! I may also say that, owing to my possessing a more definite and clearer consciousness, a state of greater peacefulness has come over me.[35]

35. Letter to Eduard Liszt, Rome, November 19, 1862.

1863

I had to remain in bed all last week—and am still pretty weak on my legs. But there is nothing further wrong: my head is free again; the rest can be imagined.[36]

36. Letter to Franz Brendel, Rome, June 18, 1863.

1864

I must tell you at once of an indisposition, which during Christmas week prevented my undertaking any other occupation or amusement than that of keeping in bed.[37]

37. Letter to Franz Brendel, January 22, 1864.

1865

My health is good, and I can unconcernedly allow people the pleasure of referring to me as 'physically broken down' and a 'decayed wreck' (as I have been described in the *Augsberger Allegemeine Zeitung*).[38]

38. Letter to Franz Brendel, The Vatican, September 28, 1865.

1871

Since our last meeting in Rome my inner sorrows have deepened. To make others share them would weigh on me as a wrong, and for the years still allotted to me I feel capable only of a kind of passive perseverance in conformity with Christian precepts.[39]

39. Letter to Olga von Meyendorff, Budapest, January 31, 1871.

It seems to me that the doctor is exaggerating causes for concern and I do not usually place much faith in recommendations of climate, baths, travel, etc., which I have only too frequently found to be foolish.[40]

40. Letter to Olga von Meyendorff, undated.

I have caught an ailment which has forced me to spend a couple of days in bed for the first time in years.[41]

41. Letter to Olga von Meyendorff, September 17, 1871.

My silly cold has improved slightly last night, and I shall probably be rid of it before the year's end.[42]

42. Letter to Marie zu Sayn-Wittgenstein, December 30, 1871.

1873

I started the year out with a bad cold which kept me in my room, more or less in bed, for several days. My friends here claim that among other faults I also have that of dressing too lightly in the winter, and they try to persuade me to wear fur coats. But my antipathy to this apparel is so strong that I am not going to resign myself to wearing one, and much prefer to catch cold and the grippe many times over.[43]

43. Letter to Olga von Meyendorff, Budapest, January 7, 1873.

For the last couple of days a stupid feverish cold in the head has kept me in bed.[44]

44. Letter to Eduard Liszt, Budapest, February 10, 1873.

M. de Korff, who was also a non-paying member of the audience yesterday morning, paid me the compliment of assuring me that I didn't look well.[45]

45. Letter to Olga von Meyendorff, May 6, 1873.

1874

On arriving here day before yesterday morning I immediately took to my bed and stayed there some fifty hours. Naturally I am not sick and do not allow people to talk to me at all about my health, as I retain my long-standing superstition on this subject. A medical oracle in Geneva used to say to me: 'Health is the basis of all progress,' and since then I have come across important people who solemnly repeated: 'Health above everything !' I have never been of their opinion, and consider many other things to be greatly preferable to health which is but a relative, secondary, and most of the time trifling blessing.[46]

46. Letter to Olga von Meyendorff, Budapest, April 10, 1874.

My cold continues to bother me; I cough a good deal, don't go out much, and when the evening comes I feel so tired that I am barely able to concentrate on reading for an hour.[47]

47. Letter to Olga von Meyendorff, Budapest, April 27, 1874.

I am resolved to ban [health] from all my conversations and correspondence, for it is only a waste of time and ink. Once again: I am not sick; my heavy and tenacious cold is at last showing signs of clearing up and I shall be going out in three or four days.[48]

48. Letter to Olga von Meyendorff, Budapest, May 6, 1874.

The question about my 'contentment' made me smile sadly. Short of wishing to be a nincompoop, one must be displeased only with one's self, and restrict to this intimate and salutary purpose the dose of discontent inherent in human nature.[49]

49. Letter to Olga von Meyendorff, Villa d'Este, August 6, 1874.

Your letter] finds me in a state of deep depression, and although I refuse to let myself worry, I feel nonetheless overwhelmed.[50]

50. Letter to Olga von Meyendorff, Rome, September 15, 1874.

On top of everything, I felt unwell, but recovered rapidly after having had to spend a day in bed.[51]

51. Letter to Olga von Meyendorff, Rome, October 5, 1874.

The patient is on the mend but still bedridden.[52]

52. Letter to Olga von Meyendorff, Rome, October 17, 1874.

It is now several weeks that I have been wanting to write to Cosima; unfortunately I can no longer hold a pen in the evening, and I don't really spend my days as I would like to. Do not ask me to explain; to go on living is enough—without any further explanation.[53]

53. Letter to Olga von Meyendorff, Villa d'Este, November 11, 1874.

1876

Hiller complimented me on my indestructible – youth! Mme Clara Schumann paid me more or less the same compliment.[54]

54. Letter to Olga von Meyendorff, Hanover, May 4, 1876.

I feel stupidly melancholic.[55]

55. Letter to Olga von Meyendorff, Hanover, May 11, 1876.

It is something of an effort for me to live through certain hours and days. Sometimes sadness envelops my soul like a shroud. This was the case last Saturday from morn till eve.[56]

56. Letter to Olga von Meyendorff, Hanover, September 27, 1876.

Several telegrams have arrived inquiring about my health. It may be that a few newspapers have mentioned my fall—not as composer, but a simple fall while getting out of a carriage. The damage was minor.[57]

57. Letter to Marie zu Sayn-Wittgenstein, Budapest, December 26, 1876.

Yes, I fell in getting out of a cab at the Hotel Hungaria; from this fall I still have a little discomfort in my right arm, nothing more.[58]

58. Letter to Olga von Meyendorff, Budapest, December 27, 1876.

1877

I am now quite recovered from my little attack. If there were nothing worse in this world than sprained legs and physical suffering, one could be quite satisfied. Moreover I belong to the very favored and happy ones, even as regards physical suffering.[59]

59. Letter to Eduard Liszt, Budapest, January 2, 1877.

So long as there is work to be done, I still feel relaxed and in fairly good form. For the rest, I am overcome by indescribable depression.[60]

60. Letter to Olga von Meyendorff, Budapest, January 28, 1877.

This is a very mild winter, but I am suffering physically and Mentally.[61]

61. Letter to Olga von Meyendorff, Budapest, February 12, 1877.

My health is adequate, my nerves and my mood are holding their own fairly well, and I would be an arch idiot not to recognize the fact that Providence has placed me among the most favored.[62]

62. Letter to Olga von Meyendorff, Budapest, February 23, 1877.

My nerves are seriously out of order.[63]

63. Letter to Olga von Meyendorff, Weimar, August 3, 1877.

My poor brain is very tired; I almost spent these last two days in bed but I am *not* sick, and you know I hate people worrying about my state of health, which is always good enough. This morning I was almost uncivil to an excellent and sympathetic young deacon who sometimes practices on my piano and who asked me 'if I was better?' This innocent question irritated me, for I consider that my health is always what it should be.[64]

64. Letter to Olga von Meyendorff, Villa d'Este, October 14, 1877.

I am desperately sad and completely incapable of finding a single ray of happiness. I'm in a kind of mental depression accompanied by physical indisposition. I've been sleeping badly for weeks, which doesn't help to calm my nerves.[65]

65. Letter to Olga von Meyendorff, Rome, November 9, 1877.

I have to go to bed early because of a bad cold which I brought with me from Rome. It seems that several newspapers say I am sick. This is not at all the case, but as I wrote you from Rome I feel I am reaching the end and even succumbing - and no longer want an extension. Keep this fairly naive confidence to yourself. Toward others I'll try to keep up a good front.[66]

66. Letter to Olga von Meyendorff, Budapest, November 28, 1877.

1878

My eyes are giving me a little trouble.[67]

67. Letter to Olga von Meyendorff, Villa d'Este, November 17, 1878.

1879

I am sad and cannot dispel my sadness.[68]

68. Letter to Olga von Meyendorff, Bayreuth, August 22, 1879.

1880

The last time I wrote was from my bed which I took to in the afternoon of Christmas day.[69]

69. Letter to Olga von Meyendorff, Villa d'Este, January 3, 1880.

Jean-Jacques Rousseau (I think it was) said that any man past forty who is not his own doctor must be considered an imbecile—an advantage to which I don't attach much importance.[70]

70. Letter to Olga von Meyendorff, January 16, 1880.

I suffer from extreme mental fatigue against which I struggle by praying and working.[71]

71. Letter to Olga von Meyendorff, Villa d'Este, October 12, 1880.

I'm writing a little poor music, but in a state of extreme depression because of my permanent conflict, for some fifteen years, with the only person who is the cause of my annual trip to Rome where I scarcely spend any time any longer.[72]

72. Letter to Olga von Meyendorff, Villa d'Este, November 13, 1880.

1881

My silly accident, from which I expected to be recovered in a week, is still dragging along. Next Wednesday I will continue with the warm baths at Bayreuth, followed by sweat-baths according to the doctor's orders.[73]

73. Letter to Marie zu Sayn-Wittgenstein, Weimar, September 12,1881. Liszt refers to a fall.

I have been ailing a good deal for the last three months. As soon as there was an improvement, something else appeared.[74]

74. Letter to Edmund von Milhalovich, Bayreuth, October 8, 1881.

My health does not preoccupy me at all; it is fairly good and only requires care, a thing which is at times irksome to me.[75]

75. Letter to Ludwig Bösendorfer, Rome, December 8, 1881.

1882

I am still detained here, partly on account of a stupid indisposition,—nothing serious, but disagreeably prolonged. I make a rule of never bothering my head about health, and I beg my friends never to trouble about it.

My eyes, without having exactly anything the matter with them, do not any longer adapt themselves either to reading or writing without reprieve; and by evening I often feel extremely tired.[76]

76. Letter to Malwine Tardieu, Weimar, November 6, 1882.

I was suffering from a twitching of the nerves that kept me from writing for a week.[77]

77. Letter to Marie zu Sayn-Wittgenstein, Venice, November 24, 1882.

1884

My eyes are growing so weak that it is becoming almost possible for me to use them for more than a few hours in the day.[78]

78. Letter to Olga von Meyendorff, Budapest, March 12, 1884.

No news from here other than the disagreeable weakening of my sight.[79]

79. Letter to Olga von Meyendorff, Budapest, April 11, 1884.

On my return [from Leipzig] I had a severe attack of illness, which prevented me for several days from writing.[80]

80. Letter to Louise de Mercy-Argenteau, October 24, 1884.

1885

My eyes are still getting weaker: my memory too, with the exception of that of my heart—described by a deaf-and-dumb person as 'gratitude.'[81]

81. Letter to Marie zu Sayn-Wittgensteint, Rome, November 19, 1885.

My weakness of sight is going from bad to worse. Soon I shall no longer be able to write.[82]

82. Letter to Olga von Meyendorff, Rome, December 23, 1885.

1886

My eyes are growing steadily weaker.[83]

Alas! I must put myself under the, to me, very disagreeable cure at Kissingen, and in September an operation to the eyes is impending for me with Gräfe at Halle. For a month past I have been quite unable to read and almost unable to write.[84]

To my physical condition, already so pleasant, has now been added these five days a most violent cough which plagues me day and night. To comfort me, the doctor says that this type of cough is very tenacious. So far, neither cough medicine nor infusions, nor mustard plasters, nor foot-baths have rid me of it.[85]

83. Letter to Olga von Meyendorff, Budapest, February 18, 1886.

84. Letter to Sophie Menter, Bayreuth, July 3, 1886.

85. Letter to Sophie Menter, Bayreuth, July 3, 1886.

Part II

Liszt View Of The World Of Music

Chapter Six

Liszt's General Outlook on Music and Art

1835

For the artist—sufferings, debasement, persecution. For art—shackles, exploitation, economic reforms, institutions, the Opera, the schools, and so on, that are either imperfect or baneful, gags and handcuffs. Everywhere, among all classes of executant musicians, professors, composers, we hear complaints, recantations, expressions of discontent or rage, vows of change or reform, aspirations towards a future that will be broader and more satisfactory that witness to the fermentation of the new leaven. More or less openly, more or less profoundly, all are suffering. Whether it be in their contact with the public or with society; the theater directors, the critics, the government clerks, the music sellers; whether it be, in a word, in their civil, their political or their religious relations … no matter *all* suffer.[1]

1. 'De la position des artistes,' *Gazette Musicale* (May-October, 1835)

1837

The work of certain artists is their life. The musician above all, who is inspired by nature but without copying it, exhales in sound his life's most intimate mysteries. He thinks, he feels, he speaks in music; but because his language, more arbitrary and less definite than all others, lends itself to a multitude of diverse interpretations. It is not unprofitable for the composer to give in a few lines the psychic sketch of his work, to explain the fundamental idea of his composition. The critic is then free to praise or blame the manifestation of his thought.

Few books appear today without prefaces, a sort of second book about the book. Often superfluous when it is a question of a book written in everyday language, does not this precaution become absolutely necessary—not for the instrumental music as conceived up till now (Beethoven and Weber excepted), music squarely ordered on a symmetrical plan—but for the compositions of the modern school, which generally aspire to be the expression of a tormented individuality?[2]

2. 'Lettre d'un bachelier ès musique à un poéte voyageur,' *Gazette Musicale* (February 2, 1837).

1840

Each day, reflection gives me deeper insight into the hidden relation that links the creations of genius. Raphael and Michelangelo make me understand Mozart and Beethoven better. Giovanni de Pisa, Fra Beato explain Marchello and Palestrina to me. The Colosseum and the Campo Santo are not as far removed from the *Eroica Symphony* and the *Requiem* as one might think. Dante found his pictorial expression in Orcagna and Michelangelo; one day perhaps he will find his musical expression in the Beethoven of the future.[3]

3. 'Lettre d'un bachelier ès musique à Berlioz,' *Gazette Musicale* (1840).

1852

External success and a certain *pleasing quality* are a secondary consideration with me in the case of works which are decidedly *above* the public.[4]

4. Letter to Richard Wagner, June 26, 1852.

All is perishable, only God's word remains forever, and God's word is revealed in the creations of genius.[5]

5. Letter to Richard Wagner, Late December, 1852.

1855

Marx is absolutely right in regarding the stage as too confined a field for the lofty passions…it lacks the indescribable magic of perspective, or mirage, or half-shade that the vision of marvelous pictures permits to the fancy. The inadequate reality of the stage can only hinder these as soon as it tries to replace the resplendent visions of the imagination by the visible scene. There cannot be any question that in many cases art does not suffer in the least when it renounces the attempt to represent everything, realize *everything*, make *everything* clear to the senses.[6]

6. 'Marx and his book, The Music of the 19th Century [1855],' in *Gesammelte Schriften*. Edited by Ramann. Leipzig, 1880–1883, V.

1856

Principles of economy are *utterly worthless* in copying, and, if you will believe my experience, always choose therefore the best, and consequently most expensive, copyists.[7]

7. Letter to Dionys Pruckner, Weimar, March 17, 1856.

Some years ago Dahlmann gave a lecture at Bonn upon immature enthusiasm. God preserve us rather from untimely pedantry![8]

8. Letter to Wilhelm Wieprecht, Weimar, July 18, 1856.

1857

The church composer is both preacher and priest, and what the *word* fails to bring to our powers of perception the *tone* makes winged and clear.[9]

9. Letter to Johann von Herbeck, Janu3ry, 1857.

1859

Music now forms an integral part of every grade of social existence. There is no one of these which, in this nineteenth century, can entirely dispense with operas and concerts, piano and singing, chamber music or part-singing; It is equally a necessity in towns during the winter, as in the country during the summer. It is in use at all solemn and public festivals, in all private family celebrations, and in the everyday habits of usual life. It is in demand for the young and gay to laugh and dance to, as an assistance to the meditations of the serious and to the reflections of the old. Each rank of society will henceforth feel its want, just as it will always need gardens and galleries. And the want must be supplied in a quantity which is frequently enormous, as well as of such exquisite quality as to render the fact of its being available often extraordinary.

......

Among the artists of all nations we must remember that it is those who are the least sure of posterity who are the most sure of themselves and of the moment.

......

To love the beautiful for its own sake became henceforth to consider the beautiful in music as an indispensable luxury for the great, the noble, and the rich; and to regard it as an indispensable article of consumption in the world, like an industrial production indispensable in commerce.

......

The Gipsies had already made their audiences understand that they should attach infinitely more importance to the quality than to the quantity, when instruments were combined. Might one not reasonably wish on behalf of many a present-day European audience (who delight in listening to military bands and to the music given at fashionable popular concerts) that they had as much good taste?

If our public were as advanced in this respect in the nineteenth century as the Gipsies already were in the fifteenth, they would willingly give up these colossal masses of instruments; for the sake of better appreciating the delicacy, individuality and expression in short, the signification of each instrument individually. In a human crowd of any description, even of instruments, there is always less euphony than clatter; in smaller numbers all men, whether virtuosi or other, know better how to express or sing whatever is sublime; instead of being constrained to shout it.

......

Dancing, being inseparable from music, lends itself naturally to singing; especially among primitive nations. Civilization eradicates and stifles this tendency by increasing the measure of what is expected from each art; and thus compelling it to adopt an isolated position, in order to become perfect. The union however always persists, until by degrees divorce becomes quite compulsory. Thus it happens that, in several countries (not by any means the least civilized) a custom survives of accompanying certain portions of the dance by choruses, interspersed with couplets, partly recited and partly sung by the principal dancer. In Poland, a neighboring country, the Krakowiaki and the Tropaki present examples, some of which have become quite celebrated in the history of national music.[10]

10. Liszt, *The Gipsy in Music*, 1859.

1860

I am writing to Schuberth by the next post to tell him (what he might know without that) how unwillingly and how seldom I meddle with dedications—especially dedications to people and societies that I don't at all know, as he would like me to do! In the somewhat numerous works of mine that have appeared of late years you will find very few dedications. The twelve Symphonic Poems have none. The *Gran Mass* is also without one—and in the Songs I have left out the earlier dedications. Therefore, before I try in America a method which I have almost given up in Europe, some time may yet elapse.[11]

11. Letter to C. F. Kähnt, Weimar, December 19, 1860.

1862

I openly confess that *in the main* Bronsart appears to me perfectly justified in vindicating his choice of new compositions for the musical directors, in spite of the fact that the two or three experiments he has made do not show in favor of the principle (as seen, by consequences). But between ourselves we must not conceal the fact that a great part of the laxity and corruption of our musical condition in Germany (as also elsewhere) is to be attributed to the too great—or too petty—yielding and pliancy of conductors and music-directors. I well know that the Euterpe Committee nourishes and cherishes quite another idea than that of Company X. Y. Z., or of the Court Theater directors A. B. C. D. Yet the question constantly arises—Shall the cook cook? Shall the coachman drive?—Ergo let the musician also have his own way. The harm that may spring from that is not so very terrible.

On the other side, I consider a change of persons in the management of a new institution is not desirable. In intellectual movements in particular the leaders of them are especially recommended to keep themselves *conservative* as regards their people. The public requires *definiteness* before all else—and just this is endangered by a change of persons.[12]

12. Letter to Franz Brendel, Rome, April 12, 1862.

1863

But of the best copyists it may be said 'Better none,' to use Beethoven's words in pronouncing his verdict upon Malzel's metronome.[13]

13. Letter to Breitkopf and Härtel, Rome, November 16, 1863.

1868

Exactitude in editions is a duty of the profession, too often neglected.[14]

14. Letter to E. Repos. Grotta Mare, August 26, 1868.

1874

Metzdorff's *Rosamunde,* well composed though it is, and even containing some brilliant passages, will have difficulty breaking into the theater circuit in view of the general prejudice (fairly well justified by experience) against new works not signed by names already made known by preceding successes, and above all against those in a serious historical vein with lofty pretensions. Pleasing and unassuming composers still have a slightly better chance of winning a few performances here and there.[15]

15. Letter to Olga von Meyendorff, Villa d'Este, June 24, 1874.

1879

A powerful, continual gale impels the Tetralogy of Wagner's Nibelings toward the summit of Sublimity. They may not easily be grasped, but who cares? Great works of human genius carry their own absolution within themselves.[16]

16. Letter to Marie zu Sayn-Wittgenstein, February 15, 1879.

Pope Gregory XVI conferred on Spontini the title of Count of San Andrea. This is the only example I know of a musician having been made a count by a sovereign. There is an equivalent in Verdi's nomination as Senator of Italy. In France, the same dignity was conferred on Auber …

I am still of the opinion that 'Intermission Music' as now played is a humiliating business for the members of the orchestra and a silly pastime for the audience. It has very sensibly already been abolished in several large theaters. The *torrent of custom* is one thing, but when it becomes a swamp it's better to do without it.[17]

17. Letter to Olga von Meyendorff, Rome, December 16, 1879.

1880

Among the Intendants I've known, Bronsart is almost the only one who is concerned with a dramatic work for the *sake of pure art*.[18]

18. Letter to Marie zu Sayn-Wittgenstein, Villa d'Este, January 1, 1880.

1881

It is not often easy for talents to succeed and this depends on capricious good luck.[19]

19. Letter to Olga von Meyendorff, Rome, November 29, 1881.

1883

Music is a tremendous burden.[20]

20. Letter to Olga von Meyendorff, Budapest, March 31, 1883.

Aesthetics

1837

It is obvious that things which can appear only objectively to the perception can in no way furnish connecting points to music; the poorest of apprentice landscape painters could give a few chalk strokes a much more faithful picture than a musician operating with all the resources of the best orchestra.[21]

21. 'Compositions pour piano de M. Robert Schumann,' *Gazette Musicale* (November 12, 1837).

1859

The word 'Evening entertainment' must, as is self-evident, be entirely dispensed with. Our business is to raise, to educate the audience, not to amuse them; and if indeed, as Goethe very pertinently says, 'deep and earnest thinkers are in a bad position as regards the public,' we will therefore not so much the less, but so much the more earnestly maintain this position.[22]

22. Letter to an Unknown Person, Spring, 1859.

1852

Since the many forms of art are only varied incantations destined to arouse sentiments and passions and make them, as it were, perceptible and tangible, since they communicate the quickenings of emotion, genius appears through the design of new shapes now and again adapted to feelings not yet embraced within the magic circle. Can it be hoped that, in those arts combining sensation with emotion unaided by thought and reflection, the very introduction of uncommon forms and styles is not already an obstacle to the immediate grasp of a work? Do not surprise and even exhaustion, caused by the strangeness of unfamiliar impressions, produce for the masses the novelty of an unknown tongue which at first seems to be uncivilized? The mere burden of accustoming the ear to it will discourage many who stubbornly refuse to study it. People of great vitality and youthfulness, those least enslaved by habit which is so respectable to its victims, are the first to be curious about, then to acquire a passion for, the new idiom. Through them it enters and takes over the resisting segments of the public which at last grasps its meaning, scope, and construction, and does justice to the qualities or riches it may enfold.

......

Let us cast out all but the noblest ambitions, to concentrate our concerns on efforts that dig a deeper furrow than the fashion of the day! Let us renounce, too, for ourselves, in the dreary time in which we live, all that is unworthy of art, all that lacks permanence, all that fails to shelter some grain of eternal and immaterial beauty which art must lighten gloriously in order to glow itself, and let us remember the ancient prayer of the Dorians, whose simple formula was so reverently poetic when they petitioned the gods: 'to give them Good through Beauty!' Instead of laboring so to attract and please listeners at any price, let us rather strive to leave a celestial echo of what we have felt, loved, and endured! Let us learn to demand of ourselves whatever ennobles in the mystical city of art rather than to seek from the present, without regard to the future, those easy crowns which, scarce assumed, are at once dulled and forgotten![23]

23. Liszt, *Chopin*, 1852.

… that sincere and earnest passion for the Beautiful without which one can never penetrate to the heart of works of genius[24]

24. Letter to Wilhelm von Lenz, Weimar, December 2, 1852.

1853

Virtuoso comes from Virtu.[25]

25. Letter to Franz Brendel, Weimar, April 30, 1853.

1855

Since in art no sect maintains a dogma on the basis of revelation and only tradition is authoritative; since music in particular does not, like painting and sculpture, recognize or adhere to an absolute model; the deciding of disputes between orthodox and heresiarchs depends not only on the court of past and present science, but also on the sense for art and for the reasonable in the coming generation. Only after a considerable lapse of time can a final decision be handed down, for what verdict of the present will be acceptable on the one hand to the older generation, which has borne from youth the easy yoke of habit, and on the other hand to the younger generation, who gather belligerently under any banner and love a fight for its own sake? Old and young must then entrust the solution of problems of this sort to a more or less distant future.

……

Music embodies *feeling* without forcing it—as it is forced in its other manifestations, in most arts and especially in the art of words—to contend and combine with *thought*. If music has one advantage over the other means through which man can reproduce the impressions of his soul, it owes this to its supreme capacity to make each inner impulse audible without the assistance of reason, so restricted in the diversity of its forms, capable, after all, only of confirming or describing our affections, not of communicating them directly in their full intensity, in that to accomplish this even approximately it is obliged to search for images and comparisons. Music, on the other hand, presents at one and the same time the intensity and the expression of *feeling*; it is the embodied and intelligible essence of feeling; capable of being apprehended by our senses, it permeates them like a dart, like a ray, like a dew, like a spirit, and fills our soul. Only in music does feeling, actually and radiantly present, lift the ban which oppresses our spirit with the sufferings of an evil earthly power and liberate us with the white-capped floods of its free and warmth-giving might from 'the demon Thought,' brushing away for brief moments his yoke from our furrowed brows. Only in music does feeling, in manifesting itself, dispense with the help of reason and its means of expression, so inadequate in comparison with its intuition, so incomplete in comparison with its strength, its delicacy, its brilliance. On the towering, sounding waves of music, feeling lifts up to heights that lie beyond the atmosphere of our earth and shows us cloud landscapes and world archipelagos that move about in ethereal space like singing swans. On the wings of the infinite art it draws us with it to regions into which it alone can penetrate, where, in the ringing ether, the heart expands and, in anticipation, shares in an immaterial, incorporeal, spiritual life. What is it that, beyond this miserable, paltry, earthly shell, beyond these numbered planets, opens to us the meadows of infinity, refreshes us at the murmuring springs of delight, steeps us in the pearly dew of longing; what is it that causes ideals to shimmer before us like the gilded spires of that submerged city, that recalls to us the indescribable recollections that surrounded our cradles, that conducts us through the reverberating workshops of the elements, that inspires us with all that ardor of thirsting after inexhaustible rapture which the blissful experience; what is it that takes hold of us and sweeps us into the turbulent maelstrom of the passions which carries us out of the world into the harbor of a more beautiful life; is it not music, animated by elemental feeling like that which vibrates in us before it manifests itself, before it solidifies and turns cold in the mold of the idea? What other art discloses to its adepts similar raptures, the more precious and ennobling in that they are veiled by a chaste and impenetrable mystery? What other art reveals to its votaries the heavens where angels lovingly hold sway and flies with them in Elijah's chariot through spheres of ecstasy?

......

Are not the arts in general, and the several arts in particular, quite as rich in variously formed and dissimilar phenomena as nature is in the vicissitudes of her principal kingdoms and their divisions? Art, like nature, is made up of gradual transitions, which link together the remotest classes and the most dissimilar species and which are necessary and natural, hence also entitled to live.

Just as there are in nature no gaps, just as the human soul consists not alone in contrasts, so between the mountain peaks of art there yawn no steep abysses and in the wondrous chain of its great whole no ring is ever missing. In nature, in the human soul, and in art, the extremes, opposites, and high points are bound one to another by a continuous series of various varieties of *being*, in which modifications bring about differences and at the same time maintain similarities. The human soul, that middle ground between nature and art, finds prospects in nature which correspond to all the shadings and modulations of feeling which it experiences before it rests on the steep and solitary peaks of contradictory passions which it climbs only at rare intervals; these prospects found in nature it carries over into art. Art, like nature, weds related or contradictory forms and impressions corresponding to the affections of the human soul; these often arise from cross currents of diverse impulses which, now uniting, now opposing, bring about a divided condition in the soul which we can call neither pure sorrow nor pure joy, neither perfect love nor thorough egoism, neither complete relaxation nor positive energy, neither extreme satisfaction nor absolute despair, forming through such mixtures of various tonalities a harmony, an individuality, or an artistic species which does not stand entirely on its own feet, yet is at the same time different from any other. Art, regarded generally and in the position it occupies in the history of mankind, would not only be impotent, it would remain incomplete, if, poorer and more dependent than nature, it were unable to offer each movement of the human soul the sympathetic sound, the proper shade of color, the indispensable form. Art and nature are so changeable in their progeny that we can neither define nor predict their boundaries; both comprise a host of heterogeneous or intimately related basic elements; both consist in material, substance, and endlessly diverse forms, each of them in turn conditioned by limits of expansion and force; both exercise through the medium of our senses an influence of our souls that is as real as it is indefinable.

Man stands in inverse relations to art and to nature; nature he rules as its capstone, its final flower, its noblest creature; art he creates as a second nature, so to speak, making of it, in relation to himself, that which he himself is to nature. For all this, he can proceed, in creating art, only according to the laws which nature lays down for him, for it is from nature that he takes the materials for his work, aiming to give them then a life superior to that which, in nature's plan, would fall to their lot. These laws carry with them the ineradicable mark of their origin in the similarity they bear to the laws of nature, and consequently, for all that it is the creature of man, the fruit of his will, the expression of his feeling, the result of his reflection, art has none the less an existence not determined by man's intention, the successive phases of which follow a course independent of his deciding and predicting. It exists and flowers in various ways in conformity with basic conditions whose inner origin remains just as much hidden as does the force which holds the world in its course, and, like the world, it is impelled toward an unpredicted and unpredictable final goal in perpetual transformations that can be made subject to no external power.

......

It sometimes happens that art blossoms like the plant which gradually unfolds its leaves and that its successive representatives complement one another in equal proportion, so that each master takes only a single step beyond what his teacher has transmitted to him. In such cases, the masses, to whom this slow progress allows ample time, whose *niveau* is only gradually elevated, are enabled to follow the quest for more perfect procedures and higher inspiration. In other cases, the genius leaps ahead of his time and climbs, with one powerful swing, several rungs of the mystic ladder. Then time must elapse until, struggling after him, the general intellectual consciousness attains his point of view; before this happens it is not understood and cannot be judged. In literature, as also in music, this has often been the case. Neither Shakespeare nor Milton, neither Cervantes nor Camoëns, neither Dante nor Tasso, neither Bach nor Mozart, neither Gluck nor Beethoven (to cite only these glorious names) was recognized by his own time in such measure as he was later. In music, which is perpetually in a formative state (and which in our time, developing at a rapid tempo, no sooner accomplishes the ascent of one peak than it begins to climb another), the peculiarity of the genius is that he enriches the art with unused materials as well as with original manipulations, of traditional ones, and one can say of music that examples of artists who have, as it were, leaped with both feet into a future time, are here to be found in greatest abundance. How could their anticipation of the, style which they recognized as destined for supremacy fail to be offensive to their contemporaries, who had not sufficient strength to tear themselves loose, as they had done, from the comfortable familiarity of traditional forms? Yet, though the crowd turn its back on them, though envious rivals revile them, though pupils desert them, though, depreciated by the stupid and damned by the ignorant, they lead a tortured, hunted life, at death they leave behind their works, like a salutary blessing. These prophetic works transmit their style and their beauty to one after another of those who follow. It often happens that talents little capable of recognizing their significance are the very first to find ways of utilizing certain of their poetic intentions or technical procedures, whose value they estimate according to their lights. There are soon imitated again and thus forced to approach more closely to what was at first misunderstood, until, in the fumbling inherent in such imitations and tentative approaches, there is finally attained the understanding and glorification of the genius who, in his lifetime, demanded recognition in vain. Not until it has become used to admiring works analogous to his, but of lesser value, does the public receive his precious bequest with complete respect and jubilant applause. The old forms, thus made obscure, soon fall into neglect and are finally forgotten by the younger generation that has grown up with the new ones and finds these more acceptable to its poetic ideal. In this way the gap between the genius, gifted with wings, and the public which follows him, snail-like and circumspect, is gradually filled out.

......

Every art is like the delicate blossom which the solid tree of a science bears at the tips of its leafy branches; the roots ought to remain hidden by a concealing coverlet. The necessity and utility of separating the material and substance in which art embodies itself into their component parts with a view to learning to know and to use their properties do not justify the confusing of science and art, of the study of the one with the practice of the other. Man must investigate art and nature; this is however not the goal of his relation to them—it is essentially a preparatory—if likewise important—moment in them. Both are given him primarily for his enjoyment; he is to absorb the divine harmonies of nature, to breathe out in art the melodies of his heart and the sighs of his soul. A work which offers only- clever manipulation of its materials will always lay claim to the interest of the immediately concerned—of the artist, student, and connoisseur -but, despite this, it will be unable to cross the threshold of the artistic kingdom. Without carrying in itself the divine spark, without being a living poem, it will be ignored by society as though it did not exist at all, and no people will ever accept it as a leaf in the breviary of the cult of the beautiful.

......

If instrumental music calls itself the summit of our art, its least constrained and most absolute manifestation, it does so either by virtue of its capacity to give to certain feelings and passions an expression intelligible to the listener, affecting his soul while his mind follows a logical development agreeing with his inner one, or by virtue of the indescribable enjoyment of indefinable impressions which, by force or in alleviation, transform our whole being into a state, incomprehensible to the unresponsive, often called contemplation of the ideal, so aptly characterized by Hegel as a sort of *liberation of the soul*, since the soul actually believes itself released from all material fetters and resigns itself unhampered to emotion's endless sea. Each musical constitution recounts to itself, if not quite clearly then at least in an approximate way, the impression which an instrumental poem should transmit from the author to the listener and is conscious of the passions and feelings and their modifications which it unfolds. Even though, in accordance with the propensity of his imagination, the individual clothes these passions and feelings with images of his own, he will be unable to deceive himself about the sort of temperamental activity which the composer intended his work to evoke. Assuredly, one cannot judge a musician's character better than by defining the mood which he leaves in the listener. The difference between the tone-poet and the mere musician is that the former reproduces his impressions and the adventures of his soul in order to communicate them, while the latter manipulates, groups, and connects the tones according to certain established rules, and, thus playfully conquering difficulties, attains at best to novel, bold, unusual, and complex combinations. Yet, since he speaks to men neither of his joys nor of his sorrows, neither of resignation nor of desire, he remains an object of indifference to the masses and interests only those colleagues competent to appreciate his facility. The rest pronounce on him the most deadly sentence of all they call him dry, meaning thereby that there flows in his work no vital sap, no noble blood, no burning passion, that it is a mere aggregation or crystallization of inorganic particles, comparable to those which scientists exclude from the science of life (biology), that is, from the realm of the living. But still—strange paradox—it is only the *composer* who can widen the boundaries of the art by breaking the chains which restrain the free soaring of his fantasy.

> Only, The Master can the moment choose
> With skillful hand to break the mold.

......

Just as marble presents artistic formulations of general concepts to the eye, so the ear, in instrumental music, desires something similar. For the cultivated listener, one symphony expresses to a supreme degree the several phases of passionate, joyous feeling, another elegiac mourning, another—heroic enthusiasm, still another—sorrow over an irreparable loss. If, then, these cultivated listeners are accustomed to seek and find in an art work the abstract expression of universal human feeling, they must experience a natural distaste for everything that aims to lend this universality concrete character, to make it particular, to derive it from a specific human figure.[26]

26. 'Berlioz and his Harold Symphony, ' *Neue Zeitschrift für Musik* (1855) XLIII.

I cherish the conviction that nothing truly good and beautiful is lost in the stream of Time, and that the pains taken by those who intend to preserve the higher and the divine in Art do not remain fruitless.[27]

27. Letter to August Kiel, Weimar, September 8, 1855.

1856

However others may judge the Symphonic Poems, they are for me the necessary developments of my inner experiences, which have brought me to the conviction that *invention* and *feeling* are not so entirely *evil* in Art. Certainly you very rightly observe that the *forms* (which are too often changed by quite respectable people into *formulas*) 'First Subject, Middle Subject, After Subject, etc., may very much grow into a habit, because they must be so thoroughly natural, primitive, and very easily intelligible.' Without making the slightest objection to this opinion, I only beg for permission to be allowed to decide upon the forms by the contents, and even should this permission be withheld from me from the side of the most commendable criticism, I shall none the less go on in my own modest way quite cheerfully. After all, in the end it comes principally to this—*what* the ideas are, and *how* they are carried out and worked up—and that leads us always back to the *feeling* and *invention*, if we would not scramble and struggle in the rut of a mere trade.[28]

28. Letter to Louis Köhler, Weimar, July 9, 1856.

Composers of my sort write, it is true, plenty of drum and trumpet parts, but by no means require the too common flourish of trumpets and drums, because they are striving after a higher aim, which is not to be attained by publicity.[29]

29. Letter to Edmund Singer, July 28, 1856.

1857

A successful performance cannot, as a rule be considered as a criterion of artistic worth.[30]

30. Letter to Fedor von Milde, Aix-la-Chapelle, June 3, 1857.

1858

Last Sunday we gave *Komala* by Sobolewski. I do not know whether you have seen a small pamphlet 'Opera, not Drama,' which he published last year as an introduction to his opera. The following beautiful comparison occurs in it: 'The words are the hard, transparent pieces of incense, the melody is the beautiful scent which emerges from the thick clouds of smoke, when the incense has been lit.'[31]

31. Letter to Wagner, November 5, 1858.

1859

It must be observed that, amongst all the arts, instrumental music is precisely that which expresses sentiment without proceeding to any direct application of it. It does not attempt to clothe the feeling it expresses with any allegory of facts, as narrated by the poem; nor does it seek to illustrate it by conflicts, as represented on the theater stage, by actual persons of the drama and their action. It brightens and charms the passions in their very essence, without endeavoring to represent them by real or imaginary personifications. It divests them of the influence of the surroundings among which they have slowly up-grown; and, like a precious sparkling diamond suddenly released from its prison, they accordingly shed their radiance. The emotions expressed by instrumental music are withdrawn from all positive assertion; neither cause nor effect being assigned to them. They are depicted only in their flow of virtual strength; thus speaking without either divulging their secret origin or their unknown extent.

Instrumental music is also the most suitable of all the arts, to release the passions from their residue in the form of hurtful applications. In this way, it enables them to be enjoyed in their purest essence; and with the most exalted motive. Manifested only in their intrinsic brilliance, they are caused by it to flow directly from the heart; just as the pure sap and most fragrant of rare essences sheds itself from a wound made in the bark of a tree.

......

To incite man to retrace the fine and noble sentiments which the manifestations of nature and art cause to unclose in him (especially in regard to desires or events which affect his fate or the misfortune and happiness of his fellow creatures) is precisely what constitutes the sublime aspect and moral sense of the benign influence which the work of God in Nature and the works of man in Art exercises upon the hearts of men, and upon the communities in which they gather.

A great artist one day expressed a thought in speaking of Art which is equally applicable to Nature. He said – 'What can Art do, more than stimulate?' By 'stimulate' he naturally meant stimulate to the *good* by the *beautiful*; according to the ancient prayer of the Dorians.

For what is the 'good,' when elevated to its utmost power, but the 'beautiful'; transported from the form in which it is known only to sentiment to the domain of action? And whence could come (if not from there) the ennobling gift of Art and Nature, the elevated character of the tastes which they inspire, and the love of which they are the objects?

Unfortunately, man is so weak, so fragile, so limited in faculty, that he cannot become absorbed in any object whatever.

Light is, for example, the very first condition of his happiness; but too much light will blind him.

Heat is the first principle of his life; but excess will soon devour him. Yet, should light fail, he is the most miserable of beings, and without heat he dies.

In the same way, he dare not totally engulf himself either in Nature or in Art; the view of the intelligence like that of the body risking to become weak by being fixed always in the same direction. Yet, he cannot in any condition disregard Nature without suffering; whilst to disregard Art, in any civilized form of society, means the death of that society, as such.

But, whatever may be the partial disorders which result for the mind from a pre-occupation too exclusive for one of these two objects—Nature or Art—the delicate chords of the hearts so devoted can never all break or become dumb; because Nature inspires and Art expresses sentiments which always *transport* the soul above the lowest regions to which it might descend—sentiments which take it *out of itself* and elevate it, on the contrary, to the highest regions to which it is capable of attaining.

……

Art being reflexible in its nature only develops under conditions which reflect. It has never been, nor will it ever be, seen to unfold itself freely in our atmosphere without resonance. Its process of germination is only accomplished under the influence of a sympathetic fluidity between artist and public. Its growth proceeds on the firm assumption of its first principle being capable of multiplication to infinity, aided by the caressing rays of a friendly warmth.

In times and places which have been remarkable for a grand development of art, artists are frequently met with who, disdaining present success or esteem, and acclamations too easily obtained, have addressed themselves more to successors than contemporaries. They have done this either by choosing for their works themes unfamiliar to those around them, or in introducing new forms. Such forms by being adapted to a new ideal promote the progress of art by hastening its inevitable transformations.

But, before arriving at the period when its vitality is sufficiently strong to withstand the coldness and indifference arising from prejudice and ignorance, or the opposition arising from hatred, art has to find a means of traversing the debilities of its infancy, and it can only do that by the fertile aid of appreciative sympathy. At this moment of its existence it resembles the sacred fig-tree of India; which only develops a rich vegetation if each branch with a downward inclination is enabled promptly to take root and become a parent-stem in its turn.

The soil is the human heart; and the productions of art are that symbolical forest in which all the trees are linked together by their upper branches, in order to provide by their living members a refreshing and delicious retreat to all hearts taking refuge there from consuming and sterilizing influences.

No people or county can be effectively illuminated by the splendors of art unless, at the appearance upon a height of its first beacon, corresponding beacons immediately appeal upon other summits. Art is not a parasitic vegetation, like the Aphides of Africa, to flower on any surf ace without root or soil or stem or even proper foliage Art, which in the eyes of positivism is the most useless of all inutilities, requires a favorable combination of conditions before it can become acclimatized; as if amongst us it were an exotic plant, having its real home in superhuman regions.

But, as the Beautiful is the splendor of the True and the charm of the Good, it follows that, though heaven makes the great gift of Art to men, it does not do so to anyone man; though it may endow an individual with the gift of creating—an approximative resemblance of its own All-power. The individual thus equipped with genius or talent, in clothing his sentiment either directly or in association with one idea, calls his work into existence out of nothing; as the Creator called the world in giving it its matter and form. But no work by anyone man constitutes an art.

Each work produced depends upon those which have preceded it; just as, according to its value, it will command those which follow it; for Art is not the inheritance of anyone individual; it is the patrimony of the people. Though it may abundantly nourish (where lips know how to taste its precious fruit), and though it may well console (where solitude of love is told to it in confidence), it can never be brought to being by the will of any individual. The individual may possess virtually in himself all the artistic faculties, but they evaporate unless joined by those of others.

The medium provided by the comprehension and enthusiasm of the body of mankind is necessary to art. It helps its progress and befriends it generally by receiving and communicating what inspiration and genius have confided to its care. Unless a nation as a whole and an entire period endow an art with their material vivifying forces, all spasmodic attempts to give it life are bound to be unavailing.

......

Music by itself does not develop the reason; but from it proceed those emotions of the heart from which the will is developed. It would avail nothing merely to *see* the True, to *know* the Good, or to *judge* the Beautiful if, in the meantime, the will to act were lacking.

Music is the intermediary which places sentiment in harmony with intelligence; enabling us to enjoy and love that which intelligence enables us to become acquainted. The Greeks, who were naturally gifted with an incomparable appreciation of the Beautiful, well understood the subtle connecting link provided by music between the perceptible and the impalpable between that which is understood and that which is felt.

......

Between *Sentiment* and *Form* there is some impalpable flame, some principle of mysterious equilibrium, the presence of which is the final authority in deciding the rank or value of any artistic production. It is that which determines whether the transparence of a sentiment is met with in a form to a sufficient degree for the sentiment to become translucent; or in other words for the sentiment to shine out in all brilliancy.

The existence of this identification between *Sentiment*:, which is the soul of every work of art, and *form*, which is the clothing of its body, constitutes the supreme reason of its existence; and is a complete and invincible reply to any objection. But this impalpable flame—this mysterious identification—does not lend itself to any verbal description; its test being that of making itself immediately perceived.

......

Let it not be forgotten that all art in general as well as each work of art taken separately is but the glorified abode of a sentiment; sometimes embodied in a thought, or sometimes acting without it by the force of its own immediate irradiation. In the latter case it gains its effect more rapidly; by showing itself more intense and always more immanent in those particular features which resemble nothing else; and in those forms the general disposition of which is stronger, and the effect more typical, because comparable to nothing else.

......

Architecture and music, moreover, are alike devoid of any prototype, and are neither of them arts of imitation. In order to be soundly judged, their works require also to be arranged in distinct families; according to the nations and to the periods to which they belong. In music as in architecture it is commonly agreed to call these great divisions by the name of *school* or *style*. In each style there are monumental works which represent its inspiration most purely—which interpret its prevailing idea most exactly. Styles which are separated from one another by a certain distance are connected by works of transition, which are of equal service to both as links; evincing in the first place the influence of the school from which they proceed and also becoming modified by the influence of the school which is about to follow; whether the latter be better or worse, or whether it be indicative of progress or decay.

But in music, as in architecture, there may also be styles; born, so to speak, away from the great royal road which art pursues. Having developed away from all observation, they seem to be of spontaneous growth, because one cannot ascertain by what means they have come into being.[32]

32. Liszt, *The Gipsy in Music*, 12, 91ff., 204ff., 289, 302ff., 329, 330ff.

Beethoven was quite right to assert *his right* to allow that which was forbidden by Kirnberger, Marpurg, Albrechtsberger, etc.![33]

33. Letter to Franz Brendel, Weimar, December 1, 1859.

1862

With notes alone nothing can be accomplished; one thirsts for soul, spirit, and actual life. Ah! composing is a misery, and the pitiful children of my Muse appear to me often like foundlings in a hospital, wandering about only as Numbers so and so![34]

34. Letter to Franz Brendel, Rome, August 29, 1862.

1869

Great manifestations of genius ought to do the part of the sun, -to illuminate and fertilize.[35]

35. Letter to Franz Servais, Rome, July 4, 1869.

1875

Music, the most communicative of the arts, is also the most lonely for those who plumb its depths. Beethoven tells us this sublimely in his last years.[36]

36. Letter to Olga von Meyendorff, Villa d'Este, October 7, 1875.

1876

To compose philosophy and politics in music appears to me an all-too-difficult task. I almost doubt whether it could be accomplished.[37]

37. Letter to Eduard Liszt, Villa d'Este, January 23, 1876.

1877

When one is at a loss what to say or write, well—one tries to help oneself with music.[38]

38. Letter to Adelheid von Schorn, Rome, September 15, 1877.

1878

Issue Nr. 2 of the *Bayreuther Blätter* (February) gives us admirable instructions by Wagner on the question, "Was ist Deutsch?' I particularly recommend pages thirty-two to thirty-five.[39]

39. Letter to Olga von Meyendorff, Budapest, March 14, 1878.

I saw in some paper or other a charming remark by Theophile Gautier: 'Music doesn't exist; it's just a sound going around.'[40]

40. Letter to Olga von Meyendorff, Rome, September 12, 1878.

1880

Supreme serenity still remains the Ideal of great Art.[41]

41. Letter to Marie zu Sayn-Wittgenstein, Weimar, July 30, 1880.

1882

Let me confess to you quite in a whisper that I am inclined rather to hold back with respect to certain love-scenes, which, it seems, are necessary on the stage, when introduced into biblical subjects. They jar on my feelings.[42]

42. Letter to Malwine Tardieu, Rome, January 20, 1882.

1883

Doubtless *form* in Art *is* necessary to the expression of ideas and sentiments; it must be adequate, supple, free, now energetic, now graceful, delicate; sometimes even subtle and complex, but always to the exclusion of the ancient remains of decrepit formalism.[43]

43. Letter to Casar Cui, Weimar, December 30, 1883.

1884

Rarely is success in a hurry to accompany *soul.*[44]

44. Letter to Louise de Mercy-Argenteau, October 24, 1884.

The New Art

1852

In the 1830s in music as in literature a new school was forming. Young talents were rising who lustily shook off the yoke of ancient Formulas. *Romanticism* was the order of the day, and it was stubbornly contested, for and against. There was no truce between those who would not admit that writing could be different from what it had been previously and those who wanted the artist to be free to choose the form and mold it to his feeling, who thought that since the rule of form was based upon agreement with the emotion demanding utterance, each different mode of feeling necessarily sanctioned a different mode of expression. The former believed in the existence of a form that was permanent, its perception representing absolute beauty, and they judged each work from this pre-established point of view. But while admitting that the great Masters had attained the ultimate limits of art and supreme perfection, they left to the artists who followed no glory other than the hope to approach them, more or less by imitation; and they denied them even the hope of equaling them, since the perfecting of technique can never rise to the level of creation. The latter denied that beauty could have an unchanging, absolute form. The various forms as manifested in the history of art appeared to them as tents pitched along the road of the ideal, momentary points which the genius reaches from epoch to epoch and which his immediate successors must go beyond. The former wished to enclose in the symmetrical frame of similar patterns the inspirations of the most dissimilar times and kinds; the latter claimed for each inspiration the freedom to create their own style, and accepted no other rule than that which springs from the direct relations of feeling and form so that one would answer for the other. (Existing models, however admirable, did not seem to have exhausted all the emotions that art can seize and all the forms that it can use.) Not stressing the excellence of form, they sought it only to the extent that its faultless perfection is indispensable to the full revelation of emotion, for they were aware that emotion is maimed as long as an imperfect form, like an opaque veil, intercepts its radiance. And so they subordinated professional craft to poetic inspiration, calling upon patience and genius to rejuvenate the form that would satisfy the demands of inspiration. They reproached their opponents for subjecting inspiration to Procrustean torture, for admitting that certain types of feeling were inexpressible in predetermined forms, and for depriving art in advance of all the works which would have tried to introduce new feelings in new shapes—feelings that come from the ever progressing development of the human spirit and the instruments and material resources of art. Those

who saw the flames of genius slowly consuming the old worm-eaten scaffolds rallied to the school of music of which Berlioz was the most gifted, most courageous, and most daring representative.[45]

45. Franz Liszt, *Chopin*, 1852, 29ff., 87ff., 116ff.

The idea of a Congress of Kapellmeisters is indeed a very judicious one, and from a satisfactory realization of it only good and better things could result for the present divided state of music. There is no question that in the insulation and paralyzing of those who are authorities in Art lies a very powerful hindrance, which, if it continues, must essentially injure and endanger Art.[46]

46. Letter to Gustav Schmidt, Weimar, May 18, 1852.

1854

The next few years will probably set our party more firmly on their legs; the invalidity of our opponents vouches pretty surely for that, apart from the fact, which is nevertheless the principal point, that powerful talent is developing in our midst, and many others who formerly stood aloof from us are drawing near to us and agreeing with us.

Do not let yourself be grieved at the ever-widening schism in Leipzig about which you write to me. We have nothing to lose by it; we must only understand how to assert our full rights in order to attain them. That is the task, which will not be accomplished in a day nor in a year. Indeed, it is written in the Gospel, 'The harvest truly is plentiful, but the laborers are few!' Therefore we are not to make ourselves over-anxious—only to remain firm, again to remain firm - the rest will come of itself![47]

47. Letter to Franz Brendel, December 1, 1854.

1855

Nothing human stands still; cult, custom, law, government, science, taste, and mode of enjoyment—all change, all are constantly coming and passing away, without rest, without respite; no country is quite like any other, and no century ends in the same atmosphere with which it began; the endeavors, tendencies, improvements, and ideals of each generation plow up the hereditary fields in order to experiment with a new kind of crop.[48]

48. 'Berlioz and his *Harold* Symphony,' *Neue Zeitschrift fürMusik* (1855) XLIII.

As far as I know, there is in London no pianist like [Klindworth]; but, on account of his determined and open sympathy with the so-called 'music of the future,' he has placed himself in a somewhat awkward position towards the Philistines and handicraftsmen there.[49]

49. Letter to Richard Wagner, Weimar, January 25, 1855.

The domain of artists is in the greater part guilty of our sluggish state of Art, and it is from this side especially that we must act, in order to bring about gradually the *reform*.[50]

50. Letter to Franz Brendel, April 1, 1855.

The English edition of Philistinism is not a whit pleasanter than the German, and the chasm between the public and ourselves is equally wide everywhere. How, in our wretched conditions, could enthusiasm, love, and art have their true effect?[51]

51. Letter to Richard Wagner, Weimar, May 2, 1855.

Yesterday we had the pleasure of swallowing huge portions of musical *Bread-soup*, under the guise of a Symphony, Overture and 'Free Fantasy' in M. Taubert's style—although for my type of mustard-lover and Grog-drinker, the *Bread-soup*, as you know, has lost all its savor.[52]

52. Letter to Marie zu Sayn-Wittgenstein, Weimar, July 21, 1855.

1858

Since [our opponents] have not succeeded in *silencing* us in a conspicuous manner, they would like to *kill* us insignificantly, for which, however, other weapons would be necessary than those which they have at their command.

Meanwhile Bronsart's form of argument ['Musical Duties,' Leipzig, Matthes, 1858] will give you a pleasant hour, and if, as you tell me, you have found in Munich a few comrades of the same mind, let the '*Musikalische Pflichten*' be recommended in their circle.

Amongst other things the assumption of the reporter of the *Allgemeine Zeitung* that Wagner himself had never conducted his *Lohengrin* better than Franz Lachner, appeared to me very droll. It is well known that Wagner has *never heard* this work, let alone conducted it! Ignorance of this kind is, moreover, not the worst on the other side, where intentional and unintentional ignorance and lies (not to mince the matter) are continually being directed against us.

But enough of that. Let us continue to go on our own way simply and honorably, and let the tame or wild beasts on our right and left behave as they like![53]

53. Letter to Dionys Pruckner, Prague, March 9, 1858.

You have struck your roots entirely in German soil; you are, and remain, the glory and splendor of German art. While theatrical affairs abroad are in their present condition, while Meyerbeer and Verdi reign supreme, while theatrical managers, singers, conductors, newspapers, and the public are under their immediate influence, there is no need for you to mix yourself up with this muddle.[54]

54. Letter to Wagner, Salzburg, October 9, 1858.

1860

Our opponents 'triumph far more than they conquer us,' as Tacitus says. They will not be able to hold their narrow, malicious, negative, and unproductive thesis much longer against our quiet, assured, positive progress in Art-works. A consoling and significant symptom of this is that they are no longer able to support their adherents among living and working composers, but devour them critically while the public is so indifferent. The *resume* of the whole criticism of the opposition may be summed up in the following words: 'All the heroes of Art in past times find, alas! no worthy successors in our day.' But our time will not give up its rights—and the rightful successors will prove themselves such![55]

55. Letter to Eduard Liszt, Weimar, September 20, 1860.

1872

Kindly return to me Hanslick's psychiatric article which I'll send off to Rome so that they should know there that if I sin out of excessive admiration for Wagner, it is not for lack of awareness of what his adversaries think. To them I would willingly say with M. de Maistre: 'From the height to which one must rise in order to encompass the totality of things, one no longer sees anything of what you see; consequently I cannot answer you, unless you should take this as an answer.'[56]

56. Letter to Olga von Meyendorff, Budapest, November 15, 1872.

1874

In spite of the legion of Dessoff, calm plains or storms, go on roaring bravely in the waters of the 'Phantom Ship.' Even should we not succeed in arriving safely in port, and should we meet no other *Senta* than Her Highness Madam Criticism, it matters not; those who follow us in the *same waters* of the Ideal will be more fortunate.[57]

57. Letter to Edmund von Mihalovich, Villa d'Este, December 29, 1874.

1877

The road already covered at Bayreuth in spite of so many obstacles makes me confident that we will finally succeed. Besides, there is something greatly comforting in the alleged exaggerations of men of great genius like Wagner; far from laughing at them, which is not difficult and may even seem almost reasonable, I attempt to rise to the height required for one not to misjudge things belonging to the higher order of inspiration. In the midst of so many theatrical indignities and filth why should it be forbidden to speak of the dignity of art? Do we have ears only for mountebanks?[58]

58. Letter to Olga von Meyendorff, Budapest, February 12, 1877.

Those who have been led astray by the common practice of theaters find it impractical that a man of extraordinary genius should speak seriously of the dignity of dramatic art, should ponder it and propose its achievement.[59]

59. Letter to Olga von Meyendorff, Budapest, February 15, 1877.

1879

I know some people more courageous, more senior, more sorely tried, and worthier than M. Richter of Dresden. Nohl, for example, has been quasi-victimized since his conversion to Wagner, which was too conspicuous for a biographer of Mozart. Let us see things as they are without indulging in rhetorical excesses. Bülow—above all others—Bronsart, Tausig, Cornelius, and a few others unknown to you have really suffered in the 'good cause' which your very humble servant flatters himself he has been defending over the last thirty years. M. Richter is still only an acolyte with no claim to martyrdom.[60]

60. Letter to Olga von Meyendorff, Rome, January 4, 1879.

On Music Literature

1849

One would say that a bad fairy, in order sometimes to counterbalance the works of genius, gives a magic success to the most vulgar works and presides over the propagation of them, favoring those whom inspiration has disdained, in order to push its elect into the shade.[61]

61. Letter to Carl Reinecke, Weimar, May 30, 1849.

1855

Kuhmstedt's oratorio *The Transfiguration of he Lord* will be given at the theater, under the very undirecting direction of the composer. After having heard it at three rehearsals, I found no satisfaction in it either for my ears or my mind: it is the old frippery of counterpoint—the old unsalted, unpeppered sausage, etc., rubbish, to the ruin of the eye and ear![62]

62. Letter to Anton Rubinstein, Weimar, April 3, 1855.

There is without doubt nothing better than to respect, admire, and study the illustrious dead; but why not also sometimes live with the living?[63]

63. Letter to the Intendant of the Court Theater in Weimar, Weimar, May 21, 1855.

Carl Evers' letter has amused me, and it will cost you but little diplomacy to conciliate the sensitive composer. You know what I think of his talent for composition. From people like that nothing is to be expected as long as they have not learned to understand that they are uselessly going round and round in what is hollow, dry, and used up. That good Flügel has also little power of imagination, although a little more approach to something more earnest, which has at least this good in itself—that it checks a really too naive productiveness.[64]

64. Letter to Franz Brendel, Weimar, June 15, 1855.

Titus Livius, composed by Sechter, will probably have to moulder away very unhistorically as waste paper.[65]

65. Letter to Moritz Hauptmann, Weimar, September 28, 1855.

1857

As far as I know, Bertini is still *living*, and according to the common idea, to which one must stick fast, only those who are *dead* can rank as classic and be proclaimed as classic. Thus

Schumann, the romanticist, and Beethoven, the glorious, holy, crazy one, have become classics. Should Bertini have already died, I take back my remark, although the popularity of his Studies is not, to me, a satisfactory reason for making his name a classic.[66]

66. Letter to L. A. Zellner, January 2, 1857.

1858

We shall perform here a comic opera, *The Barber of Bagdad* by Cornelius. The music is full of wit and humor, and moves with remarkable self-possession in the aristocratic region of art.[67]

67. Letter to Wagner, November 5, 1858.

1860

At Wiesbaden, Frankfurt, and I know not where else, they were waiting for Wagner, and wanted to see him conduct, or at least listen to, *Tannhäuser, Lohengrin*, etc., and there would certainly have been no lack of enthusiastic demonstrations; but from a work like *Tristan*, at the very first sight of the score of which every one must exclaim: 'This is something unheard of, marvelous, sublime,' they run away, and hide themselves like fools.[68]

68. Letter to Wagner, Weimar, September 21, 1860.

1869

It is long since any new composition has given me the impression of intellectual strength and musical completeness, such as I find in yours. I am convinced that wherever the 42nd and 43rd Psalms are heard every person with any depth of soul will feel their sublime beauty, and offer you something more valuable than mere ordinary applause. But allow me to tell you quite frankly: You must not hold yourself aloof and at a distance; your splendid works must be performed.[69]

69. Letter to Heinrich Schulz-Beuthen, Weimar, June 18, 1869.

1872

Are you in touch with the musical *young Russia* and its very notable leaders—Messrs. Balakireff, Cui, and Rimski-Korsakoff? I have lately read several of their works; they deserve attention, praise and propagation.[70]

70. Letter to Wilhelm von Lenz, Weimar, September 20, 1872.

1873

With such a clause as Joachim introduces for the *Novitäten-concerten*—'That only such composers shall be taken into consideration in the programs whose renown as artistic representatives of the German nation is established'—Handel, Bach, Mozart, nay even Beethoven, would have come off badly in their life-time![71]

71. Letter to Otto Lessmann, Weimar, September 24, 1873.

1874

The success of *serious* operas seems to be to be getting more and more unlikely. Offenbach and his cronies (either disguised or not) are succeeding well. Wagner survives—and predominates—in the face of farces and platitudinous works. His genius alone gives sublimity to the theater. I think, come lean years or fat, good luck or bad, all self-respecting theaters should feel it their duty to perform new works, to be chosen with discernment.[72]

72. Letter to Marie zu Sayn-Wittgenstein, Horpacs, February 1, 1874.

1875

I'm well aware that people are at their wits' end where to turn for a libretto, but is it really so essential to write scores for the stage? Couldn't young and old musicians find a better way to spend their time?[73]

73. Letter to Olga von Meyendorff, Vienna, April 8, 1875.

I insist on contemporary composers being granted their share in a spirit of intelligent generosity. So please recommend once again Metzdorff's *Rosamunde* and Saint-Saëns' *Samson* to M. de Loën, at the risk of neither of them achieving the hoped-for success. Above all, one must guard against inertia in the theater and elsewhere.[74]

74. Letter to Olga von Meyendorff, Nürenberg, September 16, 1875.

I attach *great* importance to one or two Russian symphonic works being played at the Altenburg Musikfest [Rimsky-Korsakov's *Sadko* and Borodin's *Symphony* Nr 1.[75]

75. Letter to Olga von Meyendorff, Villa d'Este, December 28, 1875.

1876

I hasten to assure you again of the strong interest which I take in the works of the new Russian composers—Rimski-Korsakof, Cui, Tschaikowsky, Balakireff, Borodine.[76]

76. Letter to the Publisher Bessel, Weimar, June 20, 1876.

In sending you today the transcription of your *Danse macabre*, I beg you to excuse my unskillfulness in reducing the marvelous coloring of the score to the possibilities of the piano. No one is bound by the impossible. To play an orchestra on the piano is not yet given to any one. Nevertheless we must always stretch towards the *Ideal* across all the more or less dogged and insufficient forms. It seems to me that Life and Art are only good for that.[77]

77. Letter to Camille Saint-Saëns, Hanover, October 2, 1876.

I have heard Bizet's *Carmen*: the music is by no means boring, and is even polished, but of a kind which is most successful in Paris.[78]

78. Letter to Olga von Meyendorff, Budapest, November 16, 1876.

1877

The new *serious* Operas are now regarded with suspicion and are in disgrace everywhere. Several trials have been made of them here and there of late years. In the happiest of them the public applauded warmly during the first performances, and abstained from attending the following ones. Consequently the coffers remained empty: ergo, it is the receipts which prove real success. If Wagner's marvelous *clef d'oeuvre* hold their own in the repertoire, it is because they make money and continue to draw even a large contingent of detractors.[79]

79. Letter to Edmund von Mihalovich, Weimar, July 20, 1877.

1878

I consider Adalbert Goldschmidt's *Todsunden* a remarkable Art-work. If the composer maintains himself on these heights in his next Opera his name will become famous in spite of all the critics.[80]

80. Letter to Eduard Liszt, Weimar, June 6, 1878.

1879

Yesterday evening Joseffy charmed me with his third Arabesque. I very much liked the second.[81]

81. Letter to Olga von Meyendorff, Budapest, January 31, 1879.

1882

Wagner is perfectly within the truth when he says that without the extraordinary munificence of H. M. the King of Bavaria the performances of *Parsifal* at Bayreuth would have been endangered, and only the sympathy of the public, outside the Wagner Societies, make the continuance of them possible. But does it follow from this that the Wagner Societies are useless, and that this is the opportunity for disbanding them? To my thinking, No, for they keep up a wholesome agitation. The *parliamentariness* of the Societies will not be averse to the absolute authority of the creator of so many immortal works. In merely minor matters variety of opinions may be made apparent; in all essentials we are really and truly one. On this account I desire the continuance, consistency, and increasing welfare of the Societies.

It goes without saying that Wagner must reign and govern as legitimate monarch, until the complete outward realization of his Bayreuth conception—namely, the model performance of his entire works, under his own aegis and directions at Bayreuth. It behooves all who sympathize in the historico-civilized culture of Art in the coming years of the closing 19th century to endeavor to promote this aim.[82]

82. Letter to Hans von Wolzogen, Venice, November 24, 1882.

I tell you again, dear Franz, that you were 'born with a silver spoon in your mouth'; after hearing of your Opera with the piano the success of a performance will follow.—Don't get impatient at a little delay; the most illustrious composers, including Meyerbeer, could not say, like Louis XIV, 'I nearly had to wait.'—But I hope that the saying, 'All comes to him who can wait' will be realized in your case without much delay. Good courage then and Mistress Patience.[83]

83. Letter to Franz Servais, Venice, November 26, 1882.

Why do you let your valuable, excellent works be so seldom heard in public? I shall reproach you further with this injustice to yourself when we come to talk over the program, and I hope that you won't continue to overdo your reserve as a composer. Without pushing one's-self forward one must still maintain one's position.[84]

84. Letter to Carl Riedel, Venice, December 9, 1882.

1883

La Jolie Fille de Perth (by Bizet), a *Carmen* that has only just blossomed, innocent of all guilt. Once and for all, I lack the taste needed to enjoy this kind of opera, even *Carmen*. I feel obtuse and often out of place.[85]

85. Letter to Olga von Meyendorff, Weimar, April 9, 1883.

1884

You have done a noble artistic deed in reinstating Cornelius's charming Opera, *The Barber of Bagdad*. I hardly know of any other comic opera of so much refined humor and spirit. This champagne has the real *sparkle* and great worth.[86]

86. Letter to Felix Mottl, Budapest, February 8, 1884.

Rimski-Korsakoff, Cui, Borodin, Balakireff, are masters of striking originality and worth. Their works make up to me for the *ennui* caused to me by other works more widely spread and more talked about.

In Russia the new composers, in spite of their remarkable talent and knowledge, have has as yet but a limited success.—The high people of the Court wait for them to succeed elsewhere before they applaud them at Petersburg. A propos of this; I recollect a striking remark which the late Grand Duke Michael made to me in 1843: "When I have to put my officers under arrest, I send them to the performances of Glinka's operas.'[87]

87. Letter to Louise de Mercy-Argenteau, October 24, 1884.

1885

I shall assuredly not cease from my propaganda of the remarkable compositions of the New Russian School, which I esteem and appreciate with lively sympathy. Their success is making a *crescendo*, in spite of the sort of contumacy that is established against Russian music. It is not in the least any desire of being peculiar that leads me to spread it, but a simple feeling of justice, based on my conviction of the real worth of these works of high lineage.[88]

88. Letter to Countess Mercy-Argenteau, Rome, January 20, 1885.

Chapter Seven

Liszt on Performance

1845

Unfortunately it is not with music as with painting and poetry: body and soul alone are not enough to make it comprehensible; it has to be performed, and very well performed too, to be understood and felt. [1]

1. Letter to Abbe de Lamennais, Marseille, April 28, 1845.

1854

This evening after the end of the third and last Concert—which parenthetically, will last from 4 to 5 hours ...[2]

2. Letter to Marie zu Sayn-Wittgenstein, Rotterdam, July 15, 1854.

1856

The chorus had studied its part well, but it is much too weak for Berlin, and in proportion to the vastness of the opera house, scarcely more efficient than ours, which always gives me great dissatisfaction. The stringed instruments, also, are not sufficiently numerous, and should, like the chorus, be increased by a good third. For a large place like this eight to ten double basses, and fifteen to twenty first violins, etc., would certainly not be too many at important performances.[3]

3. Letter to Wagner, Weimar, January 14, 1856.

[Reflecting on a performance of *Tannhäuser* in Munich] In the orchestra the wind (especially flutes, clarinets, and bassoon) is excellent. The violins and double basses (six in number) are a little hazy, and lack the necessary energy, both in bowing, which is short and easy-going, and in rhythm. The pianos and crescendos are insufficient, and for the same reason there is no fullness in the fortes. Lachner has, no doubt, studied the score with the greatest accuracy and care, for which thanks and praise are due to him. But in the drama, as you know and say best, 'we must become *wise* by means of *feeling*. Reason tells us *it is so*, but only after feeling has told us *it must be so*'; and as far as I can tell, Lackner's feeling says little about *Tannhäuser*.[4]

4. Letter to Wagner, Munich, December 25, 1856.

1857

In production the public have far more to care about the artist than he has to care about them, or indeed to let himself be embarrassed by them. At home, our whole life through, we have to study and to devise how to mature our work and to attain as near as possible to our ideal of Art. But when we enter the concert-room the feeling ought not to leave us, that, just by our conscientious and persevering striving, we stand somewhat higher than the public, and that we have to represent our portion of 'Manhood's dignity,' as Schiller says. Let us not err through *false* modesty, and let us hold fast to the *true*, which is much more difficult to practice and much more rare to find. The artist—in our sense - should be neither the servant nor the master of the public. He remains the bearer of the *Beautiful* in the inexhaustible variety which is appointed to human thought and perception—and this inviolable consciousness alone assures his authority.[5]

5. Letter to Dionys Pruckner, Weimar, February 11, 1857.

As regards the triangle I do not deny that it may give offense, especially if struck too strong and not precisely. A preconceived disinclination and objection to instruments of percussion prevails, somewhat justified by the frequent misuse of them. And few conductors are circumspect enough to bring out the rhythmic element in them, without the raw addition of a coarse noisiness, in works in which they are deliberately employed according to the intention of the composer. The dynamic and rhythmic spicing and enhancement, which are effected by the instruments of percussion, would in more cases be much more effectually produced by the careful trying and proportioning of insertions and additions of that kind.[6]

6. Letter to Eduard Liszt, Weimar, March 26, 1857.

1858

What is the good of anything that is written on paper, if it is not comprehended by the soul and imparted in a living manner?[7]

7. Letter to Rosa von Milde, Weimar, August 25, 1858.

1861

The chief thing before all else is the *conductor*;—if he be a good and reliable musician things may then be well managed in a variety of ways.[8]

8. Letter to Franz Brendel, January, 1861.

1862

As regards the performances of the Sondershausen orchestra I am quite of your opinion, and I repeat that they are not only not outdone, but are even not often equaled in their sustained richness, their judicious and liberal choice of works, as well- as in their precision, drilling, and refinement.—It is only a shame that no suitable concert hall has been built in Sondershausen. The orchestra has long deserved such an attention; should such a thing ever fall to their lot, pray urge upon Stein to spread out the platform of the orchestra as far as possible, and not to submit to the usual *limited space*, as they make the mistake of doing in the *Gewandhaus*, the *Odeonsaal* in Munich, etc. The concert hall of the Paris Conservatoire offers in this respect the right proportions, and a good part of the effect produced by the performances there is to be ascribed to this favorable condition.[9]

9. Letter to Franz Brendel, August 10, 1862.

1868

The proposed Concerto for which Wilhelmj asks has already been begged for several times from me by Sivori and Remenyi. I don't know when I shall find time to write it. There is not the least hurry for it, as long as criticism constrains violin-virtuosi to limit themselves to a repertoire of four or five pieces, very beautiful doubtless, and no less well known. Joachim naively confessed to me that after he had played the Beethoven and Mendelssohn Concertos and the Bach Chaconne he did not know what to do with himself in a town unless it were to go on playing indefinitely the same two Concertos and the same Chaconne.[10]

10. Letter to Jessie Laussot, Rome, January 13, 1868.

The Psalm [Eighteen] is very simple and massive—like a *monolith*. And, as in the case of other works of mine, the conductor has the chief part to play. He, as the chief *virtuoso* and *artifex*, is called upon to see that the whole is harmoniously articulated and that it receives a living form. Well, dear friend, you know what it is to brilliantly arouse a flaming spirit out of dead notes.[11]

11. Letter to Johann von Herbeck, Rome, June 9, 1868.

1869

[Regarding the *Elizabeth*] All possible alterations, pauses, dotted notes, ornamentations, shall be left ad *libitum* and entirely to the pleasure of the gracious singer. Do not write to me further on this subject, and endeavor merely to get Fräulein Ehnn to feel herself comfortably and pleasantly at home with my poor melodies.[12]

12. Letter to Johann von Herbeck, Weimar, January 27, 1869.

1870

With regard to the deceptive *Tempo rubato* [in Weber's Ab Major *Sonata*], I have settled the matter provisionally in a brief note; other occurrences of the *rubato* may be left to the taste and momentary feeling of gifted players. A metronomical performance is certainly tiresome and nonsensical; time and rhythm must be adapted to and identified with the melody, the harmony, the accent and the poetry. But how to indicate all this on paper? I shudder at the thought of it.[13]

13. Letter to Siegmund Lebert, Villa d'Este, January 10, 1870.

1874

What I termed 'Byzantinism' corresponds to embellishment in music. I relish them very much in Rossini and others. I employ them more or less clumsily on the piano and even with orchestra (particularly in the Hungarian rhapsodies), and only recently I spent several hours looking for some of a certain kind which seem to me pleasant. Beethoven and Chopin didn't turn up their noses at them, far from it.[14]

14. Letter to Olga von Meyendorff, Villa d'Este, December 30, 1874.

1878

With regard to *Tempi* I am very yielding in my small pieces, and gladly allow well-disposed artists to decide this.[15]

15. Letter to Walter Bache, Budapest, March 19, 1878.

1882

[On his *A magyarok istens*]: The solo trumpeter must perform his part, as a Hungarian Magnate, in a noble manner, and not blow the trumpet as though it were a trade.[16]

16. Letter to Kornel von Abrányi, Bayreuth, July 23, 1882.

1883

In the matter of concerts, those of the Meiningen orchestra, under Bülow's conductorship, are astonishing, and very instructive for the due comprehension of the works and the *rendering* of them.[17]

17. Letter to Malwine Tardieu, Weimar, December 14, 1883.

1884

Under Bülow's conducting the Meiningen orchestra accomplishes wonders. Nowhere is there to be found such intelligence in different works; precision in the performance with the most correct and subtle rhythmic and dynamic *nuances*. The result is admirable and in certain respects matchless, not excepting the Paris Conservatoire and other celebrated, concert institutions. It is said that Rubinstein and some others have expressed themselves disapprovingly about some of the unusual tempi and nuances of Bulow, but to my thinking their criticism is devoid of foundation.[18]

18. Letter to Otto Lessmann, Weimar, January 10, 1884.

Wagner was a thousand times right not to build his Bayreuth theater along the lines of the Grand Operas of Berlin, Vienna, Milan, Paris, where the singers have to exert themselves, not to the advantage of art, in halls which are far too large. Audiences of fifteen hundred are large enough. Nowadays, it is only a matter of box office receipts. Triviality and brutishness![19]

19. Letter to Otto Lessmann, Weimar, January 10, 1884.

1885

According to my opinion, without indications of expression any further editions of Palestrina and Lassus—the two great Cardinals of old Catholic Church music—would serve only for reading, and *not* for actual performances. Of course no one can fix with absolute certainty the figures to the basses of Palestrina and Lassus; yet there are determining points from which one can steer.

The best model of all is and will continue to be – Wagner's arrangement of Palestrina's *Stabat Mater*—with marks of expression and plan of the division of the voices into semi-chorus, solos, and complete chorus.

Wagner made this *model* arrangement at the time when he was conductor in Dresden. It appeared 15 years later, published by Kähnt.[20]

20. Letter to Lina Ramann, Weimar, April 27, 1885.

[Regarding a performance of *Die Götterdämmerung*]: Paur had held about a hundred rehearsals, counting partial rehearsals with voices, and bassoons.[21]

21. Letter to Olga von Meyendorff, Strasbourg, June 3, 1885.

On Pianoforte Performance

1852

It is perhaps to be regretted that Schubert's *Fantasia*, which contains many fine details, should have been played for the first time in the *Salle de Redoute*, so 'redoutable' and ungrateful a room for the piano in general; in a less vast space, such as the *salle* of the *Musik-Verein*, the virtuoso and the work would assuredly have been heard more to advantage.[22]

22. Letter to Carl Czerny, Weimar, April 19, 1852.

1854

Rubinstein cuts himself off from the thick mass of so-called *pianist composers* who don't know what playing means, and still less with what fuel to fire themselves for composing—so much so that with what is wanting to them in talent as composers they think they can make themselves pianists, and *vice versa*.[23]

23. Letter to William Mason, Weimar, December 14, 1854.

1857

The great mass of pianists is scarcely capable of *playing on* the piano, and cares very little (except sometimes for form's sake and human respect) for the interest of intelligence and feeling which might attach to the promenades of their fingers.[24]

24. Letter to Wladimir Stassoff, Weimar, March 17, 1857.

1863

The confounded pianoforte has its unmistakable significance, were it only because of the general abuse to which it is put![25]

25. Letter to Franz Brendel, Monte Mario, September 7, 1863.

1869

Up to the present time all the best-known French pianists—with the exception of Saint-Saëns—have not ventured to play anything of mine except transcriptions, my own compositions being necessarily considered absurd and insupportable. People know pretty well what to think by what they hear said, without any need of hearing the works.[26]

26. Letter to Franz Servais, Villa d'Este, December 20, 1869.

1872

I have not forgotten the recommendation the Grand Duchess deigned to make to me on the subject of artists worthy of real renown. Their number is very limited, whereas more or less clever mediocrities abound.[27]

27. Letter to Olga von Meyendorff, Budapest, January 31, 1872.

In reply to your friendly lines I beg of you earnestly no longer to think of having the barbarous operation performed upon your fingers; rather all your life long play every octave and chord wrong than commit such a mad attack upon your hands.[28]

28. Letter to Johanna Wenzel, Weimar, June 10, 1872.

1875

Here, I am staying with Bronsart, whom I have esteemed highly and been fond of for many a year. His character is of

the finest temper. The ill-bred accuse him of haughtiness, a fitting reproach from those who willingly do without dignity and distinction.[29]

29. Letter to Olga von Meyendorff, Hanover, April 27, 1875.

The entrance of the pedal after the striking of the chords as indicated by you at the beginning of page 3, and as consistently carried through by you almost to the utmost extreme, seems to me an ingenious idea, the application of which is greatly to be recommended to pianoforte players, teachers, and composers especially in slow tempi.[30]

30. Letter to Louis Köhler, Schloss Wilhelmsthal, July 27, 1875.

1876

For many long years Bülow has been habitually overdoing it and exceeding the limit in work and fatigue; witness the excessive programs which he put together for his concerts in Germany: at least a dozen pieces, among which several sonatas or suites, each with three or four movements, and which he played in 140 concerts during six or eight months. At this rate, Fasolt and Fafner would have killed themselves, without any other assistance or ceremony. A. Rubinstein, who has followed Bülow's excessive programs, and the young matadors of the piano, Zarembski, et a!., will be hard put to it to adapt their muscular and nervous systems to the task of *pantagruelizing* musically in this fashion.[31]

31. Letter to Olga von Meyendorff, Hanover, September 27, 1876.

The semi success or failure of Martha Remmert at Baden doesn't much surprise me. You were right to support her; artists of greater stature than she have had to endure harsher trials over a period of years; witness Bülow, Rubinstein, Tausig, etc. Nowadays, for one's name to become well known, one has to work hard, be patient, and endure.[32]

32. Letter to Olga von Meyendorff, Vienna, October 12, 1876.

1877

Martha Remmert is succeeding beyond my expectations. Her next goal is Vienna. There, Sophie Menter, who is in my opinion the greatest of the pianists of the fair sex in Germany or anywhere, not excepting Mme Essipoff, nor even Mme Jaell, the *impassioned* French Alsatian virtuoso and scintillating composer—where am I with all my admirations? with Sophie Menter; her presence at Vienna will not contribute to Martha Remmert's success, which will also be challenged by Vera Timanoff's fingers of steel and seductive Slavic personality.[33]

33. Letter to Olga von Meyendorff, Budapest, February 23, 1877.

1878

I am not encouraging Martha Remmert's aspirations to glory. Bad singers are able to find good engagements, since theaters are everywhere necessary. It's another thing for pianists of both sexes: 99 out of a hundred are at least superfluous, if not downright pests.[34]

34. Letter to Marie zu Sayn-Wittgenstein, Budapest, March 28, 1878.

1879

One of the wittiest pianists, Madame Raab, told her colleagues here at Budapest Music Academy: 'We are decidedly many too many: there ought to be a St. Bartholomew's massacre among pianists. Without one we shall all perish.'[35]

35. Letter to Marie zu Sayn-Wittgenstein, Budapest, January 26,1879.

Sophie Menter-Popper (the second name is becoming a nuisance) is shortly going to Russia. I often see her here and am a very devoted friend of hers. She is a pianist of exceptional virtuosity.[36]

36. Letter to Olga von Meyendorff, Budapest, January 31, 1879.

1880

For your *glissando* exercises I once again advise you to use only the nail, either of your thumb or of your index or third finger, without even the tiniest area of flesh.[37]

37. Letter to Olga von Meyendorff, December 16, 1880.

1881

[Sophie Menter] played the whole program superbly, so as to compare favorably with the three or four most famous male pianists. Her *bravura* is absolutely faultless; the rhythm and color are masterfully accented and blended. In the *Reminiscences des Huguenots*, a fantasia which in my years as a virtuoso I used to play only rarely because of the trouble it cost me, Sophie M. astonished me.[38]

38. Letter to Olga von Meyendorff, Villa d'Este, January 7, 1881.

I am quite willing to repeat my opinion that your son Alfred is a highly gifted and brilliantly aspiring pianoforte-player. [39]

39. Letter to Frau Reisenauer-Pauly, Budapest, January 29, 1881.

1882

Richter introduced me to d'Albert in Vienna last April. Since then he has worked at Weimar, without interruption, under my tutelage. Among the young virtuosi, from the time of Tausig,—Bülow and Rubinstein naturally remain the Senators and Masters—I know of none of a more gifted as well as of a more dazzling talent than d'Albert. Although he is scarcely 18, M.S., on my suggestion, called him the Weimar 'Court-pianist.'[40]

40. Letter to Marie zu Sayn-Wittgenstein, Venice, November 24, 1882.

1884

In Budapest Anton Rubinstein regaled us with two concerts, each consisting of fifteen to seventeen numbers. At the first concert, two Beethoven sonatas, and Schumann's great *Sonata* in F minor, several etudes, preludes, and nocturnes by Chopin, a few pieces by Tchaikovsky and a charming little composition by Liadoff.[41]

41. Letter to Olga von Meyendorff, Gran, February 3, 1884.

On Virtuosity

1840

Let the artist of the future renounce, then, and with all his heart, the vain and egotistical role of which Paganini was, we think, a last and illustrious example; let him fix his goal not in himself but outside himself; let virtuosity be to him a *means* and the *end*; let him always remember that *Genius Obliges*.[42]

42. Liszt, 'Sur Paganini,' *Gazette Musicale* (August 23, 1840).

1859

What is a virtuoso? Is he really no more than an intelligent machine, whose two hands are a couple of levers doing the business of a barrel-organ? Is his task so mechanical as to render it unnecessary for him to think or feel in satisfactorily performing it? Is his duty confined to producing for the ear, as it were, a photograph of the notes he is looking at?

Alas! We know only too well how many so-called virtuosi there are who are not even able to translate the thought contained in the originals they place upon their desk, or to deliver it integrally without mutilation of the sense. How many amongst them there are whose knowledge of art is confined to the mere trade—how many, indeed, who do not even know the trade!

It must be confessed that their number is legion. But usurpation, however victorious in the material sense of possession, has no effect upon the rights of a just owner. Those who make a mere business out of virtuosity are far more plentiful than it would be natural to suspect; especially by a public already depraved by these illegitimate and worse than ignorant would-be sovereigns.

As matters stand, the public is no longer in a position to judge; which is no more than might be expected after their taking pleasure in being led astray by the vulgar feats of these mountebanks, with their mechanical wonders upon the violin, piano, guitar and (most horrible of all) the cornet. When, therefore, a real master displays before them some prodigy of art, they cannot appreciate the distinction and realize that the master is acting in the name of a marvelous privilege granted to him by nature—a privilege similar to that traditional one by virtue of which the kings of France are supposed to have cured scrofula, by the mere act of touching those who suffered from it. Such powers are not acquired, being only exercised by 'divine right.'

The words virtuosity and virtue have both their origin in the Latin *vir*; the exercise of one as much as the other being an act of masculine power. Whoever has not the faculty of engendering an ideal type, fruit of the transports of his love for ideal beauty, can neither be virtuose nor virtuous. He must know how to impose respect and admiration for the beautiful; and should be the author of good works or actions—whether these belong to art or morality makes no difference; as these are but two aspects of the same thing, two sexes of the one species.

Thus, the Good, in the same way as the Beautiful, is the incarnation of the human soul due to the energy of its desires and resolves. Do we not, as a matter of act, interchange the terms, when we speak of an action belonging to the Good as a *beautiful* action, and of a production emanating from the order of thc *Beautiful* as a *good* work?

This amounts to an unconscious admission that the Good and the Beautiful can never be radically detached one from the other; every good deed being beautiful by that very fact, and every beautiful work being good by the same reasoning.

The virtuoso is not a mason; who, taking blocks of stone and with square, level and trowel in hand (a conscientious and exact proceeding), constructs the poem which the architect has already designed upon the paper. He is not a passive instrument, reproducing the thoughts and feelings of others whilst adding nothing of his own. He is not a reader, more or less expert, delivering a text; without marginal notes or glossary, and requiring no interlinear commentary.

Musical works which have been dictated by inspiration are, fundamentally, only the touching or tragic *scenario* of feeling, which it appertains to the executant to cause, by turns, to disclaim, sing, weep, sigh or adore; as also to pride himself and take pleasure in the accomplishment. The virtuoso is therefore just as much a creator as the writer; for he must virtually possess, in all their brilliancy and flagrant phosphorescence, the written passions to which he has undertaken to give life.

To him it also falls to give life and animation to the inert body of his text, as well as to vary the tints of its glances and turn the whole presentment into that of a goddess of grace: To him, again, it falls to change a mute and motionless form into a living being, a seductive Galatea; and to endow the still lifeless form with an adamantine nature into which he may infuse life at his own given moment. It follows that, of all artists, the virtuoso is not only directly called upon, but perhaps more directly than any other, to reveal the subjugating strength of the gods; and from whom it is expected that the inspiring muse can never have any secrets.

To judge by the pitch at which the science of aesthetics has arrived nowadays, there cannot be any thinker or any cultivated mind familiar with the arts, either by long and intimate practice or by theoretical speculation, who would not consider it amount to a frightful barbarism to omit Dramatic Art from the list of those entitled autonomous; which is what would practically happen in denying the comedian or tragedian the privilege of *creation*. This privilege consists in the introduction by the artist quite independently, as *by right of birth and conquest*, of graces concomitantly with his innate gift and his enthusiastic labor.

The dramatic art possesses no less than the right of life and death over those works which have only to be touched by the breath of his lips to become either eloquent and inflamed, or pale and declining, as his action may dictate. It is he also who possesses the exorbitant power of either allowing the thoughts entrusted to him to perish, or of infusing into them a life incomparably more intense than that by which he is himself animated. He pours into the dead letter that vivifying spirit which is as that which the Creator poured into the clay of Adam's body—the soul made in his own image and resemblance. Surely, then, what he does is well worthy of being called an art.

Is not the life he gives to a work one conceived after his own image and resemblance?

Could he be said to have 'created' a dramatic role unless he had conceived it in a manner so peculiar to himself that, although another might imitate it, he could never appropriate it entirely?

How can the origin of his Art in a Muse be doubted when inspiration is so evidently essential to it?

It was by reason of this being so that the Greeks, who had such a fine intuition of everything concerning the arts or proceeding from them, gave Thalia and Melpomene as patrons to interpreters as well as to genius; to Aeschylus and Sophocles as to Aristophanes and Menander.

Now the virtuoso or musical artist does for music exactly what the actor or dramatic artist does for the stage; or, in other words, for the poem, whether tragic or comic, of an author. The virtuoso possesses the same right of life and death over the works the interpretation of which is entrusted to him, with their thoughts, sentiments and emotions; for the expression of all these, being part of interpretation, is for the moment committed to his care. He can endow them with a glorious life, similar to that enjoyed by the heroes in the Elysian fields; or he can allow them, or even cause them, to die a death equally ignominious and ridiculous.

How could it possibly be maintained that the virtuoso is not the representative of an art so evidently his own; because so different from that of the author, who dictated the mere words by writing what the performing artist reproduces? The virtuoso, when addressing himself simply to the sense of hearing of his audience, does for his author precisely the same as the actor who addresses himself to both sight and hearing.

That Dramatic Art is an art apart, no person of discretion any longer denies. It is related to music by its use of the voice; to sculpture by that of gesture and attitude; to painting by employing the assistance of color; and to pantomime by depending upon movement. On the other hand, it follows that, as the musician makes no appeal to the sense of sight, upon which these last demand, his art bears no direct relation to any of them.

In return, however, the theater is fatal to each of the arts just mentioned.

It is, for example, fatal to painting, because it employs the coarsest and loudest tints as well as the most violent contrasts; besides being obliged to have recourse to illuminations which are unnatural. And it is fatal to sculpture, by the very fact of movement involving change of attitude.

The fact is that dramatic art being obliged, like all plastic art, to take Nature for its model, is nevertheless obliged to transfigure it according to its means of expression. Its own resources must be used as far as they will extend, in order to compensate for the lack of what in Nature is inimitable.

But it is a matter of common consent that any plastic art which, instead of aspiring to draw its inspiration directly from Nature, should seek to do so from the stage, would inevitably thereby become (to whatever extent this might be practiced) adulterate and degenerate; and would thereby lose all legitimate title to noble rank. The truth of this becomes evident at once if we reflect that the worst criticism which can be passed upon art a criticism implying that it has already entered upon a period of decline is to say: 'It has become *theatrical*.'

If we consider the matter from the point of view of self-sufficiency and independence, the virtuoso has every advantage over the actor; whom the painter, sculptor and mimic can alike afford to ignore and forget. And not only these; for even the dramatic poet is not confined to drama and has the power, whenever he chooses, of quitting his imaginary world and of immortalizing himself in that of poetry, unassisted by dramatic action. Moreover, such poetry, even though it may be less luminous and less emotional, is, on the other hand, less ephemeral and less subject to vicissitudes of the moment. Its faculty of dispensing with the dramatic artists is also so complete that the exercise of its control over the human heart is capable of continuing into far-off ages. Thus, in time to come, even when its language has long ceased to be that of the people, and is only understood by men of superior refinement and education, they will require no interpreters to enable them to enjoy its genius, verve or sentiment.

But the musical composer is far from being in the enjoyment of this position; for he cannot live, and therefore there can be no question of his survival without the help of the executant. Libraries are no resting-places for musical art-works, however well they may serve that purpose for thought, silent but fruitful. The special tabernacle for the musical composer's productions is the human soul, where they exist only while the soul retains their impression; for, as soon as memory allows that impression to escape, they are gone.

It would even be vain for the archaeologist to try to galvanize into life musical works of a past age; for, when acoustical means and habits have become profoundly modified—when even manners of feeling are not the same, having become more gentle or more imperious, broader or more refined—how can hearts of the present day identify themselves with those of a former generation?

In short, without the virtuoso the composer's existence would be a perpetual hell; his creative genius being unable by itself either to actuate what it conceived or to objectify that by which it is filled. It cannot make its presence evident, or show what animates its pulse, lights up its imagination, occupies it thought, or absorbs its being. Unless all this is displayed before him either by the human voice, by an instrument, or by an orchestra, the musician would be in an eternal state of travail, without hope of deliverance. He would be in the unfortunate position of experiencing a love, while being condemned never to know the object of his inspiration—the most terrible punishment of the damned.

Those who are not composers are totally unable to realize, with it is for a musician of genius to have no executants—in other words, not to be able to hear himself. It would be necessary to ask Berlioz or Wagner in their younger years (or equally any other composers before them) what it was to have felt and thought in music and to have no opportunity of judging the work evolved by their sentiment or formulated by their thought.

These reflections amply bear out our statement and show that it is rigorously true to say that both tragedy and comedy are infinitely less dependent upon the artists which represent them than music must ever be upon the executants who give it life. The virtuoso engenders the music anew and in his turn he gives it a palpable and perceptible existence, and by that act he establishes the claim of his art to be ranked with those called autonomous.[43]

43. Liszt, *The Gipsy in Music*, 1859, 264ff.

Chapter Eight

Liszt's Views on Criticism and the Public

On Criticism

1849

Would not the best results of criticism altogether be to incite to new *creation*?[1]

1. Letter to Carl Reinecke, Weimar, March 25, 1849.

1850

You are sufficiently acquainted with the habits of the Paris press to know how reluctantly it admits the entire and absolute eulogium of a work by a foreign composer, especially while he is still living.[2]

2. Letter to Richard Wagner, Weimar, September 25, 1850.

1852

If, as has often been proven, 'no man is a prophet in his own land,' is it not also known that prophets, men who sense the future and announce it by their work, are not acknowledged as such in their own age? Moreover, it would be venturesome to say that the situation can be otherwise. Young generations of artists protest vainly against the laggards whose invariable custom is to strike at the living through the dead. It is time alone, in music and in other arts, that can sometimes reveal complete beauty and full worth.[3]

3. Liszt, *Chopin*, 1852, 29.

1854

Let us only spread our wings 'with our faces firmly set,' and all the cackle of goose-quills will not trouble us at all. That your article has been rudely and spitefully criticized need not trouble you. You presuppose your reader to have refinement and educated feeling, artistic acuteness, a fine perception, and a certain Atticism. These, my dear friend, are indeed rare things. Sheep and donkeys have no taste for truffles. Moreover, dear friend, things didn't and don't go any better with other better fellows than ourselves. We need not make any fancies about it, but only go onward quietly, perseveringly, and consistently.[4]

4. Letter to Louis Köhler, Weimar, March 2, 1854.

1855

It is well known that Scudo [music critic in Paris] has, for years past, with the unequivocal arrogance of mediocrity, taken up the position of making the most spiteful and maliciously foolish opposition, in the *Revue des Deux Mondes* to our views of Art, and to those men whom we honor and back up.[5]

5. Letter to Franz Brendel, March 18, 1855.

If you believe me, my dear Rubinstein, you will not long delay making yourself of the party; for, for the few artists who have sense, intelligence, and a serious and honest will, it is really their duty to take up the pen in defense of our Art and our conviction—it matters little, moreover, on which side of the opinions represented by the Press you think it well to place yourself. Musical literature is a field far too little cultivated by productive artists, and if they continue to neglect it they will have to bear the consequences and to pay *their* damages.[6]

6. Letter to Anton Rubinstein, Weimar, April 3, 1855.

1856

Since Berlioz' stay here, which gave occasion for the Litolff cudgel-smashing newspaper rubbish …[7]

7. Letter to Louis Köhler, Weimar, May 24, 1856.

The open, straightforward sense of the public is everywhere kept so much in check by the oft-repeated rubbish of the men of the 'But' and 'Yet,' who batten on criticism, and appear to set themselves the task of crushing to death every living endeavor.[8]

8. Letter to Alexander Ritter, Munich, December 4, 1856.

1857

The musician nowadays cannot get out of the way of all the buzzing. Twenty years ago there were hardly a couple of musical papers in Europe, and the political papers referred only in the most rare cases, and then only very briefly, to musical matters. Now all this is quite different, and with my *Preludes*, for instance (which, by the way, are only the *prelude* to my path of composition), many dozen critics by *profession* have already pounced on them, in order to ruin me through and through as a composer. I by no means say that present conditions, taken as a whole, are more unfavorable to the musician than the earlier conditions, for all this talk in a hundred papers brings also much good with it, which would not otherwise be so easy to attain;—but simply the thinking and creative artist must not allow himself to be misled by it, and must go his own gait quietly and undisturbed, as they say the hippopotamus does, in spite of all the arrows which rebound from his thick skin.[9]

9. Letter to Eduard Liszt, Weimar, March 26, 1857.

1858

I played the first two portions of the Schubert *Hungarian Divertissement* with Dachs; and afterward Hanslick asked me if I wouldn't do him the honor of playing the third with him. I acceded very gracefully, and he played his part wonderfully. If only this little incident could later become a *symbol* and *omen* for the happy alliance of Art and Criticism—We could ask nothing better than to have these gentlemen play the *bass*—as long as it weren't faulty and we kept good time.[10]

10. Letter to Marie zu Sayn-Wittgenstein, Prague, April 20, 1858.

1859

The 'sneaking brood'(as you well name the people) can henceforth growl as much as they like. What does that matter to us, so long as we remain true and faithful to our task?[11]

11. Letter to Johann von Herbeck, Weimar, October 11, 1859.

1860

[On a proposed performance of *Prometheus* in Vienna]: there are certainly no powerful eagles to hack and rend in pieces the Titan's liver - but there is a whole host of ravens and creeping vermin ready to do it.[12]

12. Letter to Johann von Herbeck, January, 1860.

1861

Although, as you know, I must on principle keep myself unconcerned as regards criticism, as I cannot allow it the first word in matters of Art, yet it has long been my wish to see the 'systematic opposition' to the present incontrovertible tendency (or, better, 'development') of music not exclusively represented in the *Allgemeine Zeitung*.[13]

13. Letter to Edmund Singer, August 17, 1861.

1867

The news which reaches me fom time to time about musical matters in America is generally favorable to the cause of the progress of contemporaneous Art which I hold it an honor to serve and to sustain. It seems that, among you, the cavillings and blunders and stupidities of a criticism adulterated by ignorance, envy and venality exercise less influence than in the old continent.[14]

14. Letter to William Mason, Rome, July 8, 1867.

1873

I have lived long enough to be used to the lavishness with which the titles of 'ass, imbecile, fool, idiot'—and even worse—are conferred on those who deserve esteem and honor.[15]

15. Letter to Olga von Meyendorff, Budapest, March 19, 1873.

The grandest and most sublime work of art of the century. The glory of having created, written and published it is Wagner's intact; his detractors have only to share the disgrace of having thwarted it and delayed the bringing of it to the full light of day, by performance.[16]

16. Letter to Adelheid von Schorn, Bayreuth, July 30, 1873.

1874

Have you read Bülow's two remarkable articles (The *Augsburg General Daily*) about the performance of Glinks's opera, and the *Requiem* of Verdi at Milan? The Italian and Verdian newspapers are anathematizing and blowing Bülow to shreds.[17]

17. Letter to Marie zu Sayn-Wittgenstein, Villa d'Este, June 10, 1874.

1877

An excellent recipe against unjust criticisms is to criticize oneself thoroughly before and after and finally to remain perfectly calm and follow one's own road![18]

18. Letter to Jules de Zdarembski, Budapest, December 13, 1877.

1880

Difficult people who only wish to know things that are true should not subscribe to any newspaper. The only role of the press – in effective control—is to entertain or amuse the public with truths and falsehoods, plus, things in *between*.[19]

19. Letter to Olga von Meyendorff, Budapest, February 9, 1880.

The Public

1850

At the end of the week we shall repeat *Tannhäuser*, which, by some miracle of taste, the Weimar public and many people from the surrounding towns have demanded ever since the beginning of the theatrical season, and which has been postponed only on account of my absence.[20]

20. Letter to Richard Wagner, Weimar, January 14, 1850.

The court and the few intelligent persons in Weimar are full of sympathy and admiration for your work; and as to the public at large, they will think themselves in honor bound to admire and applaud what they cannot understand.[21]

21. Letter to Richard Wagner, Weimar, September 2, 1850.

It is not only the singers and the orchestras that must be brought up to the mark to serve as instruments in the *dramatic revolution*, but also, and before all, the *public*, which must be elevated to a level where it becomes capable of associating itself by sympathy and intelligent comprehension with conceptions of a higher order than that of the lazy amusements with which it feeds its imagination and sensibility at our theaters every day. This must be done, if need by, by violence, for, as the Gospel tells us, the kingdom of heaven suffers violence, and only those who use violence will take it.

In order to realize completely the *drama* which you conceive, it is absolutely necessary to make a breach in the old routine of criticism, the long ears and short sight of 'Philistia,' as well as the stupid arrogance of that self-sufficient fraction of the public which believes itself the destined judge of works of art by dent of birthright.

The enemy to whom, as you, my great art-hero, rightly put it, one should not capitulate - that enemy is not only in the throats of the singers, but also very essentially in the lazy and at the same time tyrannical habits of the hearers. On these as well as on the others one must make an impression if necessary by a good beating.[22]

22. Letter to Richard Wagner, September 16, 1850.

1852

They are like a sea of lead and no less heavy to move, their waves are stirred by fire. They need the strong arm of the stalwart laborer to be spilled into a mold where the flowing metal suddenly assumes thought and feeling in accordance with the imposed form.[23]

23. Liszt, *Chopin*, 1852, 83.

1854

In our stupid musical customs, often very anti-musical, it is almost impossible to appeal to a badly informed public by a second performance immediately after the first; and at Leipzig, as elsewhere, one only meets with a very small number of people who know how to apply cause and effect intelligently and enthusiastically to a piece out of the common, and signed with the name of a composer who is not dead.[24]

24. Letter to Anton Rubinstein, November 19, 1854.

1856

The Munich public is more or less neutral, more observing and listening than sympathetic. The Court does not take the slightest interest in music.[25]

25. Letter to Wagner, Munich, December 25, 1856.

1858

A well-known piece of Bazzini's, 'La Ronde des Lutins,' was by a printer's error, called 'Ronde des Cretins!' ['Rondo of Idiots']. What an immeasurably large public for such a 'Rondo!'[26]

26. Letter to Felix Draseke, Weimar, January 10, 1858.

The public is like this—that they only know what they ought to think of a work when they see it printed in black and white![27]

27. Letter to L. A. Zellner, Budapest, April 6, 1858.

1862

Considering what most people are, they require to read first, before attaining the capacity for *learning, understanding, feeling,* and *appreciating.*[28]

28. Letter to Franz' Brendel, Rome, August 29, 1862.

1868

The Panis Angelicus [by Palestrina], the Schumann *Quintet* and the sublime *Prelude to Lohengrin* are works which a well-brought-up public ought to know by heart.[29]

29. Letter to Jessie Laussot, Rome, January 13, 1868.

1869

People know pretty well what to think by what they hear said, without any need of hearing the works.[30]

30. Letter to Franz Servais, Villa d'Este, December 20, 1869.

1874

The public is a very exacting master, even in its days of favor; the more it gives the more it expects.[31]

31. Letter to Countess Marie Donhoff, January, 1874.

1875

Now-a-days an artist is reckoning without his host if he places honest faith in the public. For people now-a-days hear and judge only by reading the newspapers.[32]

32. Letter to Johann von Herbeck, Budapest, March 3, 1875.

1876

Our friend Tolstoy' s ballad, *Der blinde Sänger*, has deep significance. Courts and cities are not interested in listening to poets and musicians.[33]

33. Letter to Olga von Meyendorff, Vienna, October 12, 1876.

Pasdeloup's final argument that "music must be listened to before being hissed' is reasonable. I go even further and consider that hisses are poor company: silence suffices for a well-brought-up audience to express its disapproval.[34]

34. Letter to Olga von Meyendorff, Budapest, November 16, 1876.

The general public usually goes by what is said by the critics.[35]

35. Letter to Marianne Brandt, December 3, 1876.

1878

Nowadays, more than ever, the public thirst for Opera alone. Everything else in music is nonsense to them.[36]

36. Letter to Eduard Liszt, Weimar, June 6, 1878.

Zola's approach to divorce is perhaps slightly coarse, this being always acclaimed by the public who, as Chamfort used to say, rise only to low thoughts.[37]

37. Letter to Olga von Meyendorff, Budapest, undated.

1883

Alas! everything that is not of the *theater* and does not belong to the repertoire of the old classical masters Handel, Bach, Palestrina, etc., does not yet gain any attentive and paying consideration—the decisive criterion—of the public. Berlioz, during his lifetime, furnished the proof of this.[38]

38. Letter to Malwine Tardieu, Budapest, March 6, 1883.

1884

The Vienna performance of Sgambati's Symphony was fairly well received but in the *Presse*, Hanslick was critical. Hence it is a failure. The public is easily discouraged by a newspaper article. With few exceptions, people believe what they read.[39]

39. Letter to Olga von Meyendorff, Gran, February 3, 1884.

Chapter Nine

Liszt's Observations on Various Countries

England

1840

England is not like any other country; the expenses are enormous.[1]

1. Letter to Franz von Schober, Stonehenge, August 29, 1840.

1854

One has to get accustomed to the London atmosphere, and make one's stomach pretty solid with porter and port. For the rest, musical matters are not worse there than elsewhere, and one must even acknowledge some greatness in bestiality. If you can *stand* it, I am convinced that you will make a lucrative and pleasant position for yourself in London.[2]

2. Letter to Carl Klindworth, Weimar, July 2, 1854.

1855

The chief thing for you is to gain firm ground in London, and first of all to impress your conception of Beethoven, Gluck, etc., on the orchestra and public. When you are once accustomed to London air, it may be expected that you will settle there comfortably. Beware of the theatrical speculators, who will be sure to try and make the best of you, and might be dangerous both to your purse and to your position.[3]

3. Letter to Richard Wagner, Weimar, January 25, 1855.

Germany

1849

In the end, Wagner will be acknowledged as a great *German* composer in Germany, on condition that his works are first heard in Paris or London, following the example of Meyerbeer, to say nothing of Gluck, Weber, and Handel![4]

4. Letter to Carl Reinecke, Weimar, May 30, 1849.

1851

Köln has much good, notwithstanding its objectionable nooks. Until now the musical ground there has been choked up rather than truly cultivated! People are somewhat coarse and stupidly vain there.[5]

5. Letter to Carl Reinecke, Eilsen, March 19, 1851.

1852

Quite lately I again expressed the principle that our first and greatest task in Weimar is to give the operas of Wagner exactly *selon si bon plaisir de l'auteur.*[6]

6. Letter to Richard Wagner, Late Spring, 1852.

1853

At Karlsruhe, the Ninth Symphony, as well as the works of Wagner, Berlioz, Schumann, etc. had never been given before.[7]

7. Letter to Richard Pohl, Weimar, November 5, 1853.

1855

The Köln people have bravely swallowed *Lohengrin* without choking over it. This has delighted me. From Hamburg also I hear that the public are gradually being educated up to it.[8]

8. Letter to Richard Wagner, Weimar, February 16, 1855.

The predilection of His Majesty the King of Saxony for Beethoven's Symphonies assuredly does honor to his taste for the Beautiful in music, and no one could more truly agree to that than I. I will only observe, on the one side, that Beethoven's Symphonies are extremely well known, and, on the other, that these admirable works are performed at Dresden by an orchestra having at its disposal far more considerable means than we have here, and. that consequently our performance would run the risk of appearing rather provincial to His Majesty. Moreover if Dresden, following the example of Paris, London, Leipzig, Berlin, and a hundred other cities, stops at Beethoven (to whom, while he was living, they much preferred Haydn and Mozart), that is no reason why Weimar should keep absolutely to that. There is without doubt nothing better than to respect, admire, and study the illustrious dead; but why not also sometimes live with the living? We have tried this plan with Wagner, Berlioz, Schumann, and some others, and it would seem that it has not succeeded so badly up to now for there to be any occasion for us to alter our minds without urgent cause, and to put ourselves at the tail—of many other tails!

The significance of the musical movement of which Weimar is the real center lies precisely in this initiative, of which the public does not generally understand much, but which none the less acquires its part of importance in the development of contemporary Art.[9]

9. Letter to the Intendant of the Court Theater in Weimar, Weimar, May 21, 1855.

1876

Banish the gloomy mood of Weimar. You have to spend a certain amount of time there for your children's sake, and hence to put up with local boredom, which is fairly benign, while reflecting that the essence of human life is nothing but inexorable boredom.[10]

10. Letter to Olga von Meyendorff, Vienna, October 12, 1876.

1878

Dresden:—a town for which I hold only the musical regard it deserves, in view of the fact that its attitude toward me has always been hostile and boorish, like certain other towns of similar size.[11]

11. Letter to Olga von Meyendorff, Villa d'Este, December 27, 1878.

1879

Frankfurt am Main: a not very propitious town for musical undertakings, and pretty well smothered under the false note of the critical pundits of Leipzig and its many rivals.[12]

12. Letter to Olga von Meyendorff, Vienna, April 6, 1879.

1885

In Weimar it is wisest to keep oneself negative and *passive*.[13]

13. Letter to Alexander Siloti, May, 1885.

Hungary

1859

All native Hungarian music naturally divides itself in the first place into melodies for song and dance; amongst which there is so great a resemblance that it might almost be called identity of character.[14]

14. Liszt, *The Gipsy in Music*, 1859, 290.

1864

Every tie which unites me to our noble country is dear to me.[15]

15. Letter to the Committee of the Society for the Support of Needy Hungarian Musicians in Budapest, Rome, June 18, 1864.

1876

I can only lay claim to be the well-intentioned zealous servant of Art and of Hungary.[16]

16. Letter to Kornel von Abrányi, Villa d'Este, January 20, 1876.

I remain, until death, Hungary's true and grateful son.[17]

17. Letter to August von Trefort, Budapest, March 1, 1876.

1878

Without ever talking *twaddle about patriotism*, yet in all modesty I will not be wanting where there is something to be done for Hungary.[18]

18. Letter to Eduard Liszt, Weimar, April 26, 1878.

On the Gipsies

Preference for Instrumental Music

It must be admitted that, amongst this people, we certainly do meet here and there with ballads and romances. These rare specimens of song, rudely forged in their own language, or borrowed from others, are, however, no more than rough sketches; quite undeserving to be ranked with works of art. It may be that, for singing, inspiration alone suffices, so far as song may be considered independent of words; but, for the manipulation of words, as for the building of verse, some intellectual culture is necessary.

Contrast with the Jews

Without giving any plausible reason for it, the Gipsies have consistently resisted all temptation to participate in the prosperity of the favored nations, as well as the weakness of allowing a drop of foreign blood to mingle with their race. This last fact is sufficiently proved by the purity of their type; which, at the present day, corresponds exactly with the descriptions which have descended to us from the very earliest times. Such Gipsy women as may have become contaminated—or such as may have stolen children in order to bring them up as their own, are permanently alienated; and never recognized as stock of the race; either in the camp, or in the individual Gipsy's tent.

The Gipsy as Phenomenon

The sole object which the Gipsies pursue is constantly to delight their senses by all the enjoyments which they can derive from their great goddess, Nature—the only one whom they recognize and adore. Clearly, therefore, this is most readily obtained by an absolute liberty of existence and indifference to 'possessions.'

All notions of country, property and social institutions are specially repudiated by them. They form no local habit, deny the attraction of child reminiscence, desire no conquest, and, having no past, frankly challenge all future.

The entire earth is their country, the ground is their own, whilst every climate pleases them in which they can wander freely and move without restraint.

The tribe, formed and collected by chance though it may be, is their family; a tent, though a mere covering extended from tree to tree, their sufficient habitation; and any object of present momentary enjoyment their undisputed property.

The Gipsy as Special Votary of Nature

The intellectual enjoyments obtainable through the plastic and literary arts were accordingly destined to remain unknown to the Gipsy, as the material enjoyments of luxury and elegance are irksome and unwelcome to him.

Music, again, was the only art the exercise of which coincided with his way of feeling; being able to express a sentiment without first requiring it to be clothed in any form of thought—a condition which the Gipsy would have been incapable to carry out. It is therefore only by music; which, if need be, can be practiced without instruction, that the Gipsy has been able to proclaim his psychical fraternity with the rest of mankind.

A Visit to a Gipsy Camp

On our first return to Hungary we had a natural desire to take up the thread of our first experiences, and to revisit the hordes by whose picturesque tohu-bohu we had formerly been so much struck. We longed all the more to hear those rhythms and harmonies again on account of their appearing to us as emanating from another planet they were so completely different from anything which European art permits, or even countenances, in any way, in music.

But, however intolerable in the sight of European art, this was Music. It was most unquestionably music; for it could speak, it could narrate, it could even sing. And how it sang! How sad were the accents with which it greeted us! They seemed like the voices of men in exile; like the pleading of the imprisoned bird; like the sigh of the orphaned soul; or the plaint of bereaved affection. We understand it well—this music; for it seemed to us like a native language. But the fact is even more powerful that not we alone were in subjugation to it; for upon everyone who heard it its empire quickly fell.

Of Hungarian National Music

One thing certain is that music and dance form an integral part of the rejoicings of the Gipsies. In whatever country they are met with, a collection of sonorous musical instruments always forms part of the baggage of the camp. Another fact is that their wild whirling dances, remindful of the religious dances of the Oriental dervishes, seem also to approach in character those of a type traditional with them. The principal movements which constitute them are to be met with again and again, irrespective of any distance between the tribes concerned; a circumstance which fixes our attention when we observe that amongst customs preserved by the most miserable offshoots of the race, decrepit and forlorn creatures dwelling round the marshes of Wallachia, the leading features of dancers are precisely the same as those of the dances indulged in by the most elegant Gipsies of Moscow ...

The instruments generally considered as proper to the Hungarians, and upon which it is supposed that they originally repeated melodies which at first had been only sung (such as the Farayala, the Kust, the Tarogaso and the Duda) did not form part of the Gipsie orchestra. They have in fact never emerged from the *Pustas*, where they still rejoice the solitude of the peasant –laborer or shepherd. These instruments have never contributed outside their own rural sphere to spread the fame of a kind of music, which, by the way they interpret very badly. This music is so evidently of the Gipsies that the identity becomes quite complete the moment it is restored to its original color by the sonority of the Gipsie instruments; for the Gipsies soon make it resplendent with the luxury of ornamentation in which prismatic rays seem to play upon each note as upon the scales of a dolphin; reflecting red or gold, blue or green, violet or silver.

The Gipsy Orchestra

The orchestra of the Gipsies was composed in our time of several different instruments, associated quite *ad libitum*. The foundation was always the violin and *zymbala*, a sort of square tablet furnished with strings ranged similarly to those of square pianos and struck by sticks; causing them to give out a sound, hotly colored and highly resounding, even when the result of but little force.

The *zymbala* is evidently of Oriental origin; that is if we may judge by the samples seen in Europe of stringed instruments which have come from that direction. In Hungary it is only the Gipsies who play it; and an exact description of it, perfectly corresponding to the instrument now in use, is to be found in the earliest records of their arrival in this country—mention of this kind dating back to the fifteenth century.

This instrument is still well spread amongst the peasants of little Russia, who generally suspend it by a strap round the neck, which enables them to play without resting it upon a table. This, however, they have to do when it is desired to augment the sonority of its metallic vibrations. Like the viol in, the *zymbala* lends itself to the ornamentations of little notes, trills and runs at every organ-point.

The whole group of instruments forming a [Gipsy] orchestra generally serves only to double the harmony, mark the rhythm, and form the accompaniment. They consist, for the most part, of flutes, clarinets, a little brass, a violoncello, a double-bass, and as many second violins as can be obtained. The first violin and *zymbala* attract the principal interest; filling the great role of the musical drama about to be played; absolutely after the manner of the *primo uomo* and *prima donno* of the old Italian opera. They may be called the *soloists* of the band.

The first violin (whose technique sometimes differs materially from ours) unfolds all the wonders suggested by his imagination, whilst the *zymbala* supplies the rhythm, indicates the acceleration or slackening of time, as also the degree of movement. He manipulates with singular agility and as if it were a sleight-of-hand performance the little wooden hammers with which he travels over the strings, and which in this primitive piano perform the duty we assign to ivory keys.

The *zymbala* shares with the first viol in the right to develop certain passages and to prolong certain variations indefinitely according to the good pleasure of the moment. He is necessarily one of those who conduct the musical poem; having either created it at leisure, or being about to improvise it at the moment; and he imposes upon others the duty of surrounding him, sustaining him, even guessing him in order to sing the same funeral hymn or give himself up to the same mad freak of joy.

Form of Gipsy Music

The Gypsy musician sought an artistic form to express his most desolate sadness as well as his most unrestrainable gaiety; two emotions which have taken up their abode in the two sections of a dance beginning gravely and then passing on to a rapid movement. Has the dance constituted itself on forms already taken up by the music?

Or, has the music (finding the form of the dance already set) adapted itself to that? These are questions difficult to answer. At all events the Gypsy musicians have thrown the three principal elements of their music motive, rhythm and ornamentation—into a mold which is now, by common consent, called a 'Hongraise.' This is divided into two parts: the first corresponding to the slow dance and the second to the animated dance which follows.

Of these two movements the first has now for some time, however, not been danced; and, although its value from the musician's point of view has been constantly increasing, the dancers have regarded it merely as a sort of intensive introduction. This exordium rarely fails to acquire an importance, if not predominant, at all events more than equal to that of the other movement. This peculiarity is due to the melancholy strain in the poetic genius of the Gypsy, which prevents him from giving way to any burst of humorous fancy until he has first freely and without interruption wept all the tears accumulated, breathed all the sighs withheld, and dreamed his dreams in full.

This movement, which is generally suggestive of a mourning procession, is taken at a slow andante; and is variously called, *Lassa, Lassu,* or *Lassan*, from a word signifying the particular kind of slowness more closely indicated by *maestro, pomposo*, or *dolente*.

Under the term Frischka (corrupted from Friznu or Frisza, meaning *allegro*) the second section of the Hongraise presents us with a rapid movement, the accelerations of which, both sudden and gradual, lead up to rhythms too furious and excited ever to be applied to any of the dances used in civilized society. About a *Frischka* there is something brusque, abrupt, irregular and intermittent; it is interrupted by sudden starts, stops suddenly and then rushes off again with redoubled fury. It is never met with in triple time and its constant retention of the duple 2/4 or common time ensures a firmness of accentuation with which it sometimes rises to the terrible.[19]

19. Liszt, *The Gipsy in Music*, 1859, 12, 18, 70, 79, 90ff, 131, 291, 295ff, 312ff.

Italy

1838

I will not induce you to come to Italy. Your sympathies would be too deeply wounded there. If they have even heard that Beethoven and Weber ever existed, it is as much as they have done.[20]

20. Letter to Robert Schumann, May, 1838.

From the aristocrat to the least grocery boy, everybody takes sides for or against the prima donna. The waiter who froths your chocolate tells you that Francilla Pixis sang the rondo in the *Generentola* very well; the man who shines your shoes isn't satisfied with the ornamentation of Giuramento.[21]

21. 'Lettre d'un bachelier sur La Scala,' in *Gazette Musicale* (May 27, 1838).

1863

Here people speak of Mendelssohn and even Weber as novelties![22]

22. Letter to Franz Brendel, October 10, 1863.

1873

I haven't looked around much in Rome, and do not feel at all inclined to seek out its historical and artistic grandeurs and marvels.[23]

23. Letter to Olga von Meyendorff, Rome, October 18, 1873.

1880

Last Tuesday I attended Pinelli's orchestra concert, at which Beethoven's *Pastoral Symphony* was played for the *first time* in Rome.[24]

24. Letter to Olga von Meyendorff, Villa d'Este, December 25, 1880.

1881

Venice remains incomparably attractive to me. I saw again with rapture the church and lion of St. Mark.[25]

25. Letter to Olga von Meyendorff, Venice, October 14, 1881.

1882

Ever since my first stay in 1837 I have been enamoured of Venice.[26]

26. Letter to Adelheid von Schorn, Venice, November 20, 1882.

Paris

1859

In my opinion Paris is the most comfortable, most appropriate and cheapest place for you while things in Germany remain in their wretched state. Although you may not agree with the artistic doings there, you will find many diverting and stimulating things, which will do you more good than your walks in Switzerland, beautiful though the Alpine landscape may be.[27]

27. Letter to Wagner, Weimar, August 22, 1859.

1872

A nice remark in Hillebrand's new book: 'The Frenchman likes to pride himself on his feelings for equality: nowhere in the world is there a less well-founded pretension. This feeling exists indeed from bottom to top; each considers himself equal to the one above him, but from top to bottom, it's another matter.'[28]

28. Letter to Olga von Meyendorff, November 29, 1872.

1876

As for the idea of founding in France a theater on the model of that of Bayreuth in order to present accomplished productions of the works of Gluck, Spontini, *Les Troyens* by Berlioz, etc., it is unlikely that it will be carried out in the near future: it will be hard for the French, with all their rare, brilliant, and superior qualities, to decide to take their musical pleasures really seriously.[29]

29. Letter to Olga von Meyendorff, Szekszard, October 26, 1876.

1878

Our friend Saint-Saëns should also have been elected to the French Academy; on the first ballot he received thirteen votes, but on the second Massenet received eighteen which had been scattered on almost unknown names and had then rallied around the least debatable candidate. So Saint-Saëns will fill the next vacancy; for however immortal *ex officio* Academicians may be, there are frequently deaths among them which cause no displeasure to their heirs.[30]

30. Letter to Olga von Meyendorff, Villa, d'Este, December 7, 1878.

Poland

1863

Patria in Religione et Religio in patria might be the motto of Poland. God protect the oppressed![31]

31. Letter to Eduard Liszt, Rome, May 22, 1863.

Vienna

1841

I have just discovered a new mine of Fantaisies ... *Norma, Don Juan, Sonnambula, Maometto,* and *Moise* heaped one the top of *Freischütz* and *Robert le Diable*. When I have positively finished my European tour I shall come and play them to you in Vienna, and however tired they may be there of having applauded me so much, I still feel the power to move this public, so intelligent and so thoroughly appreciative,—a public which I have always considered as the born judge of a pianist.[32]

32. Letter to Simon Lowy, London, May 20, 1841.

1845

To tell the truth I am extremely thankful to the Vienna public, for it was they who, in a critically apathetic moment, roused and raised me.[33]

33. Letter to Franz von Schober, Gibraltar, March 3, 1845.

1856

I only cherish the wish that coming years may offer me an opportunity of devoting my poor, but seriously well-intentioned services in the cause of music to the city of Vienna, whose musical traditions shine forth so gloriously.[34]

34. Letter to the Mayor of Vienna, Weimar, February 10, 1856.

1857

To make a firm footing in Vienna as a pianoforte player is no small task, especially under the present circumstances! If one succeeds in this, one can, with the utmost confidence, make a name throughout Europe.[35]

35. Letter to Dionys Pruckner, Weimar, February 11, 1857.

1860

Spring is really delightful in Vienna. I know no better setting for the *Pastoral Symphony* than Mödling, the Brühl, and twenty other charming spots that are near by. Without casting off on the advantages of the Bois de Boulogne, the spectacular forests of Fontainebleau and St. Germain, and the superiority and charm of English Parks; still, the country around Vienna has a kind of more *natural* quality to it, and it would seem as if one might be happier there than almost any place else.[36]

36. Letter to Marie zu Sayn-Wittgenstein, Gotha, February 26, 1860.

1872

If already they are thinking of honoring the Art by another embellishment of one of Vienna's public squares, wouldn't there be a better way to do it than to erect a statue of Beethoven, in the style of the town of Bonn and 30 years later? Why not raise a collective monument Joining together the five great musicians, *born in Austria*: Gluck, Haydn, Mozart, Beethoven, Schubert?[37]

37. Letter to Marie zu Sayn-Wittgenstein, Budapest, November 28, 1872.

Chapter Ten

Liszt on the Personalities of his Day

Bach

1863

Notwithstanding all my admiration for Handel, my preference for Bach still holds good, and when I have edified myself sufficiently with Handel's common chords, I long for the precious dissonances of the Passion, the B minor Mass, and other of Bach's polyphonic wares.[1]

1. Letter to Dr. Gille, Rome, September 10, 1863.

1868

I hope to hear Berlioz's Requiem next winter in Leipzig, and also some of Bach's contrapuntal *feste Burgen*. My ears thirst for them![2]

2. Letter to Carl Riedel, Grotta Mare, August 12, 1868.

1869

You are plunging into Bach—that admirable chalybeate spring! I will bear you company, and have given myself for a Christmas present, the Peters edition of the two Passions, Masses, and Cantatas of Bach, whom one might designate as the St. Thomas Aquinas of music.[3]

3. Letter to Franz Servais, Villa d'Este, December 20, 1869.

Balakireff

1884

My admiring sympathy for your works is well known. When my young disciples want to please me they play me your compositions and those of your valiant friends.[4]

4. Letter to Mili Balakireff, Weimar, October 21, 1884.

Beethoven

1841

Beethoven—as well as many great geniuses in the history of Art – is like the ancient Janus; one of his two faces is turned towards the past, the other towards the future. The *Septet* to a certain extent marks the point of intersection, and is thus unreservedly admired both by the devotees of the past and the believers in the future.[5]

5. Letter to Freiherr von Spiegel, Paris, September 30, 1841.

1852

For us musicians, Beethoven's work is like the pillar of cloud and fire which guided the Israelites through the desert—a pillar of cloud to guide us by day, a pillar of fire to guide us by night, 'so that we may progress both day and night.' His obscurity and his light trace for us equally the path we have to follow; they are each of them a perpetual commandment, an infallible revelation. Were it my place to categorize the different periods of the great master's thoughts, I should certainly not fix the division into *three styles*, which is now pretty generally adopted, but, simply recording the questions which have been raised hitherto, I should frankly weigh the *great* question which is the axis of criticism and of musical aestheticism at the point to which Beethoven has led us—namely, in how far is traditional or recognized form a necessary determinant for the organism of thought?

The solution of this question, evolved from the works of Beethoven himself, would lead me to divide this work, not into three styles or periods,—the words *style* and *period* being here only corollary subordinate terms, of a vague and equivocal meaning,—but quite logically into two categories: the first, that in which the thought stretches, breaks, recreates, and fashions the form and style according to its needs and inspirations. Doubtless in proceeding thus we arrive in a direct line at those incessant problems of *authority* and *liberty*. But why should they alarm us? In the region of liberal arts they do not, happily, bring in any of the dangers and disasters which their oscillations occasion in the political and social world; for, in the domain of the Beautiful, Genius alone is the authority, and hence, Dualism disappearing, the notions of authority and liberty are brought back to their original identity. Manzoni, in defining genius as 'a stronger imprint of Divinity,' has eloquently expressed this very truth.[6]

6. Letter to Wilhelm von Lenz, Weimar, December 2, 1852.

1853

[On the works of Beethoven's 'last style'] which were, not long ago, with lack of reverence, explained by Beethoven's deafness and mental derangement!.[7]

7. Letter to Richard Pohl, Weimar, November 5, 1853.

1855

The predilection of His Majesty the King of Saxony for Beethoven's Symphonies assuredly does honor to his taste for the Beautiful in music, and no one could more truly agree to that than I.[8]

8. Letter to the Intendant of the Court Theater in Weimar, Weimar, May 21, 1855.

1857

Beethoven, the glorious, holy, crazy one.[9]

9. Letter to L. A. Zellner, January 2, 1857.

Yesterday I spent the day hearing Beethoven's Mass (a mediocre work by a first-rate genius) at the Cathedral.[10]

10. Letter to Marie zu Sayn-Wittgenstein, Aachen, August 3, 1857.

1859

Beethoven was quite right to assert his right to allow that which was forbidden by Kirnberger, Marpurg, Albrechtsberger, etc.![11]

11. Letter to Franz Brendel, Weimar, December 1, 1859.

1863

The more intimately acquainted one becomes with Beethoven, the more one clings to certain singularities and finds that even insignificant details are not without their value.[12]

12. Letter to Breitkopf and Härtel, Rome, March 26, 1863.

[On the Symphonies] What study is deserving of more care and assiduity than that of these *chefs d'oeuvre*? The more one gives oneself to them the more one will profit by them.[13]

13. Letter to Breitkopf and Härtel, Rome, August 28, 1863.

1875

Music, the most communicative of the arts, is also the most lonely for those who plumb its depths. Beethoven tells us this sublimely in his last years.[14]

14. Letter to Olga von Meyendorff, Villa d'Este, October 7, 1875.

1880

I frankly confess that the title of the pamphlet, 'Beethoven and Liszt,' at first frightened me. It called to my mind a reminiscence of my childhood. Nearly fifty years ago, at the *Jardin des Plantes* in Paris, I used often to notice a harmless poodle keeping company in the same cage with a majestic lion, who seemed to be kindly disposed towards the little chamberlain. I have exactly the same feeling towards Beethoven as the poodle towards that forest king.[15]

15. Letter to Anna Benfey-Schuppe, Villa d'Este, November 11, 1880.

Berlioz

1836

Genius is grandeur in novelty … thought creating its own form … Now, in what musical works do we find a higher degree of bold innovation, of profound thought and richness of form than in *Harold in Italy*?[16]

16. *Le Monde* (December 11, 1836)

1852

Berlioz, the Shakespearean genius who embraces all extremes.[17]

17. Liszt, *Chopin*, 1852, 80.

Cellini is and remains a remarkable and highly estimable work.[18]

18. Letter to Richard Wagner, Weimar, August 23, 1852.

In a fortnight's time I am expecting Mr. Berlioz here [for performances of *Benvenuto Cellini, Romeo and Juliet*, and *Faust*. I am certain that it would be a great interest to you to hear these exceptional works, of which it is a duty and an honor to me not to let Weimar be in ignorance.[19]

19. Letter to Breitkopf and Härtel, Weimar, October 30, 1852.

Berlioz was very well satisfied with his stay at Weimar, and I, for my part, felt a real pleasure in being associated with that which he experienced.[20]

20. Letter to Julius Stern, Weimar, November 24, 1852.

1853

It will be necessary for you to have several rehearsals of the *Symphonie Fantastique* - and indeed *separate* rehearsals for the [strings], and separate rehearsals for the wind instruments. The effect of Berlioz's works can only be uncommonly good when the performance of them is satisfactory. They are equally unsuited to the ordinary worthy *theater and concert maker,* because they require a higher artistic standpoint from the musician's side.[21]

21. Letter to Gustav Schmidt, Weimar, February 27, 1853.

1854

I am convinced that, when you have looked more closely into the score, you will be of my opinion, that *Cellini,* with the exception of the Wagner operas, and they should never be put into comparison with one another—is the most important, most original musical-dramatic work of Art which the last twenty years have to show.[22]

22. Letter to Wilhelm Fischer, Weimar, January 1, 1854.

Cellini is Berlioz's freshest and roundest work, and its failure in Paris and London must be attributed to low villainy and misapprehension.[23]

23. Letter to Richard Wagner, Weimar, February 21, 1854.

This almost attains to the height of *punning* of our friend Berlioz, does it not?[24]

24. Letter to Bernhard Cossmann, Weimar, September 8, 1854.

1855

The blunt antipathies, the accusations of musical high treason, the banishments for life which have been imposed on Berlioz since his first appearance these have their explanation (why deceive ourselves about it?) in the holy horror, in the pious astonishment which came over musical authorities at the principle implicit in all his works, a principle that can be briefly stated in this form: The artist may pursue the beautiful outside the rules of the school without fear that, as a result of this, it will elude him.

……

The representatives of the development to come will entertain a quite special respect for works exhibiting such enormous powers of conception and thought and will find themselves obliged to study them intensively, just as even now contemporaries approach them *nolens volens* step by step, their admiration only too often delayed by idle astonishment. Even though these works violate the rules, in that they destroy the hallowed frame which has devolved upon the symphony; even though they offend the ear, in that in the expression of their content they do not remain within the prescribed musical dikes; it will be none the less impossible to ignore them later on as one ignores them now, with the apparent intention of exempting oneself from tribute, from homage, toward a contemporary.

. . . . . .

What they will never forgive is that form has for him an importance subordinate to idea, that he does not, as they do, cultivate form for form's sake; they will never forgive him for being a thinker and a poet.[25]

25. 'Berlioz and his *Harold* Symphony,' *Neue Zeitschrift für Musik* (1855) XLIII.

He is an honest, splendid, tremendous fellow.[26]

26. Letter to Richard Wagner, Weimar, July 10, 1855.

1859

I do not possess the Overture to the Corsair (and would not recommend it for performance).[27]

27. Letter to Franz Brendel, May 23, 1859.

1862

Berlioz was so good as to send me the printed pianoforte editions of his Opera *Les Troyens*. Although for Berlioz's works pianoforte editions are plainly a deception, yet a cursory reading through of *Les Troyens* has nevertheless made an uncommonly powerful impression on me. One cannot deny that there is enormous power in it, and I certainly is not lacking in delicacy—I might almost say *subtlety*—of feeling. Berlin, or any other of the larger theaters of Germany, would certainly risk nothing of its reputation by including an opera of Berlioz in its repertoire. It is no good to try to excuse oneself, or to make it a reason, by saying that Paris has committed a similar sin of omission—for things in which other people fail we should not imitate.[28]

28. Letter to Franz Brendel, August 10, 1862.

Considering what has occurred, and what has appeared in print, it strikes me as more than doubtful whether Berlioz would make up his mind to undertake the musical conductorship of the *Tonkünstler-Versammlung*. Besides which his moral influence at the Festival and the negotiations would be hindering and disturbing.[29]

29. Letter to Franz Brendel, November 8, 1862.

1868

A fortnight ago I heard from Paris that Berlioz was failing in health and suffering greatly. When I saw him last (in the spring of 1866) he was then already physically and mentally broken down. Our personal relations always remained friendly, it is true, but on his side there was somewhat of a gloomy, cramped tone mixed with them.

Neither Schumann nor Berlioz could rest satisfied at seeing the steady advance of Wagner's works. Both of them suffered from a suppressed enthusiasm for the music of the future.[30]

30. Letter to Franz Brendel, Rome, June 17, 1868.

1874

An amateur asked him at a performance of one of Beethoven's last quartets: 'Now, Sir, does this really give you pleasure?' Berlioz responded, 'For God's sake, who do you think I am? Would I be listening to such music as this for my pleasure?' (I've rendered the gist rather than the exact language, which ran: 'Do you think that I listen to music for pleasure?')[31]

31. Letter to Olga von Meyendorff, Horpacs, January 21, 1874.

They say Flaubert spent more than twenty-five years working on La Tentation de St. Antoine, which is steeped in the substance of several hundred other volumes. Berlioz would have enjoyed more than I these saturnalia of the mind through centuries, superstitions and beliefs.[32]

32. Letter to Olga von Meyendorff, Budapest, April 27, 1874.

1876

Berlioz's Harold-Symphony is to me an old, ever-fresh recollection.[33]

33. Letter to Max Erdmannsdürfer, June 27, 1876.

1877

Berlioz sometimes used to amuse himself by rewording proverbs, and ranked among the virtuosi of this not very distinguished art.[34]

34. Letter to Olga von Meyendorff, Budapest, January 9, 1877.

1879

Le Temps was the only major Paris newspaper in 1866 who praised my *Messe de Gran*, which was at that time rejected by my closest friends—Berlioz, d'Ortigue, etc.—who were urging me to continue charming salons in the role of a celebrated pianist. Many thanks and for *not* seeing such worthless friends again.[35]

35. Letter to Olga von Meyendorff, Rome, November 8, 1879.

1882

The real title of my Transcription of the *Rakoczy March* should be—*Paraphrase symphonique*. It has more than double the number of pages of Berlioz's well-known one, and was written *before* his. From delicacy of feeling for my illustrious friend I delayed the publication of it until after his death; for he had dedicated to me his orchestral version of the Rakoczy, for which, however, one of my previous transcriptions served him, chiefly for the harmonization. Without any vanity I simply intimate the fact, which any musician can verify for himself.[36]

36. Letter to Malwine Tardieu, Weimar, November 6, 1882.

1884

Bülow is almost as lavish of rehearsals as Berlioz would have been if he had had the means to be.[37]

37. Letter to Otto Lessmann, Weimar, January 10, 1884.

In reading the first volume I was painfully affected by several passages out of Berlioz's letters, in which the discord and broken-heartedness of his early years are only too apparent. He could not grasp the just idea that a genius cannot hope to exist with impunity, and that a *new thing* cannot at once expect to please the ancient order of things!

For the rest, there lies in his complaints against the Parisian 'fools and scoundrels,' whom he might also find in other places, a large share of injustice. In spite of his exaggerated leniency in favor of a foreign country, the fact remains that up to the present time no European composer has received such distinctions from his own country as Berlioz did from France. Compare the position of Beethoven, Weber, Schubert, Schumann, with that of Berlioz.[38]

38. Letter to Richard Pohl, Weimar, September 12, 1884.

Brahms

1858

Accustomed as I am to appreciating and sometimes admiring the pieces by my friends who don't admire mine at all [and who] are not to my taste (like Joachim, Raff, Brahms, etc) …[39]

39. Letter to Marie zu Sayn-Wittgenstein, Budapest, April 2, 1858.

1884

Tomorrow we will have a Brahms concert. The most fortunate of all composers, thanks to the omnipotent protection of the critics, will himself conduct his new symphony [Op. 98], and others of his works.[40]

40. Letter to Olga von Meyendorff, Budapest, April 11, 1884.

Bülow

1855

You must enjoy yourself in *the* artist who, above all other active or dying out virtuosi, is the dearest to me, and who has, so to speak, grown out of my musical heart. I confess that such an extraordinarily gifted, thorough-bred musical organism as his has never come before me.[41]

41. Letter to Louis Köhler, Weimar, March 16, 1855.

1859

My valiant son-in-law, H. von Bülow, cannot fail to be recognized among you as an eminent musician and noble character.[42]

42. Letter to Heinrich Porges, Weimar, March 10, 1859.

1862

His individuality is such an exceptional one that its singularities must be allowed scope.[43]

43. Letter to Franz Brendel, Rome, August 29, 1862.

1867

If Bülow goes on working here for a couple of years, Munich will become the musical capital of Germany.[44]

44. Letter to Eduard Liszt, Munich, October 20, 1867.

1871

No man is as close to my heart as he. He is practically my son and has been, for some twenty years, the most spirited and intimate of my friends. The natural nobility of his character is such that heroism seems to be a familiar condition for him.

We had not seen or written to each other in two years. The painful circumstances of his separation from Cosima have greatly impaired his health; but he is now recovering his full strength and intends to start on a round of performances next winter beginning in Vienna, Budapest, Prague, Dresden, Berlin, Leipzig, and ending in London in May. In the fall he will be sailing to America.[45]

45. Letter to Olga von Meyendorff, Rome, October 23, 1871.

Bülow, more than any contemporary artist, takes the lead in celebrity. He is not only a very great virtuoso and musician, but also a veritable sovereign of music.[46]

46. Letter to Walter Bache, Rome, October 25, 1871.

His perfect mastery as a virtuoso in the finest sense of the word—is in its zenith. To him one might apply Dante's words: 'A master to those who know.'[47]

47. Letter to Marie Lipsius, Rome, October 25, 1871.

1872

No other pianist commands admiring attention to the same degree and, I would even say, respect for the ability and talent so astonishingly combined in him. He has the most intimate insight into the music, and well as the nobility and perfection of beautiful style.[48]

48. Letter to Olga von Meyendorff, Budapest, January 12, 1872.

Bülow, who had a few hours before played some fifteen pieces of Beethoven at the concert in Vienna, was sensibly in bed, and I only woke him up at ten o'clock.[49]

49. Letter to Olga von Meyendorff, Pressburg, January 20, 1872.

1873

No other man in this world is as deeply dear to me as he. Unfortunately I do not have the means of making this as clear to him as I should like.[50]

50. Letter to Olga von Meyendorff, Budapest, January 7, 1873.

1874

The whole orchestra was amazed and astounded at his fabulous memory. You will remember that not only did he not use a score, but at the rehearsal referred to numberless *letters* and *double letters* with unerring accuracy.[51]

51. Letter to Carl Riedel, Budapest, April 17, 1874.

Bülow is now going to Salzungen for a couple of months, to recover from the terrible fatigues of his concert tour.[52]

52. Letter to Walter Bache, Villa d'Este, June 21, 1874.

1875

I was troubled by Bülow's last letter in June. He was then at some village in the Tyrol, suffering strong physical and spiritual pain. How could it be otherwise, after such excessive work, fatigue,—and proud nobility? In this last respect, I know no artist who equals him; even his eccentricities, thought of as faults, arise from the highest aims, and are touched by the marks of honor and disinterestedness.[53]

53. Letter to Marie zu Sayn-Wittgenstein, Rome, September 22, 1875.

1876

To find Bülow in such a state of suffering distressed me. He feels at the end of his tether, and thinks that he is done for. I don't know how the rumor spread that Bülow had lost his mind; several people have written me about this, but nothing is more false. The fact is that his mind remains most markedly lucid, and he retains that great nobility of character with a heroic touch, which I admire and love in him. In order to satisfy your taste for specific information (which I share), I'll tell you that Bülow's mistake has been to ignore a (fairly light) stroke, which he suddenly suffered in London last year, shortly before leaving for America. For many long years he has been habitually overdoing it and exceeding the limit in work and fatigue; witness the excessive programs which he put together for his concerts in Germany: at least a dozen pieces, among which several sonatas or suites, each with three or four movements, and which he played in 140 concerts during six or eight months in America.[54]

54. Letter to Olga von Meyendorff, Hanover, September 27, 1876.

1879

Bülow is doing wonders in Hanover. Yesterday's performance of *Cellini* was admirable in precision, color, and verve. Likewise the playing of the *Ninth Symphony* and of the choruses from *Prometheus* at Sunday's concert. I have never heard the Ninth interpreted with such perfection as a whole and in detail.[55]

55. Letter to Olga von Meyendorff, Hanover, April 18, 1879.

1881

You want to know my impression of yesterday's Bülow Concert? Yet it must have been yours, that of all of us, that of the whole of the intelligent audiences of Europe. To define it in two words: admiration, enthusiasm. Bülow was my pupil in music five-and-twenty years ago, as I myself, five-and-twenty years before, had been the pupil of my much respected and beloved master, Czerny. But to Bülow it was given to do battle better and with greater perseverance than I did. His admirable Beethoven-Edition is dedicated to me as the 'fruit of my tuition.' Here however it was for the master to learn from the pupil, and Bülow continues to teach by his astonishing performances as *virtuoso*, as well as by his extraordinary learning as a musician.[56]

56. Letter to Dionys von Pazmandy, Budapest, February 15, 1881.

1882

His knowledge, ability, experience are astounding, and border on the fabulous. Especially has he, by long years of study, so thoroughly steeped himself in the understanding of Beethoven, that it seems scarcely possible for anyone else to approach near him in that respect. One must read his commentary on the pianoforte works of Beethoven (Cotta's edition), and hear his interpretations of them—(what other virtuoso could have ventured to play the five last Sonatas of Beethoven before the public in one evening?[57]

57. Letter to Otto Lassmann, Weimar, September 20, 1882.

1884

For thirty years Hans von Bülow has been expressing and actively furthering everything that is noble, right, high-minded and free-minded in the regions of creative Art. As virtuoso, teacher, conductor, commentator, propagandist—

indeed even sometimes as a humorous journalist—Bülow remains the *Chief* of musical progress, with the initiative born in and belonging to him by the grace of God, with an impassioned perseverance, incessantly striving heroically after the Ideal, and attaining the utmost possible.[58]

58. Letter to Otto Lessmann, Weimar, January 10, 1884.

Chopin

1852

In his performance Chopin delightfully imparted that sense of restlessness that gave the melody a surging effect, like a skiff on the crest of a mighty wave. Early in his writings he described this style, which lent such an individual stamp to his playing, by the phrase 'Tempo rubato': time stolen or broken, a flexible measure, both lingering and abrupt, quivering like a breath-shaken flame. In his later publications he ceased to do this, convinced that if its meaning were understood, it would be impossible to ignore this rule of irregularity. Thus all of his pieces should be played with this measured and accented alternation, the secret of which is difficult to grasp unless he himself was frequently heard. He seemed eager to teach this style to his many pupils.

His voluntary sacrifice of clamorous success concealed, we think, an internal hurt. He had a very clear sense of his great superiority, but perhaps its echo and reverberation did not suffice to bring him the quiet certainty that he was fully appreciated. Popular acclamation was lacking, and he doubtless wondered to what degree the distinguished salons compensated, in the enthusiasm of their applause, for the general public that he avoided. A discontent, perhaps quite indefinite in his mind, at least with respect to its true source, secretly undermined him. He was obviously almost shocked by eulogy. What he was entitled to claim did not arrive in great outburst, and he was inclined to be vexed by isolated praises. He often brushed them off, like annoying dust, with polite remarks, and these made it quickly evident that he felt not only slightly applauded but badly applauded, that he preferred to be undisturbed in his solitude and sentiment.

Much too subtle an expert in jesting and too clever in derision to expose himself to sarcasm, he assumed no attitude of misunderstood genius. Happily complacent in outward appearance, he so completely hid the injury to his rightful pride that its existence was scarcely suspected. But gradually increasing rarity of his concerts, could be attributed, not unreasonably, more to his desire to avoid occasions that failed to bring him deserved tributes than to his frailty.

In none of its many manifestations did Chopin's character harbor a single emotion, a single impulse, which was not dictated by the most delicate sense of honor and the noblest understanding of the affections. And yet there never was a nature more inclined to eccentricity, whim, and abrupt caprice. His imagination was passionate, his feelings tended toward violence: his physical system was weak and sickly. Who can measure the sufferings proceeding from such contrasts? They were surely heart-rending, but he never exposed them to view! He kept them hidden, screened from all glances, beneath the impenetrable calm of proud resignation.

Events for him were feelings and impressions, more striking and important than external shifts and happenings. The lessons that he gave constantly, regularly, and assiduously, were his daily and domestic obligation, discharged with satisfaction and in good conscience. He unburdened his soul in compositions as others do in prayer, pouring out those effusions of the heart, those unexpressed sorrows, those indescribable griefs that devout souls spill in their talks with God.

His whole being was harmonious and seemed to require no comment. The blue of his eye was more animated than dreamy; his fine and gentle smile did not shift to bitterness. The delicacy and transparency of his complexion caught the eye, his blond hair was silky, his nose slightly tilted, his bearing distinguished, and his manner had such an aristocratic stamp that he was instinctively treated like a prince. His gestures were many and graceful, the tone of his voice was always subdued and often dampened, he was small of stature and frail of limb.

He carried into society the evenness of mood of persons who are undisturbed because they expect no advantage. He was customarily gay. His caustic mind quickly exposed the ridiculous far beyond the surface where it makes its impact. In pantomime he displayed a near inexhaustible comic verve, and he often enjoyed reproducing, in farcical improvisation, the musical mannerisms and special idiosyncrasies of certain virtuosos, repeating their gestures and motions, and mimicking their face with a talent that betrayed their complete personality in a flash.

Everything in Italian music that is simple, glittering, and devoid of ornament as of skill; everything in German music that is stamped with vulgar, though powerful, energy displeased him equally. Among composers for the piano, Hummel was the one whom he read again and again with intense pleasure, and in his eyes Mozart was the ideal type, the poet supreme, for more rarely than any other would he deign to cross the step separating the distinctive from the commonplace.[59]

59. Liszt, *Chopin*, 1852, 81, 84ff, 107ff, 145.

1872

Don't let us forge the etymology of the word 'Virtuoso,' how it comes from the 'Cicerone' in Rome—and let us return to Chopin, the enchanting aristocrat, the most refined in his magic. Pascal's epigraph, 'One must not get one's nourishment from it, but use it as one would an essence,' is only appropriate to a certain extent. Let us inhale the essence, and leave it to the druggists to make use of it. You also, I think, exaggerate the influence which the Parisian *salons* exercised on Chopin. His soul was not in the least affected by them, and his work as an artist remains transparent, marvelous, ethereal, and of an incomparable genius—quite outside the errors of a school and the silly trifling of a salon. He is akin to the angel and the fairy; more than this, he sets in motion the heroic string which has nowhere else vibrated with so much grandeur, passion and fresh energy as in his *Polonaises*, which you brilliantly designate as 'Pindaric Hymns of Victory.'[60]

60. Letter to Wilhelm von Lenz, Weimar, September 20, 1812.

1875

Rubinstein very ingeniously explained to me Chopin's *Sonata*, Op. 35, by Heine's *Tragodien, nebst einem lyrischen Intermezzo* [Berlin, 1823] [61]

61. Letter to Olga von Meyendorff, Budapest, March 23, 1875.

1877

I remarked before how little really remains to be done to Chopin's compositions, as he himself, with praiseworthy and exceptional accuracy, added every possible instruction to the performer—even to the pedal indications, which in no other composer appear so frequently.[62]

62. Letter to Breitkopf and Härtel, Villa d'Este, September 26, 1817.

1880

Chopin is the bewitching musical genius in which the heroically chivalrous Polish nationality finds expression.[63]

63. Letter to Hermann Scholtz, Weimar, April 29, 1880.

Cui

1873

Mr. Bessel brought me the piano score of your Opera *William Ratcliff*. It is the work of a master who deserves consideration, renown and success, as much for the wealth and originality of the ideas as for the skillful handling of the form.[64]

64. Letter to Casar Cui, Weimar, May, 1873.

1883

Your musical style is raised far above ordinary phraseology; you do not cultivate the convenient and barren field of the commonplace.[65]

65. Letter to Casar Cui, Weimar, December 30, 1883.

Czerny

1828

When I think of all the immense obligations under which I am placed towards you, and at the same time consider how long I have left you without a sign of remembrance, I am perfectly ashamed and miserable, and in despair of ever being forgiven by you! 'Yes,' I said to myself with a deep feeling of bitterness, 'I am an ungrateful fellow; I have forgotten my benefactor, I have forgotten that good master to whom I owe both my talent and my success.'

......

I have been playing your admirable works here with the greatest success, and all the glory ought to be given to you.[66]

66. Letter to Carl Czerny, Paris, December 23, 1828.

1830

Among all the circles of artists where I go *in this country* I plead your cause *tremendously*: we all want you to come and stay some time in Paris. If you ever entertain this idea, *I will do for you what I would do for my father*. I have been making a special study of your *admirable* Sonata, Op. 7, and have since played it at several reunions of connoisseurs.[67]

67. Letter to Carl Czerny, Paris, August 26, 1830.

1856

Of all living composers who have occupied themselves especially with pianoforte playing and composing, I know none whose views and opinions offer so just an experience. In the twenties, when a great portion of Beethoven's creations were a kind of Sphinx, Czerny was playing Beethoven *exclusively,* with an understanding as excellent as his *technique* was efficient and effective; and, later on, he did not set himself up against some progress that had been made in *technique*, but contributed materially to it by his own teaching and works. It is only a pity that, by a too superabundant productiveness, he has necessarily weakened himself, and has not gone on further on the road of his first Sonata, Op. 6, A Flat Major, and of other works of that period, which I rate very highly, as compositions of importance, beautifully formed and having the noblest tendency. But unfortunately at that time Vienna influences, both social and publishing, were of an injurious kind, and Czerny did not possess the necessary dose of sternness to keep out of them and to preserve his better ego. Remember me to him as his grateful pupil and devoted, deeply respectful friend.[68]

68. Letter to Dionys Pruckner, Weimar, March 17, 1856.

Cesar Franck

1854

For many years past I have had a favorable opinion of Mr. Franck's talent in composition, through having heard his trios (very remarkable, as I think, and very superior to other works of the same kind published lately). His oratorio *Ruth* also contains beautiful things, and bears the stamp of an elevated and well-sustained style.[69]

69. Letter to Marie Escudier, Weimar, January 28, 1854.

Glinka

1857

Thank you for having thought of me as one of the most sincere and zealous admirers of the fine genius of your brother, so worthy of a noble glory for the very reason that it was above vulgar successes. It will be at once my pleasure and duty to do my best towards the propagation of Glinka's works, for which I have always professed the most open and admiring sympathy.[70]

70. Letter to Ludmilla Schestakoff, Weimar, October 7, 1857.

1858

[On Glinka's 'Capriccio' on the melody of the Jota Aragonese']: Even at the rehearsal the intelligent musicians whom I am proud to count among the members of our orchestra had been both struck and delighted by the lively and piquant originality of this charming piece, so delicately cut and proportioned, and finished with such taste and art! What delicious episodes … What fine *nuances* and coloring. How the happiest surprises spring constantly out of the logical developments! and how everything is in its right place, keeping the mind constantly on the watch, caressing and tickling the ear by turns, without a single moment of heaviness or fatigue![71]

71. Letter to Basil von Engelhardt, Weimar, January 8, 1858.

1874

Bülow will publish an article on *A Life for the Tsar* which the late Grand Duke Michael (in 1842) praised in this curious manner: 'When I have to punish one of my officers, I send him to Glinka's opera.'[72]

72. Letter to Olga von Meyendorff, Rome, May 22, 1874.

1879

Your illustrious brother Glinka is one of the well-chosen admirations of my youth. His genius has been known to me ever since the year 1842; and at my last concert in St. Petersburg (in 1843) I played the *Marche tscherkesse* from *Russlan and Ludmilla* in a brilliant transcription by Vollweiler of several themes from the same Opera. Glinka remains the Patriarch-prophet of music in Russia.[73]

73. Letter to Ludmilla Schestakoff, Weimar, June 14, 1879.

Goethe

1873

I am proud to be writing you, at this very moment, on the old desk bearing Goethe's name, and from the same room formerly occupied by his Olympian Excellency.[74]

74. Letter to Marie zu Sayn-Wittgenstein, Dornburg, June 25, 1873.

1875

I have never been an excessive admirer of the conventional image of Goethe: an idol, whose worship has become far too convenient for slackers; but Napoleon was right to call the real Goethe 'a great man in his own land,' and to honor him by showing him attention.[75]

75. Letter to Olga von Meyendorff, Rome, September 24, 1875.

Gounod

1873

The fall theater season opened Saturday with Gounod's *Faust* at the Apollo. Faust had been to all intents and purposes hooted off the stage when it was first produced here. This time it was fairly well received. However, I was told yesterday that as people were leaving, a connoisseur said, 'For bad music, it's not so bad!'[76]

76. Letter to Olga von Meyendorff, Rome, October 8, 1873.

1880

Gounod had also sent me from London his *Marche funèbre*, together with a good many of his new vocal compositions. I don't remember the other pieces, but they probably include naive and piquant things.[77]

77. Letter to Olga von Meyendorff, Villa d'Este, January 3, 1880.

1882

And Gounod's *Redemption*! Ought one to speak of success or non-success in a work of that kind? Gounod has always kept the Catholic religious incentive with a turn towards the sublime.[78]

78. Letter to Malwine Tardieu, Weimar, September 12, 1882.

Grieg

1868

The Sonata, Op. 8, bears testimony to a talent of vigorous, reflective and inventive composition of excellent quality,— which has only to follow its natural bent in order to rise to a high rank.[79]

79. Letter to Edvard Grieg, Rome, December 29, 1868.

Handel

1855

'Zadok the Priest and Nathan the Prophet anointed Solomon King,' is a glorious ray of Handel's genius, and one might truly quote, of the first verse of this anthem, the well-known saying *C' est grand comme le monde.*[80]

80. Letter to Moritz Hauptmann, Weimar, September 28, 1855.

1857

You will not expect of me, dear Herr Kapellmeister, that I should go off into a great panegyric about Handel, and, if you caught me doing it, you might stop me immediately with the words of the ancient Greek who did not want any more praises of Homer—'You praise him but who is thinking of blaming him?' The fullness and glory of this musical majesty is as uncontested as the pleasant, emulating, easily attainable performance of the *Messiah, a chef-d'oeuvre,* which has been for years the 'daily bread,' so to speak, of great and small vocal societies both in England and Germany.[81]

81. Letter to Herr von Turanyi, Weimar, January 3, 1857.

Haydn

1872

I admire the literature of Mme Recamier somewhat in the same way that I admire the sonatas and symphonies of Haydn—as long as I don't have to hear them often.[82]

82. Letter to Olga von Meyendorff, November 29, 1872.

Bravissimo! for your charming comparison of a parrot cage with the frequent thematic repetitions in Haydn's symphonies. I share this impression in spite of the great respect due to the creator of the modern symphony and quartet.[83]

83. Letter to Olga von Meyendorff, undated, c. 1885.

1885

Ninety years ago my father was preparing for his duties as bookkeeper to Prince Nikolaus Esterházy in Eisenstadt. At that time he often took part, as an amateur, among the violoncellos in the Prince's frequent court concerts, under the conductorship of the happy great *master* Josef Haydn. My father often told me about his intercourse with Haydn, and the daily parties he made up with him.

. . . . . .

May the simple, artless genius of Haydn ever rule over the Eisenstadt Kindergarten conducted by your daughter.[84]

84. Letter to J. P. von Kiraly, Antwerp, June 5, 1885.

Heine

1874

A fascinating poet, too much celebrated and tainted by the triviality of vulgar applause.[85]

85. Letter to Edmund von Mihalovich, Villa d'Este, December 8, 1874.

Henselt

1838

May I confess to you that I was not very much struck with Henselt's Studies, and that I found them not up to their reputation? I don't know whether you share my opinion, but they appear to me, on the whole, very *careless*. They are pretty to listen to, they are very pretty to look at, the effect is excellent, the edition is most carefully done; but, all counted, I question whether Henselt is anything but a distinguished mediocrity.[86]

86. Letter to Robert Schwnann, May, 1838.

1878

The original works of Adolf Henselt's are the noblest jewels of Art. One longs for more of them.[87]

87. Letter to Adolf von Henselt, Weimar, June 5, 1878.

Hiller

1876

Now Hiller deserves to be treated as a musical figure; he has been enormously industrious and has produced a quantity of works of all kinds: operas, oratorios, symphonies, Lieder, chamber music (somewhat lacking in spirit at times), etc.: as a polygraph he could be ranked with Raff and Rubinstein; but each one of these three composers cares little for a common link and would prefer being ranked with Beethoven, or at least with Meyerbeer and Mendelssohn combined.[88]

88. Letter to Olga von Meyendorff, Villa d'Este, January 12, 1876.

Hummel

1885

Rubinstein and Lescheitizky will play the Sonata in A flat [Op. 92], one of the best works of the celebrated late Kapellmeister, whose piano compositions were formerly far more prized and played in salons and in public than those of Beethoven.[89]

89. Letter to Olga von Meyendorff, Budapest, April 11, 1885.

Joachim

1852

You know what high esteem I profess for Joachim's talent … my praises of him latterly are by no means exaggerated.[90]

90. Letter to Julius Stern, Weimar, November 24, 1852.

1854

Joachim is making a considerable step in advance as a composer; and if he goes on like this for a few years, he will do something out of the way.[91]

91. Letter to Richard Wagner, May 20, 1854.

Joachim sent me two remarkable scores composed with lion's claws and lion's jaws![92]

92. Letter to J. W. von Wasielewski, Weimar, December 14, 1854.

1880

Of all my old former friends, Joachim is the *only* one with whom it has been hard to keep up. He has stayed the classic chief of all contemporary violinists for the past thirty years.[93]

93. Letter to Marie zu Sayn-Wittgenstein, Budapest, January 23, 1880.

As for Joachim's talent as a virtuoso, I have been of the same opinion for thirty years; no other violinist produces such an impression of accomplished perfection as he does. Certainly, charm and attractiveness are hardly absent, but they are not scattered here and there indiscriminately. In some respects Bülow who, in his execution and in other respects, has a far more individual and bold genius nonetheless resembles Joachim in masterly concentration and a superior sense of style.[94]

94. Letter to Olga von Meyendorff, Budapest, February 1, 1880.

Cosima Liszt

1862

The letters in which she has written to me here and there of musical events in Berlin and elsewhere are really charming, and full of the finest understanding and striking wit.[95]

95. Letter to Franz Brendel, August 10, 1862.

1872

Although the stay of the Wagners at Dammallee is only temporary, Cosima has given proof there of her remarkable talents of Mistress of the House in the installation, the running, and the staffing of the house. No noise, no indecisiveness, nothing lacking.[96]

96. Letter to Olga von Meyendorff, Bayreuth, October 20, 1872.

1874

For a number of years, I have felt more than in harmony with Cosima—quai-identical—and when she happens to take an initiative, it is always with the best and most constructive intentions.[97]

97. Letter to Olga von Meyendorff, Rome, May 22, 1874.

On every occasion she has the gift of telling me specifically and exclusively those things I like to hear.[98]

98. Letter to Olga von Meyendorff, Rome, October 17, 1874.

1879

Lenbach recently painted a second or third portrait of Cosima. He expresses admirably without any mannerism the ideal of my daughter's personality.[99]

99. Letter to Olga von Meyendorff, Bayreuth, August 28, 1879.

1883

I suggested to my daughter that I join her in Venice and escort her back to Bayreuth. She replied in the negative. Between her and me there are bonds and dates far removed from ordinary relations.[100]

100. Letter to Olga von Meyendorff, Budapest, February 20, 1883, after the death of Wagner.

Litolff

1854

His Fourth *Symphonic Concerto* is a very remarkable composition, and he played it in such a masterly manner, with so much verve, such boldness and certainty, that it gave me very great pleasure.[101]

101. Letter to William Mason, Weimar, December 14, 1854.

Ludwig II of Bavaria

1872

People told of some oddities and flights of poetic fancy of the King of Bavaria, sailing about on the lake he has created in his winter garden at the castle, and planning the construction of a Vesuvius somewhere or other. This latter idea seems to me to have originated with others than the King, whose deeds and behavior I am in no way disposed to criticize in view of the extraordinary nobility of his feelings toward Wagner.[102]

102. Letter to Olga von Meyendorff, Schillingsfürst, October 9, 1872.

Mendelssohn

1839

Would you send me Mr. Mendelssohn's 'Preludes and Fugues?' It is an extremely remarkable work.[103]

103. Letter to Breitkopf and Härtel, Milan, June, 1839.

1880

Mendelssohn's excellent Concerti, always hold their ground without risk, especially since Berlioz's witty article (published nearly 30 years ago), according to which they are occasionally performed by the pianos alone, without further trouble on the part of the pianist.[104]

104. Letter to Frau Reisenauer-Pauly, Budapest, January 30, 1880.

Meyerbeer

1851

I should be delighted if you would help me to fill up this gap in the recognition I owe to Meyerbeer.[105]

105. Letter to Breitkopf and Härtel, Weimar, December 1, 1851.

1852

Meyerbeer has long since exhausted all admiring exclamations.[106]

106. Franz Liszt, *Chopin*, 1852, 94.

1859

Meyerbeer never dreamed of emancipating himself from the Italian school, which he started off by copying; nor from the German school, to which he gave his attention at a later period. All he did was to unite them—to place them in juxtaposition.

That, however, was a new combination; one which had never before been seen. But, although it enabled Meyerbeer to reap an unexampled popularity, it was nothing more than a combination. He could not assimilate the prodigious melodic energy of Rossini; because he lacked that inexhaustible source of inspiration which appertained to the Southern Italian feeling. Nor could he rise to any equality with Beethoven; for want of that composer's endless fund of Northern German sentiment. All he could do, therefore, was to improve on Mercadente in the one case and on Weber in the other.[107]

107. Liszt, *The Gipsy in Music*, 1859, 47ff.

1860

The Duke of Gotha made me the very handsome gift of the piano and vocal score of *Diana of Solanges*, published in German and French by Brandus, in Paris. The double dedication to the 'author of the Huguenots and Tannhäuser,' with which the eminent composer had originally planned to adorn his work, was finally omitted. When I commented to him about it, he told me that *Giacomo* had appeared only mildly flattered by the compliment of yoking together two names in such clashing harmony! As for our good friend Richard Wagner, he would have doubtlessly had at least a touch of fever from it. Beethoven, Schumann, Berlioz, all would have shown themselves the same—since, alas! in our artistic world, every star plays at being Jehovah, and tells himself very seriously: I am that I am![108]

108. Letter to Marie zu Sayn-Wittgenstein, Gotha, February 26, 1860.

Michelangelo

1877

No one, perhaps, knew and experienced the loneliness of human genius as much as he in the course of a long life. Before this great figure I feel a sad modesty combined with shame. This too is a form of vanity![109]

109. Letter to Olga von Meyendorff, Villa d'Este, October 14, 1877.

1881

Michelangelo used to say: 'He who follows others will never move ahead of them.'[110]

110. Letter to Olga von Meyendorff, Budapest, February 26, 1881.

Mozart

1855

In the program which has been sent to me I am pleased with the prospect before us, that the glories which Mozart unfolds in the different domains of Art—Symphony, Opera, Church, and Concert music—are taken into account, and that thus the manifold rays of his genius are laid hold of.[111]

111. Letter to Ritter von Seiler, Weimar, December 26, 1855.

1856

According to my ideas, an edition of Mozart's works, critically explained, equally beautifully printed, and revised by a committee appointed for it, a universally useful, lasting, and living monument to the glorious Master will be formed.[112]

112. Letter to Eduard Liszt, February 9 1856.

1872

As for the collective monument [in Vienna] of the five Austrian Musician-Geniuses, Gluck, Haydn, Mozart, Beethoven, and, Schubert, I dared risk the *idea* only in very humble confidence to Your Highness. If you don't altogether reject it, perhaps some day it too will have its happy moment. Schubert's very successful statue, in the Stadt-Park, doesn't seem to me to be a definite obstacle against the quintuple-monument: the chief difficulty rests in the composition of the group. To my way of thinking the place in the center belongs to Mozart, due to the universality of his genius; but how should the others be grouped and shown?[113]

113. Letter to Marie zu Sayn-Wittgenstein, Budapest, December 10, 1872.

Without being solemn I repeat to you that the *Symphony* in G minor, the one known as Jupiter, together with the superb *Zauberflöte* overture by Mozart are the peaks of instrumental music before Beethoven. Let us admire them in an appropriately respectful manner, or let us not discuss any music any more.[114]

114. Letter to Olga von Meyendorff, undated, c. 1872.

Nietzsche

1872

Today's mail brought me a letter from Friedrich Nietzsche, whom I do not have the advantage of knowing, a professor in Basel and author of the work about which I spoke to you recently. Forgive my seeming vanity in quoting to you the last paragraph of his letter: 'When I look around me for the few people who have truly and instinctively grasped the phenomenon I have described, and which I call *Dionysiac,* my eyes turn again and again primarily to you: you in particular must be familiar with the most recondite mysteries of that phenomenon to such a degree that I see in you one of its most remarkable exemplifications and have observed you time and time again with the highest theoretical interest.'[115]

115. Letter to Olga von Meyendorff, Budapest, January 21, 1872.

Between ourselves it will be fairly hard for me to reply to the author so as to please him. His work is more brilliant than clear; and you justly note that many things in it run 'counter to my feelings and to my manner of thinking and acting.'[116]

116. Letter to Olga von Meyendorff, Budapest, January 31, 1872.

1874

I have read Nietzsche; I find his impassioned and flashing tone sympathetic. Since he strikes without intermittence, he often hits the nail on the head, and his campaign against *Bildungs-Philisterium* is as courageous as it is justified.[117]

117. Letter to Olga von Meyendorff, Budapest, May 6, 1874.

Paganini

1832

What at man, what a violin, what an artist! Heavens! What sufferings, what misery, what tortures in those four strings! As to his expression, his manner of phrasing, his very soul in fact![118]

118. Letter to Pierre Wolff, Paris, May 2, 1832.

Remenyi

1864

Remenyi, who has played here … with *extraordinary* success. Of all the violinists I know, I could scarcely name three who could equal him as regards effect.[119]

119. Letter to Franz Brendel, Rome, May 28, 1864.

Rimsky-Korsakof

1878

Russian national music could not be more felt or better understood than by Rimsky-Korsakoff.[120]

120. Letter to B. Bessel, Budapest, March 11, 1878.

Rossini

1850

Comte Ory is a charming work, brimming over and sparkling with melody like champagne, so that at the last rehearsal I christened it the 'Champagner-Oper.'[121]

121. Letter to Breitkopf and Hartel, February 24, 1850.

1854

Yesterday evening I took my siesta at the *Barber of Seville*, since it's had neither charm nor interest for me for a long time; for I've heard it too often before, and too well done for me to get used to the mediocre performances such as Weimar, Leipzig, or Gotha offer.[122]

122. Letter to Marie zu Sayn-Wittgenstein, Gotha, March 23, 1854.

Rubinstein

1854

Rubinstein is a clever fellow the most notable musician, pianist, and composer, indeed, who has appeared to me from among the newer lights. He possesses tremendous material, and an extraordinary versatility in the handling of it.[123]

123.Letter to Carl Klindworth, Weimar, July 2, 1854.

My appreciation of the value that I recognize in your works will not vary, for it is not without a well-fixed *criterion*, quite apart from the fashion of the day, and the high or low tide of success, that I estimate your compositions highly, finding much to praise in them, except the reservation of some criticisms which almost all sum up as follows—that your extreme productiveness has not as yet left you the necessary leisure to imprint a more marked individuality on your works, and to *complete* them. For, as it has been very justly said, it is not enough to *do* a thing, but it must be *completed*. This said and understood, there is no one who admires more than I do your remarkable and abundant faculties, or who takes a more sincere and friendly interest in your work.[124]

124. Letter to Anton Rubinstein, November 19, 1854.

I am glad that you have come together again with the pseudo-Musician of the Future, Rubinstein. He is a clever fellow, possessed of talent and character in an exceptional degree, and therefore no one can be more just to him than I have been for years. Still I do not want to preach to him—he may sow his wild oats and fish deeper in the Mendelssohn waters, and even swim away if he likes. But sooner or later I am certain he will give up the apparent and the formalistic for the organically Real, if he does not want to stand still.[125]

125. Letter to Franz Brendel, December 1, 1854.

1859

You know that I am truly interested in what he is doing, considering that he has all that is wanting to compose good and beautiful things, provided that he does not persist in writing straight off too hurriedly, and guards a little against excess in the very exercise of these grand qualities.[126]

126. Letter to Ingeborg Stark, Weimar, November 2, 1859.

1884

Rubinstein has just given half a dozen concerts with large box office receipts and enthusiastic audiences. He will soon play in Paris, Lyon, Bordeaux, and then in Sweden. It is astonishing how he continues to be an extraordinary virtuoso, but his personality definitely betrays fatigue. His eyes are growing weak and he is to undergo a cataract operation.[127]

127. Letter to Olga von Meyendorff, Gran, February 3, 1884.

Saint-Saëns

1866

I must mention the name of Camille Saint-Saëns in Paris, as especially deserving of notice in the *Neue Zeitschrift* as a distinguished artist, virtuoso and composer. Last year he was in Leipzig, so he told me, and played his Concerto at the Gewandhaus there. But people could not make anything out of him, and in dignified ignorance allowed him to pass.[128]

128. Letter to Franz Brendel, Rome, June 19, 1866.

1869

I want to thank you again for your second Concerto, which I greatly applaud. The form of it is new and very happy; the interest of the three portions goes on increasing, and you take into just account the effect of the pianist without sacrificing anything of the ideas of the composer, which is an essential rule in this class of work.[129]

129. Letter to Camille Saint-Saëns, Rome, July 19, 1869.

At last your compositions have come, and I spent all yesterday in their amiable society. Let us speak first of the Mass: this is a capital, grand, beautiful, admirable work so good that, among contemporary works of the same kind, I know perhaps of none so striking by the elevation of the sentiment, the religious character, the sustained, adequate, vigorous style and consummate mastery. It is like a magnificent Gothic Cathedral in which Bach would conduct his orchestra![130]

130. Letter to Camille Saint-Saëns, Rome, August 4, 1869.

1874

Saint-Saëns will not, however, be able to come,—the less so as a few years ago his appearance in quite a harmless concert in Baden-Baden brought down upon him hideous rebukes and reproaches from the Parisian Press.

……

Among modern composers I regard Saint-Saëns as the ablest and most gifted.[131]

131. Letter to Carl Riedel, Budapest, May 5, 1874.

1877

I know no one among contemporary artists who, all things considered, is his equal in talent, knowledge, and variety of skills—except for Rubinstein. However, the latter does not have the advantage of being an organist, in which capacity Saint-Saëns is not merely in the first rank but incomparable, as is Sebastian Bach as a master in counterpoint.[132]

132. Letter to Olga von Meyendorff, Budapest, December 9, 1877.

1879

I venture to recommend him as the best musician I know of all France and Navarre.[133]

133. Letter to Marie zu Sayn-Wittgenstein, Budapest, January 26, 1879.

Saint-Saëns was here. He is worth still more than his great reputation.[134]

134. Letter to Marie zu Sayn-Wittgenstein, Budapest, March 8, 1879.

1882

I am still quite struck with wonder at your *Predication aux oiseaux de St. François*. You use your organ as an orchestra in an incredible way, as only a great composer and a great performer, like yourself, could do.[135]

135. Letter to Saint-Saens, Weimar, May 14, 1882.

George Sand

1852

She brought the full power of her ardent genius, which had the rare quality, reserved only for a few elect, of perceiving beauty in any form of art and nature, a quality that might be that 'second sight' the superior gifts of which all nations acknowledge in women who are inspired.

……

Dark and olive-hued Lelial! thou hast trod in lonely ways, depressed like Lara, shaken like Manfred, rebellious like Cain, but fiercer, more pitiless, more comfortless than they, for no man's heart has been found feminine enough to love thee as they were loved, to pay thine assertive charms the homage of blind and implicit submission, of silent and deep devotion, to shelter its obedience beneath thine amazonian strength! Woman-hero like unto those woman warriors, thou hast been valiant and eager for combat, like them thou has not feared to expose the satiny fineness of they countenance to sun and harsh wind, to harden thy frail limbs by fatigue and so remove the strength of their weakness. Like them thou must needs have donned a cuirass, wounding and tearing, to protect a woman's breast which, as vital as life and as secret as the grave, man adores when his heart is its sole and impenetrable shield!

Blunting her chisel in polishing this image—its haughtiness and condescension, its glance tortured and darkened by the approach of, a pure gaze, its locks waving with electric life, reminding us of ancient cameos with magnificent features demanding admiration, a fine fatal brow and the lordly smile of the Gorgon whose look benumbed and stopped the heart—Mme Sand vainly sought another form for the feeling that gnawed her unsatisfied soul. Having fashioned with infinite art this proud image, which assumed the masculine virtues in place of what she rejected—the supreme virtue of abasement in love, that virtue which the poet of vastest intellect placed at the pinnacle of the empyrean and called 'the eternal feminine,' that virtue which is love existing before its joys and surviving all its griefs—having called curses upon Don Juan and having her [Lelia] sing a hymn to Desire (and she, like Don Juan, spurning the one sensuality that crowns desire: sacrifice); having avenged Elvina by creating Stenio; having scorned men more than Don Juan had degraded women.[136]

136. Letter to Liszt, *Chopin*, 1852, 151ff.

Sarasate

1878

With regard to Sarasate, I recall having said to Princess Elsi that his successes were not inferior to his talent. I gladly applaud them and am happy at the enthusiasm displayed for Sarasate by courts and towns. However *his* Nocturne in E flat minor by Chopin, which is so generally admired, is a travesty in the worst of taste. How can one thus climb on the very first page to the higher octave like squirrels or acrobats, and then go down rapidly to the low strings, then climb and fall again, and finally swoon on a most trivial cadenza? Had you been paying attention, you would have found these acrobatics horrible.[137]

137. Letter to Olga von Meyendorff, Budapest, January 19, 1878.

Schubert

1850

With regard to Schubert's opera, *Alfonso and Estrella*, a recent experience has entirely confirmed me in the opinion I had already formed at the time of the first rehearsals, namely, that Schubert's delicate and interesting score is, as it were, crushed by the heaviness of the *libretto*! Nevertheless, I do not despair of giving this work with success; but this success appears possible only on one condition—namely, to adapt another libretto to Schubert's music.[138]

138. Letter to Breitkopf and Härtel, February 24, 1850.

1868

Our pianists scarcely realize what a glorious treasure they have in Schubert's pianoforte compositions. Most pianists play them over en *passant*, notice here and there repetitions, lengthinesses, apparent carelessnesses… and then lay them aside. It is true that Schubert himself is somewhat to blame for the very unsatisfactory manner in which his admirable pianoforte pieces are treated. He was too immoderately productive, wrote incessantly, mixing insignificant with important things, grand things with mediocre work, paid no heed to criticism, and always soared on his wings. Like a bird in the air, he lived in music and sang in angelic fashion.

O never-resting, ever-welling genius, full of tenderness! O my cherished Hero of the Heaven of Youth! Harmony, freshness, power, grace, dreamings, passion, soothings, tears and flames pour forth from the depths and heights of thy soul, and thou makest us almost forget the greatness of thine excellence in the fascination of thy spirit![139]

139. Letter to S. Lebert, Villa d'Este, December 2, 1868.

Clara Schumann

1839

How much I am rejoicing at the thought of hearing you again soon in Leipzig![140]

140. Letter to Clara Schumann, Budapest, December 25, 1839.

1854

I have again heard her with that sympathy and thoroughly admiring esteem which her talent commands.[141]

141. Letter to William Mason, Weimar, December 14, 1854.

Robert Schumann

1838

Mademoiselle Wieck, whom I have been so happy as to meet here, will express to you, better than I can, all the sympathy, all the admiring affection I have for you. We have been talking so much of you, day and night, that it hardly occurred to me to write to you.

......

The *Carneval* and the *Fantasiestücke* have interested me excessively. I play them really with delight, and God knows that I can't say as much of many things. To speak frankly and freely, it is absolutely only Chopin's compositions and yours that have a powerful interest for me. The rest do not deserve the honor of being mentioned.[142]

142. Letter to Robert Schumann, May, 1838.

Schumann, a young composer of very great merit.[143]

143. Letter to M. Pacini, Padua, September 30, 1838.

1839

I must again tell you that the last pieces you were so kind as to send me to Rome appear to me admirable both in inspiration and composition. The Fantaisie Op. 17 dedicated to me is a work of the highest kind—and I am really proud of the honor you have done me in dedicating to me so grand a composition. I mean, therefore, to work at it and penetrate it through and through, so as to make the utmost possible effect with it. As to the *Kinderscenen*, I owe to them one of the greatest pleasures of my life.[144]

144. Letter to Robert Schumann, Albano, June 5, 1839.

1849

No one honors and admires you more truly than my humble self. Manfred is glorious, passionately attractive![145]

145. Letter to Robert Schumann, Weimar, June 5, 1849.

1852

I believe you would not have been dissatisfied with the musical preparation and performance of *Manfred* (which I count among your greatest successes). The whole impression was a thoroughly noble, deep, and elevating one, in accordance with my expectations.[146]

146. Letter to Robert Schumann, Weimar, June 26, 1852.

1855

[Regarding Schumann' s *Genoveva*]: It is a work in which there is something worthy of consideration, and which bears a strong impress of the composer's style. Among the Opera which have been produced during the last fifty years it is certainly the one I prefer (Wagner excepted that is understood), notwithstanding its lack of dramatic vitality—a lack not made up for by some beautiful pieces of music, whatever interest musicians of our kind may nevertheless take in hearing them.[147]

147. Letter to Anton Rubinstein, Weimar, April 3, 1855.

1857

I should like to tell you truly with what sincere, heartfelt, and complete reverence I have followed Schumann's genius during twenty years and faithfully adhered to it.

……

At the beginning of the winter of 1840 we traveled together to Leipzig. Wieck, afterwards Schumann's father-in-law, had at that time a lawsuit against him to prevent his marriage with Clara. I had known Wieck and his daughter from Vienna days, and was friendly with both. None the less I refused to see Wieck again in Dresden, as he had made himself so unfriendly to Schumann; and, breaking off all further intercourse with him, I took Schumann's side entirely, as seemed to me only right and natural. Wieck without delay richly requited me for this after my first appearance in Leipzig, where he aired his bitter feelings against me in several papers.

……

Since my first acquaintance with his compositions, I have played many of them in private circles in Milan, Vienna, etc., but without being able to win over my hearers to them. They lay, happily, much too far removed from the insipid taste, which at that time absolutely dominated, for it to be possible for anyone to thrust them into the commonplace circle of approbation. The public did not care for them, and the majority of pianists did not understand them. In Leipzig even, where I played the *Carneval* at my second concert in the *Gewandhaus*, I did not succeed in obtaining my usual applause. The musicians, together with those who were supposed to understand music, had (with few exceptions) their ears still too tightly stopped up to be able to comprehend this charming, tasteful *Carneval*, the various numbers of which are harmoniously combined in such artistic fancy. I do not doubt that, later on, this work will maintain its natural place in universal recognition by the side of the *Thirty-three Variations on a Waltz of Diabelli* by Beethoven (to which, in my opinion, it is superior even in melodic invention and importance).[148]

148. Letter to J. W. von Wasielewski, Weimar, January 9, 1857.

1860

In the notices of Brendel's next-to-last number you will find the program of the Zwickau *Schumann Festival*. I have decided to go to it. Brendel, David, Martha Schumann, E. Genast, and other acquaintances of ours are going too,—and all the more because Mme Schumann and her friends want nothing of our company, and their dislike of us makes one more reason for joining this commemoration in Schumann's honor. Mme Schumann and Joachim have made their excuses to the Committee for their absence, motivated for the wife's part by the excessive emotion she would undergo, and for Joachim's by the absence of the wife.[149]

149. Letter to Marie zu Sayn-Wittgenstein, June 2, 1860.

1868

Neither Schumann nor Berlioz could rest satisfied at seeing the steady advance of Wagner's works. Both of them suffered from a suppressed enthusiasm for the music of he future.[150]

150. Letter to Franz Brendel, Rome, June 17, 1868.

1875

Schumann's *Genoveva* a work which has been taken up again with marked success this year (after it had been prudently ignored for twenty years). At the time of the performance which I conducted, and that is some twenty years ago, I said: *Genoveva* is musically the sister of *Fidelio*.[151]

151. Letter to Adelheid von Schorn, Weimar, May 17, 1875.

Sgambati

1862

I have fished out here a very talented young pianist, Sgambati by name, who makes a first-rate partner in duets, and who, for example, plays the *Dante Symphony* boldly and correctly.[152]

152. Letter to Franz Brendel, August 10, 1862.

1865

Sgambati has done wonders this winter at his four concerts, which have had a success both of fashion and of real good taste. I, for my part, have gained a *thorough* affection for Sgambati, and the remarkable development of his talent of so fine and noble a quality interests me keenly.[153]

153. Letter to Jessie Laussot, Rome, March 6, 1865.

1868

Sgambati is very much in fashion this winter, and the fashion is perfection right in this.[154]

154. Letter to Walter Bache, Rome, January 30, 1868.

Sgambati is decidedly not an artist for a *watering-place*, although as a virtuoso his talent is extraordinary and undoubtedly effective. He plays Bach, Beethoven, Chopin, Schumann, and my most troublesome things with perfect independence and in a masterly style. His artistic tendencies and sympathies are altogether *new-German*.[155]

155. Letter to Franz Brendel, March 31, 1868.

Sgambati is quite a phenomenal pianist for Italy, and is certain to do himself credit elsewhere on account of his sterling qualities, and his rare excellence as a virtuoso is combined with a personality of the greatest amiability and *reliable artistic feeling*.[156]

156. Letter to Franz Brendel, Rome, June 17, 1868.

1879

Sgambati regaled us with several of his compostions—among others a nocturne and an etude worthy of Chopin. What greater praise can one bestow?[157]

157. Letter to Olga von Meyendorff, Rome, November 8, 1879.

Smetana

1884

I write in haste to tell you that Smetana's death has moved me deeply. He was a genius.[158]

158. Letter to Carl Navratil, Weimar, May 30, 1884.

Spohr

1852

For the head of the proposed Congress of Kapellmeisters, Liszt proposes Spohr to you as the proper head. The master Spohr is our *senior*; he has always furthered the cause of music as far as circumstances at Cassel permitted—the *Fliegender Holländer* was given at Cassel under his direction earlier than *Tannhäuser* was given at Weimar.[159]

159. Letter to Gustav Schmidt, Weimar, May 18, 1852.

1857

Spohr, in the course of the winter, regularly plays quartets at the homes of several of the city's *finest*; but ordinarily his repertory is limited to quartets of Spohr and to a few of Mozart—and the latter in the proportion of a double dose of Spohr to a single one of Mozart. As for Beethoven, they claim that he can't play a single one of his quartets without committing some obvious mistake; and he takes his revenge by stating that no matter how lovely one wishes to find these works, they absolutely lacked *form*.[160]

160. Letter to Marie zu Sayn-Wittgenstein, Cassel, May 19, 1857.

Tausig

1855

About 6 o'clock a little piano-playing *prodigy,* age 13, from Warsaw, and named Tausig, came to see me. He's an amazingly gifted boy whom you will enjoy hearing. He plays everything by heart, composes (fairly well) and seems to me destined to make a brilliant reputation for himself very quickly.[161]

161. Letter to Marie zu Sayn-Wittgenstein, Weimar, July 21, 1855.

1857

If it is possible for you to take an opportunity of bringing out my dear and *extraordinary* budding genius Carl Tausig at the Court, I promise you that he will do honor to your recommendation.[162]

162. Letter to Hofkapellmeister Stein, Weimar, December 6, 1857.

1858

The young Titan sometimes gives way to an absence of mind and a state of overexcitement, against which those who wish him well should warn him. His exceptional talent and his genial and prepossessing manner generally incline me towards being overindulgent with him, and I do not deny my genuine love and partiality for this remarkable specimen of a 'Liszt of the future,' as Tausig has been called in Vienna. But for that very reason I expect him to be a good and steady fellow in all respects.[163]

163. Letter to Wagner, July 18, 1858.

1871

Tausig has died in Leipzig. This is a great loss for me, both in terms of friendship and of art. He was an individual of great quality and skill. Men such as he are so rare that one does not know where to come across them.[164]

164. Letter to Olga von Meyendorff, Weimar, July 20, 1871.

In what year of the fifties his father brought him to Weimar, I do not now recollect; but I do remember how greatly astonished I was at his extraordinary talent when I first heard him play. The intellectual claws and pinions were already giving signs of mighty power in the youth who was scarcely 14 years of age, and somewhat delicate in appearance. I felt some compunction in undertaking to give him further instruction, determined not to undertake the task, and therefore informed the father that in the case of such a stupendous organization the wisest plan was to leave it free, independent development without a teacher. However Tausig insisted upon remaining with me. He studied immoderately; as a rule kept very much to himself while in Weimar, and got into various little scrapes in consequence of his quick, ironical humor. I was accused of being over-indulgent with him, and of thus *spoiling* him; but I really could not have acted otherwise, and I loved him with all my heart. On various occasions when I had to undertake short journeys in connection with the performances of my works he accompanied me; among other places to Dresden, Prague and Vienna. As far as I know, no one has understood Tausig's genius, his demoniacally ideal nature, with so quick a perception, so refined and—I might say with womanly intuition.[165]

165. Letter to Marie Lipius, Schloss Wilhelmsthal, July 23, 1871.

Tolstoy

1886

This work [*Ma Religion*] may please people who enjoy fuzzy thinking.[166]

166. Letter to Olga von Meyendorff, Venice, January 27, 1886.

Wagner

1849

Herr van Zigesar has lately written to you to say with how much zeal and with what ever-increasing admiration and sympathy we are studying your *Tannhäuser*.[167]

167. Letter to Richard Wagner, February 9, 1849.

So much do I owe to your bold and high genius, to the fiery and magnificent pages of your *Tannhäuser*, that I feel quite awkward in accepting the gratitude you are good enough to express with regard to the two performances I had the honor and happiness to conduct.[168]

168. Letter to Richard Wagner, February 26, 1849.

Richard Wagner, a Dresden conductor, has been here since yesterday. That is a man of wonderful genius, such a brain-splitting genius indeed as beseems this country,—a new and brilliant appearance in Art.[169]

169. Letter to 'B,' Weimar, May 14, 1849.

He is a man of genius, who must of necessity obtrude himself on the general admiration, and hold a high place in contemporary art. His *Tannhäuser*, which is for me the most lyric of dramas, the most remarkable, the most harmonious, the most complete, the most original and *selbstwürdig*, both in foundation and form, that Germany has produced since Weber.[170]

170. Letter to Heinrich Ernst, May 30, 1849.

Could not you, on your part, arrange some concerts at Zürich, the proceeds of which would enable you to get through the winter tolerably? Why should you not undertake this? Your personal dignity, it seems to me, would not in the least suffer by it. Yet another thing, another string to your bow. Should you think it inconvenient to publish a book of vocal compositions,—Lieder or ballads, melodies or lyrical effusions, anything? For a work of this class signed with your name I can easily find a publisher and insist upon a decent honorarium, and there is surely nothing derogatory in continuing in a path which Mozart, Beethoven, Schubert, and Rossini have not disdained.[171]

171. Letter to Richard Wagner, Buckeburg, October 28, 1849.

1850

If the work succeeds at Leipzig, a publisher will easily be found; but I must not conceal from you that the success of *Lohengrin* seems to me somewhat doubtful, unless the necessary preliminary precautions with regard to study, rehearsals, and the press are taken. In leaving it to its fate—although, no doubt, it deserves a propitious fate—I have serious apprehensions from the ill-will which attaches to you personally and from the envy and stupidity which still combat your genius.[172]

172. Letter to Richard Wagner, Summer, 1850.

Lohengrin is to my idea a *chef-d'oeuvre* of the highest and most ideal kind! Not one of the operas which has entertained the theaters for the past twenty years can give any approximate idea of it.[173]

173. Letter to Simon Löwy, Weimar, August 5, 1850.

Your *Lohengrin* is a sublime work from one end to the other. The tears rose from my heart in more than one place. The whole opera being one indivisible wonder, I cannot stop to point out any particular passage, combination, or effect. The duet between Elsa and Lohengrin in the third act, to my thinking is the acme of the beautiful and true in art.[174]

174. Letter to Richard Wagner, Weimar, September 2, 1850.

1852

Of the conclusion of the preface to the three operatic poems of the Ring I say nothing. It has hit me in my heart of hearts, and I have shed a manly tear over it.[175]

175. Letter to Richard Wagner, Weimar, January 15, 1852.

It will be the task of my life to be worthy of your friendship. The little that so far I have been able to do for you and through you for the honor of art has chiefly this merit: that it encourages me to do still better and more decisive things for your works in the future.[176]

176. Letter to Richard Wagner, Weimar, August 23, 1852.

Your last letter, of about six weeks ago, has made your whole sorrow and misery clear to me. I have wept biter tears over your pains and wounds. Suffering and patience are unfortunately the only remedies open to you. How sad for a friend to be able to say no more than this.[177]

177. Letter to Richard Wagner, Late December, 1852.

1853

Wagner has a truly incredible fiery energy and rebound, and is the only one I know who is capable of sustaining in this manner six to eight hours of solid conversation which very often turns into monologues.[178]

178. Letter to Marie zu Sayn-Wittgenstein, Zürich, July 3, 1853

At the beginning of July I enjoyed several *Wallhalla*-days with Wagner, and I praise God for having created such a man.[179]

179. Letter to Louis Köhler, Carlsbad, August 1, 1853.

I like to remain in communication with people who prove real friends of yours. We form a little Church of our own, and edify each other by singing your praises. Take note, dear Richard, and make up your mind to it, for it cannot be otherwise. You are now, and will be still more, the concentric focus of every high endeavor, high feeling, and honest effort in art. This is my true conviction, without pedantry and charlatanism, both of which I abhor.

……

Our friend Köhler has latterly been severely attacked by several individuals who have the arrogance to think that they stand in opposition to you, while in reality they move in a low and *bottomless* region. [180]

180. Letter to Richard Wagner, Carlsbad, August 7, 1853.

1855

I am delighted at your friendly relations with Berlioz. Of all contemporary composers he is the one with whom you can converse in the simplest, openness, and most interesting manner. Take him for all in all, he is an honest, splendid, tremendous fellow; and, together with your letter, I received one from Berlioz, in which he says amongst other things: 'Wagner will, no doubt, tell you all about his stay in London, and what he has had to suffer from predetermined hostility. He is splendid in his ardor and warmth of heart, and I confess that even his violence delights me.' [181]

184. Letter to Richard Wagner, Weimar, July 10, 1855.

Write to me, at the first opportunity, whether ten thousand or twelve thousand dollars, with proper guarantee, would be a sufficient honorarium if you were to act as conductor in America for six months. [182]

181. Letter to Richard Wagner, Weimar, September 23, 1855.

I am looking forward to *Lohengrin*, that wonderful work, which, to me, is the highest and most perfect thing in art—until your *Nibelungen* is finished. At Berlin, at Count Redern's, I heard a few pieces from *Lohengrin* splendidly executed by several regimental bands. [183]

182. Letter to Wagner, December 24, 1855.

1856

Your last letter was very sad and bitter. Your illness must have put you out still more, and, unfortunately, your friends can do little to relieve you. If the consciousness of the most sincere and cordial comprehension of, and sympathy with, your sufferings can be of any comfort to you, you may rely upon me in fullest measure, for I do not believe that there are many people in this universe who have inspired another being with such real and continual sympathy as you have me. [184]

183. Letter to Wagner, Weimar, January 14, 1856.

Wagner and I see each other every day, and are together the livelong day. His *Nibelungen* are an entirely new and glorious world, towards which I have often yearned, and for which the most thoughtful people. will still be enthusiastic, even if the measure of mediocrity should prove inadequate to it! [185]

185. Letter to a Dr. Gille Zürich, November 14, 1856.

In spite of my illness I am spending glorious days here with Wagner, and am satiating myself with his Nibelungen world, of which our business musicians and chaff-threshing critics have as yet no suspicion. It is to be hoped that this tremendous work may succeed in being performed in the year 1859, and I, on my side, will not neglect anything to forward this performance as soon as possible—a performance which certainly implies many difficulties and exertions. Wagner requires for the purpose a special theatre built for himself, and a not ordinary acting and orchestral staff. [186]

186. Letter to Adolf Stern, Zürich, November 14, 1856.

I had some glorious days with Wagner; and Rheingold and the Wälküre are incredibly *wonderful works*. [187]

187. Letter to Alexander Ritter, Munich, December 4, 1856.

1857

The princess and her daughter will arrive this evening. The child is mad about your *Tristan* but, by all the gods, how can you turn it into an opera for *Italian singers*, as, according to B., you intend to do? Well, the incredible and impossible are your elements, and perhaps you will manage to do even this. [188]

188. Letter to Wagner, November 3, 1857.

1858

I cannot tell you how deeply *Lohengrin* moves me every time. The last time we performed it I felt proud of my century, because it possessed such a man as you show yourself to be in this work. With *Lohengrin*, the old opera world comes to a close; the spirit moves upon the face of the waters, and there is light. [189]

189. Letter to Wagner, January 30, 1858.

A certain one (who is indeed someone) of our friends sometimes embarrasses me as to what I can do for him, seeing that he has a peculiar talent for managing his affairs badly … With his immense genius, which becomes more incontestable in all the silly combats he has to engage in, he unfortunately doesn't manage to free himself from the most grievous domestic upsets, to say nothing of the evil consequences of his fantastic calculations. He resembles those high mountains that are radiant at the summit, but wrapped in mist up to the shoulder—with the difference that imaginary mists are more truly inconvenient than real ones. [190]

190. Letter to his Daughter, May, 1858, quoted in 'Lettres d'un pere et de sa fille,' *Revue des Deux Modes* (December' 15, 1935.

Härtel has sent me a divine Christmas present. All the children in the world cannot be so delighted with their trees and the golden apples and splendid gifts suspended thereon as I, in my own person, am with your unique *Tristan*. Away with all the cares and tribulations of everyday existence! Here one can weep and glow again. What blissful charm, what undivined wealth of beauty in this fiery love-potion! What must you have felt while you created and formed this wondrous work? What can I tell you about it beyond saying that I feel with you in my heart of hearts![191]

191. Letter to Wagner, December 26, 1858.

1859

If your operas have elsewhere been given for the purpose of getting money, the responsibility lies with those concerned; but here, where these works have been guarded and watched with so much love, I cannot make myself an accomplice of the brutal mercantile spirit in which they are now regarded.[192]

192. Letter to Wagner, January 1, 1859.

My confidence in you is unshaken. Hamlet's dilemma does not apply to you, for *you are* and cannot help being. Even your mad injustice towards yourself in calling yourself a 'miserable musician and blunderer' is a sign of your greatness. It is true that your greatness brings you little comfort and happiness, but where is happiness, in the narrow monotonous sense which is absurdly given to the word? Resignation and patience alone sustain us in this world.[193]

193. Letter to Wagner, Weimar, May 14, 1859.

1860

This evening is Wagner's first concert in Paris. I expect little good to him from it, and consider such a step on Wagner's part as a mistake. In consequence of this opinion our correspondence is for the time suspended.[194]

194. Letter to Franz Brendel, Weimar, January 25, 1860.

Among our Art-comrades of the day there is one name which has already become glorious, and which will become so ever more and more—Richard Wagner. His genius has been to me a light which I have followed—and my friendship for Wagner has always been of the character of a noble passion.[195]

195. Letter toPrincess Caroline Sayn-Wittgenstein, Weimar, September 14, 1860.

1861

In *Tristan* and the *Ring des Nibelungen* Wagner has decidedly attained his zenith![196]

196. Letter to Peter Cornelius, Weimar, April 18, 1861.

1862

Tristan and Isolde are my 'soul's longing!'[197]

197. Letter to Franz Brendel, Rome, August 29, 1862.

Ah, it is a pity that we cannot procure a stream of gold for him, or have some palaces of gold built for him! What can he do with admiration, enthusiasm, devotion, and all such non-essential things?

Nevertheless it is our indebtedness and duty to remain faithful and devoted to him. The whole German *Musik-Verein* shall raise up a brazen wall in his honor! He is verily worthy of it![198]

198. Letter to Franz Brendel, November 8, 1862.

My endeavors to secure him comfortable quarters in Weimar seem for the time being to be useless, because of his dislike of an insignificant appointment, and the adverse circumstances of life in a small town.[199]

199. Letter to Eduard Liszt, Rome, November 19, 1862.

1864

Of Wagner's wondrous fortune you are sure to have heard. No such star has ever before beamed upon a poet or composer.[200]

200. Letter to Eduard Liszt, Weimar, September 7, 1864.

1871

There is no need for you to make an effort to feel carried away by *La Muette de Portici* on the basis of Wagner's reminiscences. It merely acts for him as a nail on which to hang some bauble of his golden doctrine, which I follow with conviction and zeal – aside from some reservation of common sense.[201]

201. Letter to Olga von Meyendorff, Budapest, November 20, 1871.

1875

The performances (announced for the month of August, 1876) of the Tetralogy, *Der Ring des Nibelungen*, will be the chief event of dramatic Art, thus royally made manifest for the first time in this century in its *ensemble* and unification of

Poetry, Music, Acting, and their decorations of Painting and *mise-en-scene*.

There is not merely the chance, but the guarantee of a grand and striking success, in view of the sublimity of the work itself, and also of the enthusiasm which it already excites amongst the numerous staff of artists chosen to interpret it. In spite of the difficulties of this new transcendental style of Wagner, the preparatory study and rehearsals are an enchantment for the singers and the musicians of the orchestra. [202]

202. Letter to Carl Hillebrand, Bayreuth, August 2, 1875.

Here we are sailing in the full tide of the marvels of art. Every day, morning and evening, one act of the *Ring des Nibelungen* is rehearsed in Wagner's new theater. The enthusiasm of the whole staff of singers and orchestral players, to the number of about 150, is as sincere as it is abundant, and everything augers for next year some prodigious performances of the immense and sublime work which royally dominates all contemporary Art, including the former works of Wagner.[203]

203. Letter to Adelheid von Schorn, Bayreuth, August 7, 1875.

The most laudatory epithets such as admirable, wonderful, gigantic, unheard of, sublime, all grow pale before the grandeur and beauty of Wagner's work, the *Nibelungen*.

. . . . . .

Never has there been so much enthusiasm shown at rehearsals for any other work whatsoever. Here they've been going on for more than a month, twice a day: the singers, virtuosi, orchestra musicians, set-designers, technicians, costumers,—almost 200 persons are gathered here,—are all full of zeal, and they understand that something extraordinary and of the very highest order is taking place.

I congratulate M. Jauner for convincing Wagner to get up several of his works again for the Vienna stage. Besides his huge genius, Wagner has additional abilities in dramatic and artistic production, as well as in poetry, music, and stagecraft and all to the highest degree. Under his personal direction, the Viennese performances will gain noticeably in their tone and intensity of effect.[204]

204. Letter to Marie zu Sayn-Wittgenstein, Bayreuth, August 9, 1875.

1876

M. Pasdeloup should have particularly refrained from uttering a coarse insult such as: 'Today it is as a man that M. Wagner is judged.'—By whom, in what way, if you please? [205]

205. Letter to Olga von Meyendorff, Budapest, November 16, 1876.

My Wagner Transcriptions, by-the-by, were not in any way a matter of speculation to me. Appearing at the beginning of the fifties, when only the Weimar theater had the honor of performing Tannhäuser, Lohengrin and the Flying Dutcbman, such transcriptions only served as modest propaganda on the inadequate Piano for the sublime genius of Wagner, whose radiating glory now and henceforth belongs to the Pride of Germany.[206]

206. Letter to Breitkopf and Härtel, November 23, 1876.

1877

Cosima read me *Parsifal* Sunday evening. In the third act there is a sublime religious page. I don't know whether it's possible to stage this miraculous work. No matter; Wagner's genius overcomes even the impossible.[207]

207. Letter to Olga von Meyendorff, Weimar, August 1, 1877.

What a miracle is contained within *Parsifal*! I read the poem last night in an ecstasy of joy. Your comment on the feelings of obscurity which the uninitiated will experience at certain mystical passages is very true. However, with the aid of the music, the 'luminous darkness' will fire the public.[208]

208. Letter to Olga von Meyendorff, Budapest, December 31, 1877.

1878

What could I write to you about Wagner's *Parsifal*? The composition of the first act is finished: in it are revealed the most wonderous depths and the most celestial heights of Art.[209]

209. Letter to Kornel von Abrányi, Bayreuth, April 14, 1878.

After Vienna, I spent a week in Bayreuth at Wagner's. His genius is not at all waning: on the contrary, he climbs with *Parsifal* from the sublime to the miraculous, for which the first act music and a third of the second act is completed. There only remains to write the orchestration,—a rather long job but an easy one, since the chief instruments for it are already established within the context of the present score for piano and voice.[210]

210. Letter to Marie zu Sayn-Wittgenstein, Weimar, May, 1878.

The day after your departure we turned back again to *Parsifal* for a while; but Wagner didn't much enjoy it, and I understand this perfectly. The creation of such a work must give one a distaste for performances in general, and a particular revulsion for those with piano accompaniment. We therefore limited ourselves to rereading thirty pages or so; and to amuse ourselves we played a few hands of whist for three. To my surprise Wagner knows very well indeed the rules and fine points of this game, which he never plays.[211]

211. Letter to Olga von Meyendorff, Munich, September 1, 1878.

The October issue of your *Bayreuther Blätter,* [with Wagner's article, 'The Public in Time and Space,' brought me the highest intellectual gift. No temporal ruler can bestow one like it. The estimation of it lays me all the more under an obligation to that true humility with which I have long and most devoutly paid homage to our incomparable master, Richard Wagner.[212]

212. Letter to Hans von Wolzogen, Villa d'Este, November 15, 1878.

1879

Of Wagner I'll only say to you that my deep and lovingly passionate admiration for his genius continues to increase. I leave it to others to criticize and haggle. To me he is the equal of Dante. King Ludwig of Bavaria and my daughter have the right perspective adoration.[213]

213. Letter to Olga von Meyendorff, Bayreuth, August 22, 1879.

The third act of *Parsifal* is absolutely sublime. It makes the soul quiver and weep …

In the next issue of the *Bayreuther Blätter* Wagner's alarm bell against the all-pervading musical and literary *mediocrity* will ring out. He wants, once and for all, to settle matters with mishmash tripe, high and low. My role of privy-counselor at Wahnfried forbids me to vex Wagner, all the more so since I share his opinion in almost every respect—theology excepted.[214]

214. Letter to Olga von Meyendorff, Bayreuth, August 28, 1879.

With *Parsifal*, Wagner climbs still higher on that mysterious Jacob's Ladder with which art links heaven and earth.[215]

215. Letter to Marie zu Sayn-Wittgenstein, Villa d'Este, September 12, 1879.

1880

Wagner has shown and taught us triumphantly "what style is.'[216]

216. Letter to Hans von Wolzogen, Weimar, July 28, 1880.

Wagner hasn't worked much at the orchestral score of *Parsifal*, but he has the whole thing complete in his head. I reread this most highly sublime work, first in my room without a piano, and yesterday we went through the last part of the third act with Wagner; he singing and I accompanying—There is in the third act an idealized flower garden watered with the blood and tears of the Mystery of Good Friday, which is absolutely *incredible*. I know nothing comparable in music.[217]

217. Letter to Olga von Meyendorff, Siena, September 24, 1880.

The piano and voice score of *Parsifal* is written and copied; there remains to put the orchestra score down on paper. It is now ready and already vibrating in Wagner's head; but he seems anxious to go on neither with this work nor with the performance. As for me, I can only consider that he is right not to hand *Parsifal* over to the present theatrical repertory, and to demand thoroughly exceptional terms for such an extraordinary work.[218]

218. Letter to Marie zu Sayn-Wittgenstein, Villa d'Este, September 30, 1880.

1881

Wagner goes out only to get some air in his brougham with a jump seat, which he bought recently, and to which are harnessed two white horses of Hungarian origin. In general he retains the good humor of a great, a very great man, outwardly caustic and with the myriad coils of genius within. He is ill at ease with others and his relations with them are to him superfluous. He loves his wife and children; it is up to his true friends to understand the life style he requires and to take care not to bore him.[219]

219. Letter to Olga von Meyendorff, Bayreuth, October 7, 1881.

Wagner is finishing the instrumentation of the second act of *Parsifal*, and gives it his most passionate attention. We shall have something new, marvelous, unheard of, to hear.[220]

220. Letter to Edmund von Milhalovich, Bayreuth, October 8, 1881.

1882

Wagner's *Parsifal* far surpasses the masterworks which the theater boasts up to the present time. May the public be educated up to it.[221]

221. Letter to Kornel von Abrányi, Bayreuth, July 23, 1882.

Both at and after yesterday's performance of Wagner's *Parsifal* it was the universal feeling that about this wonderful work it is impossible to speak. It has indeed struck dumb those who were so deeply impressed by it; its sacred pendulum swings from the sublime to the sublimest.[222]

222. Letter to Hans von Wolzogen, Bayreuth, July 27, 1882.

His work is already becoming immortal.[223]

223. Letter to Malwine Tardieu, Weimar, September 12, 1882.

1883

I have become the most complete stay-at-home. Wagner is still a more thorough one, and he calls on nobody; his wife succeeds with great difficulty in persuading him that he must, however, make a pretense of rubbing up against a few human beings at infrequent intervals, even if they are very unpleasant. His bitter and ironic exclusiveness is related to his supremely absolute genius. In such a most extraordinary case, to reproach him would be to make a mistake.[224]

224. Letter to Marie zu Sayn-Wittgenstein, Budapest, February 14, 1883.

Your sad news of the death of Wagner pierces my heart. Worthily have you said of the great, undying hero of Art, 'May the memory of him lead us on the right road to truth!'[225]

225. Letter to Otto Lessmann, Budapest, February 18, 1883.

The press is full of obituary notices on the great poet-musician, the supreme dramatist of an Ideal never realized before him in *complete art*: poetry, music, and the stage. Compared with this triple achievement the colossi, Beethoven and Goethe, are sublime fragments. From *Tannhäuser* and *Lohengrin* to the *Nibelungen* and *Parsifal*, complete art has been revealed. To see Wagner only as a celebrity or showpiece strikes me as a somewhat silly misconception. The branches of his genius rise from deeper roots. In him the superhuman dominates.[226]

226. Letter to Olga von Meyendorff, Budapest, February 20, 1883.

To great grief silence is best suited. I will be silent on Wagner, the prototype of an initiatory genius.[227]

227. Letter to Malwine Tardieu, Budapest, March 6, 1883.

As to the Nibelungen tetralogy of Wagner—it shines with an immortal glory.[228]

228. Letter to Malwine Tardieu, Weimar, December 14, 1883.

1884

My admiration remains unlimited for the sublime genius of Wagner ... the *Art* of our century finds its foundation and glory therein.[229]

229. Letter to Hans von Wolzogen, Weimar, June 18, 1884.

Weber

1852

With one stroke a man of genius restored the polonaise's vigorous brilliance. Weber turned the Polonaise into a dithyramb wherein all the vanished magnificence and its dazzling deployment were suddenly rediscovered. To echo the past in a formula become diluted, he brought together the varied resources of his art. Without seeking to recall the nature of ancient music, he infused into it the very essence of the ancient Polonaise. He emphasized rhythm. He dramatized the melody, coloring it through modulation with a lavishness that the subject not only suggested but absolutely demanded. He injected into the Polonaise life and warmth and passion, without ignoring the haughty air, the formally pompous dignity, the majesty both natural and affected that are it inherent characteristics. The cadences were marked by chords calling to mind the sound of sabers shaken in their scabbards. The murmur of voices, instead of relaying pallid twitterings of love, resounded with bass tones, full and deep, like those accustomed to command. Such voices attract the fiery, distant neighing of those desert steeds, so nobly and elegantly built, that fretfully paw the ground and gaze with gentle, intelligent and flashing eye—and carry so gracefully the long trappings, trimmed with turquoises or rubies, which the Polish lords would pile upon them. Did Weber know the Poland of old? Had he evoked a picture already contemplated in order thus to establish the association? Idle questions! Does not Genius have its intuitions, and does Poetry ever fail to reveal to Genius what lies in its domain?[230]

230. Liszt, *Chopin*, 1852, 58ff.

1868

Send me a copy of the *Invitation to the Dance* that is so drummed at everywhere. You forgot to let me have this piece of salon-fireworks … years ago I had to play this over and over again, times innumerable—without the smallest 'invitation' on my part and it became a detestable nuisance to me.[231]

231. Letter to S. Lebert, Villa d'Este, December 2, 1868.

Part III

Liszt's Reflections On His Own Music

Chapter Eleven

Liszt on his own Musical Studies

1832

Here is a whole fortnight that my mind and fingers have been working like two lost spirits,—Homer, the Bible, Plato, Locke, Byron, Hugo, Lamartine, Chateaubriand, Beethoven, Bach, Hummel, Mozart, Weber, are all around me. I study them, meditate on them, devour them with fury; besides this I practice four to five hours of exercises (3rds, 6ths, 8ths, tremolos, repetition of notes, cadences, etc.). Ah! provided I don't go mad, you will find an artist in me![1]

1. Letter to Pierre Wolff, Paris, May 2, 1832.

1839

[On the Schumann *Fantaisie*, Op. 171] I mean to work at it and penetrate it through and through, so as to make the utmost possible effect with it.[2]

2. Letter to Robert Schumann, Albano, June 5, 1839.

1847

Send me Bach's six Pedal Fugues, in which I wish to steep myself more fully.[3]

3. Letter to Carl Haslinger, Woronino, December 19, 1847.

1869

I shall spend two or three days at Regensburg in order to hear the Cathedral choir there, which has a great reputation in Germany. There also I shall find a manuscript of the highest interest, and one which up to now has been almost unknown: it is the *opus musicum magnum* of Orlandus Lassus.[4]

4. Letter to E. Repos, Weimar, March 3, 1869.

1873

If the flight of your genius should find itself somewhat trammeled, for the time being, before the tribunal of counterpoint and fugue, it will soar all the more proudly afterwards.[5]

5. Letter to Franz Servais, June 5, 1873.

1878

My self-dissatisfaction finds ample consolation in the ever-fresh joy of the master-works of the Past and Present: most of all in Wagner's majestic creations.[6]

6. Letter to Kornel von Abrányi, Villa d'Este, September 13, 1878.

1881

I had been the pupil of my much respected and beloved master, Czerny.[7]

7. Letter to Dionys von Pazmandy, Budapest, February 15, 1881.

Chapter Twelve

Liszt on his own Creative Process

1839

I worked immensely hard in Italy. Without exaggeration I think I have written four to five hundred pages of pianoforte music.[1]

1. Letter to Clara Schumann, Budapest, December 25, 1839.

1852

I should have liked to be able to send you some of my new works for Piano, but, as I have been altering them and touching them up, the publication of them has been delayed.[2]

2. Letter to Carl Reinecke, Weimar, April 16, 1852.

What you tell me of the prodigious activity of your Muse obliges me to make a somewhat shameful acknowledgment of my relative slowness and idleness. The pupil is far from the master in this as in other points. Nevertheless I think I have made a better use of the last three years than of the preceding ones; for one thing I have gone through a rather severe work of revision, and have remodeled entirely several of my old works. I have been continuing writing in proportion as ideas came to me, and I fancy I have arrived at last at that point where the style is adequate to the thought.[3]

3. Letter to Carl Czerny, Weimar, April 19, 1852.

You have only to assimilate Palestrina and Bach—then let your heart speak.[4]

4. Letter to Peter Cornelius, Weimar, September 4, 1852.

1855

In literature the production of very much altered, increased, and improved editions is no uncommon thing. In works both important and trivial, alterations, additions, varying divisions of periods, etc., are a common experience of an author. In the domain of music such a thing is more minute and more difficult—and therefore it is seldom done. None the less do I consider it very profitable to correct one's mistakes as far as possible, and to make use of the experiences one gains by the editions of the works themselves.[5]

5. Letter to Alfred Dorffel, January 17, 1855.

During these last weeks I have spun myself into my mass. I do not know how it will sound, but may say that I have prayed it rather than *composed* it.[6]

6. Letter to Richard Wagner, Weimar, May 2, 1855.

1857

By the many performances (of the *Gran Mass*), which have been of great use to me in this work, many additions, enlargements, and details of performance have occurred to me, which will enhance the effect of the whole, and will make some things easier in performance.[7]

7. Letter to Joachim Raff, February, 1857.

That in composing I do not quite work at haphazard and grope about in the dark, as my opponents in so many quarters reproach me with doing, will be gradually acknowledged.

......

Binding together and rounding off a whole piece at its close is somewhat my own idea, but it is quite maintained and justified from the standpoint of musical form.

......

In face of the most wise proscription of the learned critics I shall, however, continue to employ instruments of percussion, and think I shall yet win for them some effects little known.[8]

8. Letter to Eduard Liszt, Weimar, March 26, 1857.

1858

The Dresden performance was a necessity to me, in order to realize its effect. As long as one has only to do with lifeless paper one can easily make a slip of the pen. Music requires tone and resonance!

......

The chief thing is that my present works should prove themselves to be taking a *firm footing* in musical matters, and should contribute something towards doing away with what is corrupt.[9]

9. Letter to Felix Draseke, Weimar, January 10, 1858.

1859

To practice art and even to practice it successfully is, however, not the same as possessing the supreme power of creation. To create is to call into being from nothing; it is to give a new form to a feeling already known; an aspect as yet unknown to an expression which is familiar. To 'practice' art is simply to vary the tonality of sentiments already expressed, the contexture of forms already existing, the modulation of tints which are already there. The genius sings by virtue of a personal inspiration in whatever way it dictates and suggests;

but talent can only retouch what others have already said. The talent may be extraordinary, but it is not an initiator. Between creating and innovating there is the same difference as between genius and talent; the same as between Bach and Mendelssohn, or Beethoven and Meyerbeer.

......

Being unable by nature to confine himself to mere receptivity, man is possessed by an involuntary desire to communicate, in his turn, the impressions by which he has been suddenly and unexpectedly charmed. He is inwardly moved to incorporate, in some act of his own, the moral emanations which have penetrated to him by outside means, and the emotions which he has sought and found; either in the spectacles of nature or in the contemplation of art. Both the one and the other cause his heart to palpitate, without any immediate agency; bring him to tears, without any misfortune having overtaken him; and provoke him to smile, without any subject for mirth being at hand. It is a generous tendency which inclines him to reproduce the impressions drawn from these two divine sources, though vague and without direct application. His desire is to bring them into active life, to seek their return in scenes—not fictional but real—where destinies are decided; to experience them afresh in the episodes which incite and develop his individual passions and personal sentiments, on the very battle-ground of real existence.

Everything that imagination can picture can be called up at the Artist's will. It may be lugubrious or charming, grandiose or delicious; that depends upon whether the master makes his appeal to the laughing or weeping faculties of the listener, whether he wishes to darken his soul by enveloping it in sombre shrouds through which terrifying visions are to be discerned, or whether he chooses to inundate it with light and cradle it in azure bands fringed with transparent droplets; for the soul is capable of being transported into an atmosphere of sensations nearly approaching a state of ravishment—sensations which inject into the veins some unknown beneficial influence, the pulsations of which render the body lighter, communicating to all its articulations an elasticity thought to be the attribute only of demi-gods.[10]

10. Liszt, *The Gipsy in Music*, 1859, 40, 91, 309.

I require my whole time for my further works, which must go on incessantly.[11]

11. Letter to Felix Draseke, Weimar, October 20, 1859.

Our own winter here will be wan and grey—for consolation, I shall let the ink fairly snow on my Music paper![12]

12. Letter to Marie zu Sayn-Wittgenstein, November 25, 1859.

1860

In these latter weeks I have been completely absorbed in my composing. If I mistake not, my power of production has materially increased, while some things in me are made clear and others are more concentrated.[13]

13. Letter to Eduard Liszt, Weimar, July 9, 1860.

The three *Chansons* and arrangement of the three Quartets for men's voices are all completed in my head; you shall have them as a new manuscript at the end of the week.[14]

14. Letter to C. F. Kähnt, Weimar, December 2, 1860.

1861

Unfortunately I have been able to do but very little work this winter. Revisions and proof-correcting took up almost my whole time.[15]

15. Letter to Peter Cornelius, Weimar, April 18, 1861.

1862

I am firmly resolved for some length of time to continue working on here undisturbed, unremittingly and with an object. After having, as far as I could, solved the greater part of the *Symphonic* challenge set me in Germany, I mean now to undertake the *Oratorio* challenge. The Legend of Saint Elizabeth, which was altogether finished a couple of months ago, must not remain an isolated work, and I must see to it that the society it needs is forthcoming! To other people this anxiety on my part may appear trifling, useless, at all events thankless, and but little profitable; to me it is the one object in art which I have to strive after, and to which I must sacrifice everything else.[16]

16. Letter to Franz Brendel, November 8, 1862.

'O friends, to these tones, rather let us strike up *pleasanter* ones,' sings Beethoven. The *Elizabeth*, it is to be hoped, contains something of the sort. At least, as far as possible,

I have labored carefully at the work, and, so to say, *lived it through* for more than a year.[17]

17. Letter to A. W. Gottschalg, Rome, November 15, 1862.

1863

To find myself in a net of social civilities is vexatious to me; my mental activity requires absolutely to be free, without which I cannot accomplish anything.[18]

18. Letter to Franz Brendel, Rome, April 14, 1863.

1865

My old musical weaknesses have not left me! The weakest and worst thing about them is perhaps that I never cease composing; but such wondrous things go wandering about in my head that I cannot help putting them down on paper.[19]

19. Letter to Breitkopf and Härtel, The Vatican, May 27, 1865.

1868

In Grotta mare I wrote about 20 pages of the technical exercises. Unfortunately a host of correspondence prevents my making progress with the work I have already begun and which is finished in my head.[20]

20. Letter to Siegmund Lebert, Rome, September 10, 1868.

1871

Now I have become terribly scrupulous and cautious in discharging my profession of musician. In order to go on writing I have to put everything else aside, and the setting down of my ideas, as such, takes an amount of time vastly disproportionate to their slight value.[21]

21. Letter to Olga von Meyendorff, Budapest, March 7, 1871.

1872

Regensburg being on the way to Vienna I prefer to stop there. The cathedral is grandiose. In the past I dreamed there of a Music which I know now how to write.[22]

22. Letter to Olga von Meyendorff, Bayreuth, October 20, 1872.

1874

So long as I am engaged in composing music, it absorbs me passionately; then, when it is a matter of performing it, of publishing it, etc., I have to make an effort to reinvolve myself even slightly in it, and generally I prefer to forget it completely.[23]

23. Letter to Olga von Meyendorff, Villa d'Este, November 11, 1874.

1875

I am especially pleased with the conclusion of an article by Külke: 'In the same way as Sebastian Bach could not conceive a musical thought in any other way than from a contrapuntal point of view, Liszt cannot conceive a theme in any other way than from a thematic point of view.'[24]

24. Letter to Eduard Liszt, Villa d'Este, October 31, 1875.

1876

My *Via Crucia* is barely sketched, and is still more in my head than on paper.[25]

25. Letter to Olga von Meyendorff, Villa d'Este, February 4, 1876.

1877

A well-disposed *program composer* uses such hints 'as prefaces and poems' more than is generally supposed.[26]

26. Letter to Breitkopf and Härtel, Villa d'Este, September 26, 1877.

I have spent this week here very much absorbed in the silly things I am writing on music paper continually scraping, changing, and rechanging, without managing to express what I feel, and yet would like more or less to express musically.[27]

27. Letter to Olga von Meyendorff, Rome, October 27, 1877.

I pursue my labors while trying not to become too much discouraged in my musical work, which I have resolved not to give up short of either total infirmity or death. A few more pages have been added...no less boring and redundant than the previous ones! To tell the truth I sense in myself a terrible lack of talent compared with what I would like to express; the notes I write are pitiful. A strange sense of the infinite makes me impersonal and uncommunicative.[28]

28. Letter to Olga von Meyendorff, Rome, November 9, 1877.

1878

A harmonic combination or progression may be against the rules of a system.[29]

29. Letter to Walter Bache, Budapest, March 19, 1878.

I am often quite anxious about further writing of music, but I do not give it up, although I do not imagine at all that I can express that which floats before my mind.[30]

30. Letter to Abrányi, Villa d'Este, September 13, 1878.

I have hardly opened a magnificent Erard piano installed in my sitting room. I am absorbed in the composition of the *Via Crucis* and in order not to spoil it I refrain from playing it until the manuscript is completed.[31]

31. Letter to Olga von Meyendorff, Villa d'Este, September 22, 1878.

These last two weeks I have been completely absorbed in my *Via Crucis*. It is at last complete (except for the indications of the fortes, pianos, etc.) and I still feel quite shaken by it. Day after tomorrow I will go back to writing letters, a task impossible for me to undertake so long as music torments my brain. I am barely able to keep up a few indispensable though brief conversations during pauses in my work; and in the evening I feel very tired. I go to bed at 9:30 and read for another half an hour; then the wretched notes of the morning and of the day to come enter my mind and disturb my slumber. In music as in moral matters one rarelv does the *good* one would wish, but often the *evil* which one would not wish[32]

32. Letter to Olga von Meyendorff, Rome, October 23, 1878.

I'm working feverishly six or seven hours a day on a task which is not suited to drawing rooms.[33]

33. Letter to Olga von Meyendorff, Rome, October 29, 1878.

I have been dreadfully industrious with my music writing since the middle of September. I sit and walk in it like one possessed![34]

34. Letter to Eduard Liszt, Villa d'Este, November 21, 1878.

1879

I'm so weary and even so harassed by the music I am writing, while composing it, revising the copy and the proofs, that afterwards I don't like to talk about it.[35]

35. Letter to Olga von Meyendorff, Villa d'Este, December 26, 1879.

1880

Formerly, people never looked at *libretti* very closely; today more care and poetic rapport have become necessary, particularly for Oratorios.[36]

36. Letter to Marie zu Sayn-Wittgenstein, June 11, 1880.

Zola's study on Flaubert is most remarkable. What interested me most is Flaubert's lengthy method of work in eager search of the *mot juste*, suitable, expressive, simple, and unique. I know similar torments in music. This or that chord, or even pause, have cost me hours and numerous erasures.

Those who know the meaning of *style* are a prey to these strange torments.[37]

37. Letter to Olga von Meyendorff, Villa d'Este, December 25, 1880.

1881

There is so much admirable music written that one is ashamed to write any more. With me it only happens in cases of urgency and from inner necessity.[38]

38. Letter to Otto Lessmann, Weimar, September 8, 1881.

1882

One can rub out easily on this paper, which is one of the most important things - that is to say, unless one tears up the whole manuscript, which would often be advisable.[39]

39. Letter to Carl Riedel, Venice, December 9, 1882.

1883

In the last couple of weeks I've been doing nothing but write music. The oars of a *Gondole Lugubre* beat on my brain. I have tried to write them and had to rewrite them twice, whereupon other lugubrious things come back to mind and, willy-nilly, my scrawls on music sheets continued to the exclusion of all else.[40]

40. Letter to Olga von Meyendorff, Venice, January 7, 1883.

1884

Still writing music, as I am, I sometimes ask myself at such and such a passage, 'Would that please Saint-Saëns?' The affirmative encourages me to go on, in spite of the fatigue of age and other wearinesses.[41]

41. Letter to Camille Saint-Saëns, end of 1884.

Chapter Thirteen

Liszt on his own Composition

Fantasiestücke
[1834–1838]

1838

I shall send you a half-dozen *Fantasiestücke* ('Impressions et Poemes ')—I consider them less bad than others of my making. [1]

1. Letter to Robert Schumann, May, 1838.

Festkantate zum Enthüllung des Beethoven-Denkmals in Bonn

1845

It is a sort of *Magnificat* of human Genius conquered by God in the eternal revelation through time and space,—a text which might apply equally well to Goethe or Raphael or Columbus, as to Beethoven. [2]

2. Letter to Abbé de Lamennais, Marseille, April 28, 1845.

First Concerto in Eb
[1849]

1858

In the Eb Major I have now hit on the expedient of striking the triangle (which aroused such anger and gave such offense) quite lightly with a tuning-fork and in the Finale I have pretty nearly struck it out altogether, because the ordinary *triangle-virtuosi* as a rule come in wrong and strike it too hard. [3]

3. Letter to Dionys Pruckner, Prague, March 9, 1858.

The Hungarian Rhapsodies [1851–]

1858

By the word 'Rhapsody' the intention has been to designate the fantastically *epic* element which we deem this music to contain. Each one of these productions has always seemed to us to form part of a poetic cycle, remarkable by the unity of its inspiration, eminently national. The conditions of this unity are fulfilled by the music belonging exclusively to the one people whose soul and intimate sentiments it accurately depicts; sentiments moreover which are nowhere else so well

expressed and which are cast in a form proper to this one nation; having been invented and practiced exclusively by them. [4]

4. Liszt, *The Gipsy in Music*, 1858, 337.

The Symphonic Poems

1856

Whatever fate may be in store for my *Symphonic Poems*, however much they may be cut up and pulled to pieces and found fault with through their performances and reviews everywhere, yet the sight of the beautiful manner in which these first six numbers are published will always be a pleasant satisfaction to me. [5]

5. Letter to Breitkopf & Härtel, Weimar, May 15, 1856.

The proofs have taken up a great deal of my time; for although I had not omitted, in the first proofs, to have things altered in the scores many times, yet many things looked different to me in print from what I wished them to be, and I had to try them over again plainly with the orchestra, have them written out again, and ask for fresh proofs. At last the six first numbers have come out, and even if they are very badly done I can no longer do them otherwise or better. I have labored too much in order to realize the requisite proportion and harmony, for them to be able to give me any other pleasure if some sympathy, and also some understanding of the spirit of them on the part of my few friends, does not fall to my share. [6]

6. Letter to Louis Köhler, Weimar, May 24, 1856.

Härtel will send you in a couple of days the first seven numbers of the arrangements for two pianofortes of my *Symphonic Poems* which have already appeared. An arrangement of that kind is not so easy to make use of as a four-hand one. Nevertheless, after I had tried to compass the score of *Tasso* plainly into *one* pianoforte, I soon gave up this project for the others, on account of the unadvisable mutilation and defacement by the working into and through one another of the four-hand parts, and submitted to doing without tone and color and *orchestral light and shade,* but at any rate fixing an abstract rendering of the musical contents, which would be clear to the ear, by the two-piano arrangement (which I could arrange tolerably freely). [7]

7. Letter to Louis Köhler, Weimar, July 9, 1856.

Tasso *[1849]*

1856

I learn from several Berliners that you have had the great kindness to orchestrate my march *Vom Fels zum Meer* splendidly, and have had it performed several times. Permit me to express my warmest thanks to you for this new proof of your friendship, and at the same time to remind you of a promise the fulfillment of which is very much desired by me.

It is that, in my last visit to Berlin, you were so kind as to say that the Symphonic Poem *Tasso* would not be amiss arranged by you for a military band, and you, with your well-known *readiness for action*, expressed your willingness to arrange the instrumentation accordingly. Allow me today to lay claim to half your kind offer, and to beg you to strike out forty-two pages of this long score, and so to dispose your arrangement that, after the last bar of page 5 (score), you make a skip to the second bar of page 47 (Lento assai), by this means shortening the *Lamento* of *Tasso* and of the public also.

......

I have not the slightest objection to simplifying rhythms, and beg you altogether, dear friend, to feel *quite free* to do as you like in the matter. The flattering thing for me would be just *this*—that the work should please you sufficiently for you to be allowed to take what liberties you wish with it.

Some years ago Dahlmann gave a lecture at Bonn upon immature enthusiasm. God preserve us rather from untimely pedantry! Certainly no one shall have to suffer from this from my side. Behold in this only the joy which the fulfillment of your promise will give me. If, as I imagine, the Finale from *Tasso* could be so arranged that moderate military bands could play it fairly well, I should of course be glad. However I leave it entirely in your hands to do with it whatever seems best to you. [8]

8. Letter to Wilhelm Wieprecht, Weimar, July 18, 1856.

Prometheus *[1850]*

1860

The *Prometheus* choruses, together with the *Symphonic Poem* which goes before them were composed in July, 1850 for the Herder Festival, and were performed in the theater here on the eve of that festival. My pulses were then all beating feverishly, and the thrice-repeated *cry of woe* of the Oceanides, the Dryads, and the infernals echoed in my ears from all the trees and lakes of our park.

In my work I strove after an ideal of the antique, which should be represented, not as an ancient skeleton, but as a living and moving form. A beautiful stanza of Andre Chenier, 'On modern thoughts let us fashion verses antique,' served me for precept, and showed me the way to musical plastic art and symmetry. [9]

9. Letter to Johann von Herbeck, January, 1860.

Hungaria *[1854]*

1848

Since my Beethoven Cantata I have written nothing so striking and so spontaneous. [10]

10. Letter to Franz von Schober, April 22, 1848.

Die Hunnenschlacht *[1857]*

1857

As I already intimated to Kaulbach in Munich, I was led by the musical demands of the material to give proportionately more place to the solar light of Christianity, personified in the Catholic chorale 'Crux fidelis,' than appears to be the case in the glorious painting, in order thereby to win and pregnantly represent the conclusion of the Victory of the Cross, with which I, both as a Catholic and as a man, could not dispense. [11]

11. Letter to Frau von Kaulbach, Weimar, May 1, 1857.

1876

I absolutely wrote the *Hunnenschlacht* for the sake of the hymn 'Crux fidelis.' [12]

12. Letter to Eduard Liszt, Villa d'Este, January 23, 1876.

1879

Kaulbach's world-renowned picture presents two battles—the one on earth, the other in the air, according to the legend that warriors, after their death, continue fighting incessantly as spirits. In the middle of the picture appears the *Cross* and its mystic light: on this my *Symphonic Poem* is founded. The chorale 'Crux fidelis,' which is gradually developed, illustrates the idea of the final victory of Christianity in its effectual love to God and man. [13]

13. Letter to Walter Bache, Weimar, May 25, 1879.

An die Künstler
[1853]

1868

It has hitherto been more *screamed* at than heard, for it has been accounted one of my most culpable heresies to have set these words of Schiller's to music after Mendelssohn did, and indeed without copying Mendelssohn and without humoring the customary taste of Vocal Societies. Parenthetically be it said that Schiller and 'Manhood's dignity' forbade me to make this composition any pleasanter. I dreamt of a temple and not a kiosk!

If you run the risk of giving this Artists Chorus in Altenburg I must beg the conductor to take all possible care in rehearsing it—and to aim at the most dignified *composure* in the performance. Like reverberating marble-pillars must be the effect of the singing! [14]

14. Letter to Franz Brendel, March 31, 1868.

Berceuse
[1854]

1854

The thing ought properly to be played in an American rocking-chair with a Nargileh for accompaniment, in *tempo comodissimo con sentimento*, so that the player may, willy-nilly, give himself up to a dreamy condition, rocked by the regular movement of the *chair-rhythm*. [15]

15. Letter to Louis Kohler, Weimar, June 8, 1854.

Missa solemnis (for Gran)
[1855]

1855

In five or six weeks I hope to have finished this work, at which I am working heart and soul. [16]

16. Letter to Anton Rubinstein, Weimar, April 3, 1855.

The Mass will not take up an excessively long time, either in performance or studying. But it is indispensable that I should conduct the general rehearsal as well as the performance myself; for the work cannot be ranked among those in which ordinary singing, playing, and arrangement will suffice. It is a matter of some not usual trifles in the way of accent, devotion, inspiration, etc. [17]

17. Letter to Edmund Singer, August 1, 1855.

1856

Yesterday's performance of my Mass was quite according to my intentions, and was more successful and effective by far than all the preceding ones. Without exaggeration and with all Christian modesty I can assure you that many tears were shed, and that the very numerous audience, as well as the performers, had raised themselves, body and soul, into my contemplation of the sacred mysteries of the Mass. [18]

18. Letter to Eduard Liszt, Budapest, September 5, 1856.

It has sprung from the truly fervent faith of my heart, such as I have felt it since my childhood. [19]

19. Letter to a Dr. Gille, Zürich, November 14, 1856.

1857

If I am not quite mistaken, the Church element, as well as the musical style of this work, will be better understood and more spiritually felt after frequent performances than can be the case at first in the face of the prevailing prejudice against my later compositions, and the systematic opposition of routine and custom which I have to meet with on so many sides. Thus much I may in all conscientiousness affirm, that I composed the work, from the first bar to the last, with the deepest ardor as a Catholic and the utmost care as a musician, and hence I can leave it with perfect comfort to time to form a corresponding verdict upon it. [20]

20. Letter to Georg Schariezer, Weimar, April 25, 1857.

Psalm Thirteen [1855]

1863

This is one of those compositions I have worked out most fully, and contains two fugue movements and a couple of passages which were written with tears of blood. Were anyone of my more recent works -likely to be performed at a concert with orchestra and chorus, I would recommend this Psalm. Its poetic subject welled up plenteously out of my soul. It requires a lyrical tenor; while singing he must be able to pray, to sigh and lament, to become exalted, pacified and biblically inspired. Superficial or ordinarily careful study would not suffice. [21]

21. Letter to Franz Brendel, November 11, 1863.

1871

Psalm 13 should not be sung by a female voice; it calls for a virile register combined with the feminine sentiment of the anguish of things divine. [22]

22. Letter to Olga von Meyendorff, Budapest, March 27, 1871.

Mass for Male Voices

1857

Before all else it requires the utmost certainty in intonation and then, above all, *religious* absorption, meditation, expansion, ecstasy, shadow, light, soaring - in a word, *Catholic devotion and inspiration*. The *Credo* as if built on a rock, should sound as steadfast as the dogma itself; a mystic and ecstatic joy should pervade the *Sanctus*; the *Agnus Dei* (as well as the *Miserere* in the *Gloria*) should be accentuated, in a tender and deeply elegiac manner, by the most fervent sympathy with the *Passion* of Christ; and the *Dona nobis pacem*, expressive of reconciliation and full of faith, should float away like sweet-smelling incense. If the extent of the chorus allows it, it might perhaps be desirable to add a few more wind instruments (clarinets, bassoon, horns, indeed even a couple of trombones) to support the voices more. [23]

23. Letter to Johann von Herbeck, January, 1857.

1859

In the performance last year at Jena (at the secular celebration of the University) I had the opportunity of convincing myself how capital your instrumentation of the Mass sounds, and I especially beg that you will not leave out one *iota* of it in the oboes or trombones. The organ is not sufficient, especially if there is a large chorus. [24]

24. Letter to Johann von Herbeck, Weimar, October 11, 1859.

Die Legende von der heiligne Elisabeth [1857–1862]

1862

The tenor part is a very important one;—I have made *myself* sing it, and thus had King David's feelings poured into me in flesh and blood! [25]

25. Letter to Franz Brendel, Rome, August 29, 1862.

Marches [1857]

1857

By the end of this week, I shall have finished my Marches, which, if I am not wrong, are most successful. In the Goethe March there is a 'cultural-historical' second Trio that has a serene quality, and is calm and majestically sweet. For M.

Sach's March, I discovered a motif from a *non-Protestant* Chorale, yea-saying and as if overflowing with love; and it blends in marked contrast with the militant and warrior spirit of the first motif - I should like a courageous, daring, almost reckless Prince, who announces his reign with this ray of love and faith should shine on royal heads like the sun glowing on mountain peaks! [26]

26. Letter to Marie zu Sayn-Wittgenstein, Aachen, July 28, 1857.

Psalm One Hundred Thirty-Seven [1859]

1864

The violin accompaniment which on several occasions is in unison, as well as the concluding chorus, 'Jerusalem, Jerusalem,' are written exclusively for women's (or boys') voices, and thus demand a female soloist. Besides which it seems to me that the sentiment and spiritual tonality of the Psalm do not move in the masculinum. Israeli gentlemen must not be called upon to sigh, to dream and to abandon themselves to their grief in any such way. [27]

27. Letter to an Undesignated Person, Rome, August 7, 1864.

1865

What lady takes the solo?—mind and soul are indispensable in it. [28]

28. Letter to Franz Brendel, April 3, 1865.

Beatitudes

1861

I have written few things that have so welled up from my innermost soul. [29]

29. Letter to Franz Brendel, Weimar, March 4, 1861.

1863

[Regarding a reviewer in the *Neue Zeitschrift*] He has formed the most correct estimate of my endeavors by pointing to the result, namely, to throw life into the truly Catholic, universal and immortal spirit - hence to develop it—and to raise the 'culture that has been handed down to us from the remote Middle Ages, out of the heavy atmosphere of the monasteries and, as it were, to weave it into the life-giving ether of the free spirit pervading the universe.' I also perfectly agree with the extremely applicable close of the same article: 'Our age has not yielded its right to feel itself connected with the Infinite.'[30]

30. Letter to Franz Brendel, November 11, 1863.

Hungarian Coronation Mass [1867]

1867

The Mass fulfilled its object in Budapest on the Coronation Day. If it should be given on any future occasion, I would recommend the conductor to take the tempi solemnly always, but *never dragging*, and to beat the time throughout *alla Breve*. And the *Gloria,* more especially towards the middle and before the commencement of the *Agnus dei* up to the Prestissimo, must be worked up brilliantly and majestically. [31]

31. Letter to Eduard Liszt, Rome, November 6, 1867.

Liszt's Arrangements of Beethoven

Symphonies

1839

It is essential that I should correct the last proof, so that the edition may be *absolutely* correct. I also wish to add the fingering to several passages, to make them easier for amateurs. [32]

32. Letter to Breitkopf and Härtel, Florence, January 3, 1839.

Forgive me for having kept them so long, and for having corrected them with so much care. Allow me to ask you for a second proof (for it is of great consequence to me that the edition should be as correct as possible). I shall take advantage of this opportunity [a trip to England] to let the Symphonies be heard at my concerts, so as to give them a certain publicity. [33]

33. Letter to Breitkopf and Härtel, Milan, June, 1839.

1863

A pianoforte arrangement of these creations must, indeed, expect to remain a very poor and far-off *approximation*. How to instill into the transitory hammers of the piano breath and soul, resonance and power, fullness and inspiration, color and accent?—However I will, at least, endeavor to overcome the worst difficulties and to furnish the pianoforte-playing world with as faithful as possible an illustration of Beethoven's genius.[34]

34. Letter to Breitkopf and Härtel, Rome, March 26, 1863.

Whilst initiating myself further in the genius of Beethoven, I trust I have also made some little progress in the manner of adapting his inspirations to the piano, as far as this instrument admits of it; and I have tried not to neglect to take into account the relative facility of execution while maintaining an exact fidelity to the original. Such as this arrangement of Beethoven's Symphonies actually is, the pupils of the first class in the Conservatoires will be able to play them off fairly well on *reading them at sight*, save and except that they will succeed better in them by working at them, which is always advisable. What study is deserving of more care and assiduity than that of these *chefs d'oeuvre*? The more one gives oneself to them the more one will profit by them, firstly in relation to the sense and aesthetic intelligence, and then also in relation to the technical skill and the attaining of perfection in virtuosity—of which one should only despise the bad use that is sometimes made.

......

I wish to indicate my intention of associating the spirit of the performer with the orchestral effects, and to render apparent, in the narrow limits of the piano, sonorous sounds and different nuances. With this in view I have frequently noted down the names of the instruments: oboe, clarinet, timpani, etc., as well as the contrasts of strings and wind instruments. It would certainly be highly ridiculous to pretend that these designations suffice to transplant the magic of the orchestra to the piano; nevertheless I don't consider them superfluous. Apart from some little use they have as instruction, pianists of some intelligence may make them a help in accentuating and grouping the subjects, bringing out the chief ones, keeping the secondary ones in the background, and—in a word—regulating themselves by the standard of the orchestra.[35]

35. Letter to Breitkopf and Härtel, Rome, August 28, 1863.

1864

After various endeavors one way and another, I became inevitably and distinctly convinced of the impossibility of making any pianoforte arrangement of the final movement of the Ninth Symphony for two-hands, that could in any way be even approximately effective or satisfactory. I trust you will not bear me any ill-will for failing in this. [36]

36. Letter to Breitkopf and Härtel, Schloss Löwenberg, September 14, 1864.

In compliance with the wish you so kindly express, I will again make an attempt to 'adapt' the final movement of the Ninth Symphony to the piano. Let us hope that the variation of the proverb: 'So often goes the pitcher to the water that at last it is filled' may prove true. [37]

37. Letter to Breitkopf and Härtel, Wilhelmsthal, October 1, 1864.

Quartets

1863

I would gladly, next summer, proceed in working out a former pet idea of mine; to make pianoforte transcriptions of Beethoven's Quartets 'for the home circle,' and, as it were, to make them a link in the Master's *catena aurea*, between his Sonatas and Symphonies. [38]

38. Letter to Breitkopf and Härtel, Rome, November 16, 1863.

1866

It is very mortifying to me to have to confess that I have most awkwardly come to a standstill with the transcription of the Beethoven Quartets. After several attempts the result was either absolutely unplayable or insipid stuff. Nevertheless I shall not give up my project, and shall make another trial to solve this problem of pianoforte arrangement. [39]

39. Letter to Breitkopf and Härtel, Rome, October 4, 1866.

Concerti

1879

I keep a long-standing promise today, by sending you the three last Concerti by Beethoven arranged for two pianos. This arrangement is distinctly different from all other existing arrangements of the same Concerti for two pianos. Till now it has been the habit of arrangers to content themselves with setting the Tutti (or better, the orchestral parts) for the second piano only, leaving the first to rest entirely or to support the second according to inclination. By this a grievous disproportion in the effect of the orchestral parts is induced, let alone the fact that some of the arrangements are exceedingly scanty.

In my opinion this sort of proceeding belongs to the past and is *hackneyed*. What good is there in the first player sitting there at all, if he does not know how to take part in the whole? Ergo, I had to occupy him almost constantly. [40]

40. Letter to Sigmund Lebert, Rome, September 25, 1879.

Chapter Fourteen

Liszt's Views on the Acceptance of his Music

1852

I will send you shortly my Catalog, which you will greatly oblige me by bringing out without much delay. The dispersion and confusion through which my works have had to make their way hitherto have done them harm, over and above any wrong that they already had by themselves; it is therefore of some importance to classify them, and to present to the public a categorical insight into what little I am worth. [1]

1. Letter to Breitkopf and Härtel, Weimar, October 30, 1852.

1853

In the first week of the new year I shall send you the score of my *Künstler* chorus. Tell me plainly your opinion of the composition, which of course I look upon only as a stepping-stone to other things. If you find it bad, bombastic, mistaken, tell me so without hesitation. You may be convinced that I am not in the least vain of my works; and if I do not produce anything good and beautiful all my life, I shall none the less continue to feel genuine and cordial pleasure in the beautiful and good things which I recognize and admire in others. [2]

2. Letter to Richard Wagner, Weimar, December 29, 1853.

1855

I want to inform you about my minor success this winter. I confess that for the time being I have no exact opinion about it. They clapped after each number on the Program—and there was one encore after the *Preludes* and the *Concerto* which Bülow played superbly ... the *Tasso* seems to have made a fairly good impression (even at the rehearsals); but it was less warmly applauded—and after the *Psalm*, which went perfectly, there were several 'St's' or 'Szt's' (the last letter s of my name), and these occasioned a roar of Bravo's, amid whose noise I climbed down once more the steps of this hall which formerly I knew so well. Needless to say, the most tense silence filled the hall during the performance; and I conducted it with apparently the necessary calmness. All are unanimous about its success. [3]

3. Letter to Marie zu Sayn-Wittgenstein, Berıin,December 7, 1855.

1856

For many years, since I became firmly resolved to live up to my artistic vocation, I have not been able to count upon any additional money from the music publishers. My *Symphonic Poems*, of which I shall send you a few in full score in a fortnight's time, do not bring me in a shilling, but, on the contrary, cost me a considerable sum, which I have to spend on the purchase of copies for distribution amongst my friends. My *Mass* and my *Faust* symphony, etc., are also entirely *useless works*, and for several years to come I have no chance of earning money. [4]

4. Letter to Wagner, March, 1856.

Yesterday evening's concert made too great an impression on me to begin again right away—The *Preludes* ought to have been played right through again; and as for the *Hungaria*, which was the last piece on the program, there was better than applause—all wept, both men and women! 'Tears are the joy of the Hungarians,' is a proverb of this country and yesterday evening proved to me that I made no mistake in style when I wrote the *Hungaria*, which I now do not wish to hear again.

……

A toast that followed called me 'the regenerator of Church music.'

The idea is starting to take hold among the intelligent portion of this country's clergy. [5]

5. Letter to Marie zu Sayn-Wittgenstein, Budapest, September 9, 1856.

Whether a production of his Symphonic Poems would be possible in Stettin I much doubt, in spite of your friendly advances. The open, straightforward sense of the public is everywhere kept so much in check by the oft-repeated rubbish of the men of the 'But' and 'Yet,' who batten on criticism, and appear to set themselves the task of crushing to death every living endeavor, in order thereby to increase their own reputation and importance, that I must regard the rapid spread of my works almost as an imprudence. You desire *Orphus, Tasso* and *Festklänge* from me, dear friend! But have you considered that *Orpheus* has no proper development section, and hovers quite simply between bliss and woe, breathing out reconciliation in Art? Pray do not forget that *Tasso* celebrates no *psychic* triumph, which an ingenious critic has already denounced (probably mindful of the 'inner camel,' which Heine designates as an indispensable necessity of German aestheticism!), and the *Festkläng* sounded too confusedly noisy even to our friend Pohl! And then what has all this *canaille* to do with instruments of percussion, cymbals, triangle, and drum in the sacred domain of Symphony? It is, believe me, not only confusion and derangement of ideas, but also a prostitution of the species itself! [6]

6. Letter to Alexander Ritter, Munich, December 4, 1856.

1857

I have read with attention and interest the discussions in the Vienna papers, to which the performance of the *Preludes* and the concert gave rise. As I had previously said to you, the *doctrinaire* Hanslick could not be favorable to me; his article is perfidious, but on the whole seemly. Moreover it would be an easy matter for me to reduce his arguments to ill, and I think he is sharp enough to know that. On a better opportunity this could also be shown to him without having the appearance of correcting him. I suppose the initials C.D. in the Vienna paper mean Dörffl—or Drechsler? No matter by whom -the critique is written, the author convicts himself in it of such intense narrowness that he will be very welcome to many other people less *narrow* than himself. His like has already often existed, but is constantly in demand.

……

I hear from Paris that at all the street corners they are selling a little pamphlet for a sou entitled 'The only means how not to die on the 13th of June at the appearance of the comet.' The only means is to drown oneself on the 12th of June. Much of the good advice which is given to me by the critics is very like this *seul moyen*. Yet we will not drown ourselves not even in the lukewarm waters of criticism - and will also for the future stand firm on our own legs with a good conscience. [7]

7. Letter to Eduard Liszt, Weimar, March 26, 1857.

The essential thing is that you love me, and consider my honest efforts as a musician worthy of your sympathy. This you have said in a manner in which no one else could say it. I confess candidly that when I brought my things to you at Zürich, I did not know how you would receive and like them. I have had to hear and read so much about them, that I have really have no opinion on the subject, and continue to work only from persistent inner conviction, and without any claim to recognition or approval. Several of my intimate friends—for example, Joachim, and formerly Schumann and others—have shown themselves strange, doubtful, and unfavorable towards my musical creations. I owe them no grudge on that account, and cannot retaliate, because I continue to take a sincere and comprehensive interest in their works.

Imagine then, dear Richard, the unspeakable joy which the hours at Zürich and St. Gallen gave me when your beaming glance penetrated my soul and lovingly encompassed it, bringing life and peace. [8]

8. Letter to Wagner, April 19, 1857.

They are also planning music for the Jubilee fêtes of the Grand Duke Carl August; and I predict to you beforehand that you will be able to read all sorts of unflattering things on this subject, as the music in question will be in great part my composition. However that may be, I shall try to have always something better to do than to trouble myself with what is said or written about me. [9]

9. Letter to Countess Rosalie Sauerma, Weimar, June 22, 1857.

You, dear friend, will have to bear some of the responsibility if I go on writing more such 'confused,' 'formless,' and, for the every-day critic, quite 'fathomless' things. [10]

10. Letter to Hofkapellmeister Stein, Weimar, December 6, 1857.

1858

How long this curious comedy of criticism will last I am unable to determine; anyhow I am resolved not to trouble my head about the cry of murder which is raised against me, and to go on my way in a consistent and undeterred fashion. Whether I shall be answerable for the scandal, or whether my opponents will entangle themselves in the scandal, will appear later. Meanwhile they can hiss and scribble as much as they please. [11]

11. Letter to Louis Köhler, Weimar, February 1, 1858.

The last chords of *Tasso* have just resounded—and I treated myself to the small pleasure of having the final march played again, which pleased the public exceedingly. This piece, which was *acquitted* and accepted in advance by the *big-wigs* here, was a great success afterwards. At yesterday's rehearsal, during a pause between the two Adagio's, a dog started to howl – 'another critic,' I said to myself *under my breath*!. Everyone takes his pleasure where he finds it, and they all find so much fault with me, that I wouldn't dream of picking on everyone else in the same way! [12]

12. Letter to Marie zu Sayn-Wittgenstein, Prague, March 14, 1858.

When the Princess informed me of your kind intention I wrote to her that a performance of my things in Leipzig appeared to me *untimely*, and that I was resolved to let them fall into oblivion rather than to importune my friends with them. I still think it is better not to have the *Preludes* performed now in Leipzig; but I thank you none the less warmly for the kind interest you take in my compositions—in spite of their bad name. [13]

13. Letter to Dr. Steche, Vienna, March 20, 1858.

My Symphonic Poems may obtain a hearing in Budapest sooner than in Vienna, because I may expect much more susceptibility to them here.[14]

14. Letter to L. A. Zellner, Budapest, April 6, 1858.

As regards the choruses to *Prometheus*, I confess to you candidly that, much as I thank you for thinking about them, I think it is wiser to wait a little bit. I am not in the slightest hurry to force myself on to the public, and can quietly let a little more of the nonsense about my *failure in attempts at composition* be spread abroad. Only in so far as I am able to do something lasting may I place some modest value upon it. This can and will be decided by time alone. But I should not wish previously to impose on any of my friends the disagreeables which the performance of my works, with the widespread presuppositions and prejudices against them, brings with it. In a few years I hope things will go better, more rationally, and more justly with musical matters.[15]

15. Letter to Johann von Herbeck, Weimar, November 22, 1858.

1859

And now if it isn't my poor old symphonic poems, marching out triumphantly just like Esther, and followed by the most illustrious cortege of contemporary names that one could imagine! I felt a child-like joy at reading the letter of invitation, and to see my poor works attain their *true* goal for the first time: that of 'being performed in your honor.'[16]

16. Letter to Marie zu Sayn-Wittgenstein, Weimar, May 17, 1859.

Dietrich plays Op. 106 and the Schumann *Sonata* capitally—as also the 'Invitation to hissing and stamping,' as Gumprecht designates that work of ill odor—my *Sonata*.[17]

17. Letter to Peter Cornelius, Weimar, August 23, 1859.

Do me the kindness to be perfectly free and open and regardless of consequences in the discussion of my works. Do not imagine that the slightest vanity comes over me or impels me. I have long ago done with all that sort of thing. So long as you allow that I possess the necessary musical equipment to create freely in Art, as I gather from your letter that you do, I can but be grateful to you for all else, even were it severe blame. I have often expressed my opinion to my friends that, even if all my compositions failed to succeed (which I neither affirm nor deny), they would not on that account be quite without their use, owing to the stir and impetus which they would give to the further development of Art. This consciousness so completely satisfies me that I can consistently persevere and go on composing.[18]

18. Letter to Louis Köhler, Weimar, September 3, 1859.

Experience having taught me to regard as a fate attached to my name the impossibility of publishing anything which does not instantly gather round it opinions as contrary as they are forcibly enunciated, I am, although quite accustomed to these little storms, very sensitive to the kindly judgment of those who, not letting themselves be influenced by this transitory impulse, desire to take into consideration what I have written, with sobriety and composure, just as you have done in your account of my book 'The Gipsies.'[19]

19. Letter to Eduard Hanslick, September 24. 1859.

My intimate friends know perfectly well that it is not by any means my desire to push myself into any concert program whatever.[20]

20. Letter to Johann von Herbeck, Weimar, October 11, 1859.

[Several letters have arrived for me from Vienna on the occasion of the performance of my first Mass (for men's voices). According to what I am told, both the work and its performance made an equally good impression. [21]

21. Letter to Marie zu Sayn-Wittgenstein, Weimar, October 27, 1859.

Prometheus will present himself to you by the end of this month. If after looking through the score, dear friend., you think the work suitable for a performance in Vienna, I shall be glad. If not, I beg you to tell me so *with perfect candour* and without the slightest scruple of thereby wounding my vanity. Whether the *stomach* of the critics and of the public will be able to digest such a liver cut out of the vulture as this of my *Prometheus,* or whether at the very first bars all will not be lost, I cannot determine. [22]

22. Letter to Johann von Herbeck, November 18, 1859.

The songs can hold their ground in their present form (regardless of the criticism of our choking and quarrelling opponents which will infallibly follow!); and if a few singers could be found, not of the *raw* and superficial kind, who would boldly venture to sing songs by the notorious *non-composer*, Franz Liszt, they would probably find a public for them.

……

In consequence of the performance of my Mass in Munich (on the King's birthday), which, as I am told on many sides, was well given and—which seems wonderful—was acknowledged by many musicians there to be a work of importance—so that even Lachner spoke favorably of it—the *Allgemeine Zeitung* against breathes forth poison and gall. [23]

23. Letter to Franz Brendel, Weimar, December 6, 1859.

1860

The performance of new works on the part of so renowned an orchestra as that of Munich must ever remain a mark of special attention for the composers. But I must rate it still higher that, in face of the strong prejudice against my name, one of my *ill-famed* Symphonic Poems should have been included in the program of the concerts of the Munich Hofkapelle. The more unseemly and malicious factiousness may show itself against new works, the more am I laid under a grateful obligation to those who do not accept as their artistic criterion the injustice inflicted on me.

Time levels all things, and I can quietly wait until people are more occupied in learning to know and to hear my scores than in condemning and hissing them. Mean-spirited, blackguard tricks, even when played in concert-rooms and newspaper reports, are no arguments worthy of a lasting import. [24]

24. Letter to the Secretary of the Concerts of the Hofkapelle in Munich, Weimar, January 15, 1860.

Excuse me if I speak to you so often of this musical crowd [his Tone Poems]; but they have me by the heart – and *by the throat*, as Pascal says. Apart from the feeling that dominates my whole life and for whose honor I would gladly give all ten of my fingers – one after the other and all my worldly possessions, I have no other passion save that for my task. The contradictions, nay even the injustice occasioned by my work, far from thwarting me, arouse me still further; and they confirm me completely in the attitude I have had since my youth: that is, in the field of Music I have something to say; and no one else can say it for me. [25]

25. Letter to Marie zu Sayn-Wittgenstein, Weimar, June 4, 1860.

1862

Although I have long been prepared to bear the *fiasco* of my works quietly and unmoved, yet still it is pleasant to me to learn that the *Faust* Symphony in Leipzig did not have such a very bad fate. [26]

26. Letter to Franz Brendel, Rome, April 12, 1862.

In spite of all good precepts and *friendly* counselors (who mean it much better by me than I can ever understand!) I go so far as to maintain that for several years past and in many yet to come I have not done and shall not do anything more ingenuous than cheerfully to go on composing. And what more harmless occupation could there be? especially as I never force my little works upon anyone, nay, have frequently begged persons to refrain from giving certain too unconscientious renderings of them,—and that I ask no further appreciation or approval than can, in fact, be granted according to taste and disposition. [27]

27. Letter to Eduard Liszt,. Rome, November 19, 1862.

1863

Unfortunately, however, I must make up my mind that only by way of an exception can I expect to find friends for my compositions. The blame is mine; why should one presume to feel independently, and set the comfortable complacency of other folks at defiance? Everything that I have written for several years past shows something of a pristine delinquency which is as little to be pardoned as I am unable to alter it. This fault, it is true, is the life-nerve of my compositions, which, in fact, can only be what they are and nothing else. [28]

28. Letter to A. W. Gottschalg, Rome, April 14, 1863.

Ample experience has taught me that my compositions more readily rouse estrangement than attraction. [29]

29. Letter to Eduard Liszt, Rome, May 22, 1863.

With regard to performances of my works generally, my disposition and inclination are more than ever completely in the *negative*. My friends, and you more especially, dearest friend, have done their part in this respect fully and in the kindest manner. It seems to me now high time that I should be somewhat forgotten, or, at least, placed very much in the background. My name has been too frequently spoken of; many have taken unbrage at this, and been uselessly annoyed at it. While 'paving the way for a better appreciation,' it might be advisable to regard my things as a reserve corps, and to introduce new works by other composers. [30]

30. Letter to Franz Brendel, Rome, June 18, 1863.

From the Committee of the Association for the Completion of the Köln Cathedral I have received an invitation to the Festival. The worthy gentlemen seem absolutely not to have considered how my activity could now appropriately be of service, and they wisely guard against mentioning any of my ecclesiastical compositions, although it might have occurred to them that I could manage something in that species of music. However, the worthy Committee find the old story of the 'period of my brilliancy,' and the 'bewitching strains I drew from the keys,' etc., more voluble and convenient. [31]

31. Letter to Franz Brendel, Monte Mario, September 7, 1863.

I found much pleasant and encouraging in the issues of the *Neue Zeitschrift*. I could verily not have imagined that so mild and kindly a ray of light could have been shed over my compositions discussed there. I promise not to divulge the secret—and meanwhile present my as yet unknown, reviewer with my sincerest thanks for his appreciation of my nature, which he manifests in so kind and sympathetic a manner in his commentary on the *Beatitudes*.

……

The St. Petersburg Philharmonic Society has invited me to direct two of their concerts, giving performances of my own compositions. The letter certainly reads somewhat more rationally than that of the Köln Cathedral Committee; but the good folks can nevertheless not refrain from referring to the trash about "my former triumphs, unrivaled mastery as a pianist,' etc, and this is utterly sickening to me—like so much stale, luke-warm champagne. [32]

32. Letter to Franz Brendel, November 11, 1863.

1864

No complaint whatever can be made about the performances at the *Tonkünstler-Versammlung* in Karlsruhe, and the reception accorded by the audience, especially to my Psalms, was extremely favorable. I assuredly never expected to meet with such sympathetic appreciation, after my experiences of former years. [33]

33. Letter to Eduard Liszt, Weimar, September 7, 1864.

1865

Knowing by experience with how little favor my works meet, I have been obliged to force a sort of systematic heedlessness on to myself with regard to them, and a resigned passiveness. Thus during the years of my foreign activity in Germany I constantly observed the rule of never asking anyone whatsoever to have any of my works performed; more than that, I plainly dissuaded many persons from doing so who showed some intention of this kind—and I shall do the same elsewhere. There is neither modesty nor pride in this, as it seems to me, for I simply take into consideration this fact – that 'Mr. Litz' is, as it were, always welcome when he appears *at the Piano* (especially since he has made a profession of the contrary) but that it is not permitted to him to have anything to do with thinking and writing according to his own fancy.

The result is that, for some fifteen years, so-called friends, as well as indifferent and ill-disposed people on all sides, sing, enough to split your head, to this unhappy 'Mr. Litz,' who has nothing to do with it, 'Be a pianist, and nothing but that.'

Possibly they are right—but it would be too much to expect me to sign my own condemnation. [34]

34. Letter to Jessie Laussot, Rome, March 6, 1865.

Owing to the *crooked* way in which my works have been listened to in past years, I have felt oppressed; and in order that my freedom in my work might remain unaffected, I was obliged wholly to disregard their outward success. Hence my absolute distrust of performances of my own compositions, and this was not to be accounted for my any exaggerated modesty on my part. As for the *Battle of the Huns* I was specially doubtful; the Christian significance of Kaulbach's picture—as represented in the *Chorale*—seemed to me a stumbling-block in the way of favorable criticism. Besides, at the time of the *Battle of the Huns* the organ was *not* yet invented! This last sweeping argument was triumphantly hurled at me in Weimar by the infallible censors. Since then I have hesitated to allow the work to be performed. [35]

35. Letter to Franz Brendel, Villa d'Este-Tivoli, July 21, 1865.

With regard to the *Elizabeth* I have received offers from Vienna and a few other places; but it is in no way my intention to wage war in a hurry with this work. It cannot be given in Jena without the co-operation of the Weimar performers. And why plague our dear and excellent Weimar singers and artists, and how—with their many theatrical engagements—could they find the necessary time for studying the parts, for rehearsals?—etc., etc. [36]

36. Letter to Franz Brendel, The Vatican, September 28, 1865.

You know how much against my wish it is to put the *Elizabeth* into circulation. And, however flattering it may be to me to receive offers from various places about it, still I think it advisable to avoid precipitancy, and not to expose my friends so soon again to unpleasantnesses such as my earlier works brought upon them. Considering the various kinds of abuse which my works have had to endure, silence would seem to be most becoming.

Therefore be good enough, dearest Eduard, to tell those kindly disposed 'Musical Friends,' *emphatically* that I cannot make up my mind to the proposed performance of the *Elizabeth*, and beg them to pardon this small-mindedness in me. [37]

37. Letter to Eduard Liszt, Rome, November 1, 1865.

1878

You know that the Coronation Mass has met with the most kind reception in Budapest. None of my works up to the present time had been so favorably accepted.[38]

38. Letter to Eduard Liszt, Rome, June 20, 1867.

I have heard the highest praises of the capability of Mr. Theodore Thomas, whom I have to thank particularly for the interest he takes in my Symphonic Poems. Artists who are willing to take the trouble to understand and to interpret my works cut themselves off from the generality of their fraternity.[39]

39. Letter to William Mason, Rome, July 8, 1867.

I do not share your rosy hopes of this work proving a success in towns where my earlier works not only met with little appreciation, but even received unseemly rebuffs. In Vienna, Leipzig, Berlin and even larger cities, the hisses of half a dozen stupid boys or evil-disposed persons were always sufficient to delude the public, and to frustrate the best intentions of my somewhat disheartened friends. In the newspaper criticisms these hissing critics are sure to find numerous supporters and pleasant re-echoes as long as the one object of the majority of my judges of this species is to get me out of their way. The improvement, which is said of late to have shown itself in regard to my position, may be interpreted somewhat thus: 'For years in his Symphonic Poems, his Masses, Pianoforte works, Songs, etc., Liszt has written mere bewildering and objectionable stuff; in his *Elizabeth* he appears to have acted somewhat more rationally—still, etc., etc.' However it is possible that my resolute friends may, in the end, be right in asserting that my things are not so bad as they are made out to be! Meanwhile what I have to do is to go on working quietly and undismayed, without in the smallest degree urging the performance of my works—nay in restraining some friendly disposed conductors from undertaking them.

……

Much as I appreciate and admire Herbeck's talent as a conductor, still I cannot know in advance whether he likes my work or not, or how far he agrees with my intentions. At all events I should have to come to some personal understanding with him on the subject before a performance is given in

Vienna, just because this is a matter of importance to me, and the performance ought not to be a dementi of the preceding ones. It is much more to my advantage not to have my works performed at all, than to allow them to be performed in a half-and-half or unsatisfactory manner.—I may say quite frankly that it would certainly be very agreeable to me to stand in a somewhat better light in Vienna as a composer than I have hitherto done. But the time has not come for that. [40]

40. Letter to Eduard Liszt, Munich, October 16, 1867.

It seems to me that it would not be of any use for you to undertake to publish now one or two large works of my composition. In order to be somewhat accredited, they must first of all be performed and heard, not *en passant*, but seriously and several times. For this I have no support in France, and should even expose myself to unpleasant dispositions and interpretations if I in the least endeavored to bring myself forward there. It is only in Germany, Hungary, and Holland that, in spite of frequent and lively opposition, my name as a composer has acquired a certain weight. In those countries they continue performing my music by inclination, curiosity, and interest, without my asking anybody to do so. [41]

41. Letter to E. Repos, Rome, November 8, 1867.

1868

As to the *Beatitudes* I *entirely* approve of your not having exhibited them a second time. You know, moreover, that I usually dissuade my friends from encumbering concert programs with my compositions. For the little they have to lose they will not lose it by waiting. Let us then administer them in homoeopathic doses—and rarely. [42]

42. Letter to Jessie Laussot, Rome, January 13, 1868.

How did the performance of the *Elizabeth* go off? Ask Kähnt to let me have one or two of the notices of it—especially the unfavorable ones. [43]

43. Letter to Franz Brendel, Rome, January 26, 1868.

The *An die Künstler* has hitherto been more *screamed at* than heard, for it has been accounted one of my most culpable heresies to have set these words of Schiller's to music after Mendelssohn did, and indeed without copying Mendelssohn. [44]

44. Letter to Franz Brendel, March 31, 1868.

I am quite aware that the performance of the *Elizabeth* in Vienna—which is considered a mark of honorable distinction to me—I owe to you. My not having complied with your offer before was mainly due to my desire to spare you any embarrassments which I, owing to my peculiar position and my distance from active circles of the Press, can readily ignore without the slightest 'bitterness of feeling.' To return to the Elizabeth performance in Vienna; I should like to be present. I must tell you beforehand, in confidence, that on this occasion I should not be able to remain in Vienna beyond a couple of days, and that I wish especially to keep quiet while there, and to meet as few people as possible. It is no longer in any way appropriate that I should appear anywhere in person; it suits me much better, when necessary, to be *trodden down in effigy* by all the different chatter. [45]

45. Letter to Johann von Herbeck, Villa d'Este, December 1, 1868.

1869

I have judiciously made up my mind not to trouble myself about my compositions any further than the writing of them, without in the least thinking of spreading them. Supposing that they have any value it will always be found out soon enough either during my life or afterwards. The sympathy of my friends (a very well chosen sympathy, I flatter myself) amply suffices me; the rest of the world may talk in its own way. [46]

46. Letter to Camille Saint-Saëns, Rome, July 19, 1869.

1870

To be displayed [in Vienna] now on posters, does not at all enter into my little personal program;—to put it otherwise, I am asking for no performance of my compositions in Vienna this winter, and if people play them, I prefer not to be present.[47]

47. Letter to Marie zu Sayn-Wittgenstein, Budapest, November 30, 1870.

1875

Owing to critical circumstances and negativings I have, as a rule, to dissuade people everywhere from giving performances of my scores. All the more pleasantly am I affected by the goodwill of the few friends who carefully and courageously march on in front. [48]

48. Letter to Julius Stern, Rome, February 4, 1875.

To say 'nay' to my friends always comes hard to me. But how can I act otherwise in face of the negativings of critics? And why should I not prefer abiding my time *in peace* alone?

Now-a-days an artist is reckoning without his host if he places honest faith in the public. For people now-a-days hear and judge only by reading the newspapers.

I mean to take advantage of this in so far that the leading and favorite papers of Vienna, Budapest, Leipzig, Berlin, Paris, London, etc.—which abhor my humble compositions and have declared them worthless and objectionable—shall be relieved of all further outward trouble concerning them. What is the good of performances to people who only care to read newspapers?

Hence, dear good friend, let the *Gran Mass* and the *Glöcken* remain unperformed in Vienna. [49]

49. Letter to Johann von Herbeck, Budapest, March 3, 1875.

The performance of the *Christus Oratorium* at Munich was extremely satisfying. The public received the work well, and this makes my acceptance of the newspaper criticism easier. [50]

50. Letter to Marie zu Sayn-Wittgenstein, Weimar, April 15, 1875.

Proud of my Königsberg title of doctor, and anxious to do it credit, I willingly refrain from giving performances of my humble compositions anywhere. [51]

51. Letter to Louis Köhler, Schloss Wilhelmsthal, July 27, 1875.

I am very anxious that this *Prometheus* - who is ready to 'unchain' himself next summer in Düsseldorf and at the Music Festival at Altenburg—should not again be a failure in Vienna, after his late lack of success there. [52]

52. Letter to Eduard Liszt, Villa d'Este, October 31, 1875.

I almost doubt whether the *Hunnenschlacht* could be performed amongst the *Philharmoniker* without defeat to me. [53]

53. Letter to Eduard Liszt, Villa d'Este, November 26, 1875.

As have several other old friends of mine (Joachim at their head), Hiller thought it better to ignore, even to bury me, after a fashion, under criticism. Far from resenting this, I am almost tempted to praise their prudence, which has never prevented me from frankly recognizing their talents, nor from deriving pleasure from their works. [54]

54. Letter to Olga von Meyendorff, Villa d'Este, December 28, 1875.

1876

To tell the truth, I have an increasingly poor opinion of my compositions, and it is only through my reaction to the indulgence of others that I manage to find them acceptable. On the other hand, I greatly enjoy many of the compositions of my colleagues and masters. They amply repay me for the tediousness and shortcomings of my own. [55]

55. Letter to Olga von Meyendorff, Villa d'Este, February 4, 1876.

The two concerts in Düsseldorf were a complete success. Ratzenberger deserves all praise for this; he conducted in a remarkable manner, with perfect understanding and assurance, the choruses of *Prometheus*, and the *Messe de Gran*, etc. [56]

56. Letter to Olga von Meyendorff, Hanover, May 4, 1876.

I have become altogether somewhat shy as regards the performance of my compositions. Although I quietly endure their foregone want of success with prevailing criticism, it is my duty not to let my friends be injured by it. [57]

57. Letter to Hans Richter, November 10, 1876.

You know my habit of not involving myself in the performance of my works (which are always too long, even when they consist only of two or three pages) and of urging my friends to ignore them entirely. Recently, I again had to write a few letters in this vein to Vienna and Berlin. It is not a question of spite but, rather, of wise and slightly condescending resignation. [58]

58. Letter to Olga von Meyendorff, Budapest, December 4, 1876.

1877

Truly, dear Bache, you are a *wonder-working* friend. Your persevering trouble, exertions, expenditure of time and money for the production of my bitterly-criticized compositions in London during the past fifteen years; are among the most uncommon occurrences in the annals of Art. [59]

59. Letter to Walter Bache, Budapest, March 9, 1877.

In spite of the much criticizing, ignoring, and denunciation, which the Symphonic Poems have had to suffer for 20 years, they are perhaps not yet quite done to death. [60]

60. Letter to Breitkopf and Härtel, Villa d'Este, September 26, 1877.

1878

The program of your fourteenth 'Annual Concert' is again an act of courage; particularly in London, where my compositions meet with all manner of obstructions—almost more than elsewhere.

……

It stands clearly written, a hundred times over, that I cannot compose; without indulging in unseemly protests against this, I quietly go on writing. [61]

61. Letter to Walter Bache, Budapest, March 19, 1878.

1879

I owe a debt of gratitude to the public of Saint Petersburg and of Moscow, which received favorably several of my works either ignored or flayed elsewhere. [62]

62. Letter to Olga von Meyendorff, Rome, January 4, 1879.

The best part of my religious compositions is the emotion evoked by them in a few fine souls. [63]

63. Letter to Marie zu Sayn-Wittgenstein, Budapest, January 26, 1879.

Saint-Saëns played my *La Predication de St. Françoix aux oiseau* on Cavaille-Coll's wonderful organ at the Trocadero last summer during the Paris Exhibition at a great concert attended by several thousand persons. How he managed this I could not explain, but the fact remains that Saint-Saëns success was complete. Since then people have spoken to me about it in the affably surprised tone of those who assume that all my feeble compositions must be hissed, or at least ignored. [64]

64. Letter to Olga von Meyendorff, Budapest, March 24, 1879.

My modest ordination as Honorary *Canon* will probably take place on Sunday, October 12 under the auspices of Cardinal Hohenlohe. Calderon and Copernicus were *full* Canons. Why haggle with me over the title Honorary? Could it be because I have written more than a thousand sheets of religious music which do not please the great majority of the Canons who are addicted to what they call in Italian 'gratt' orecchio'? In spite of this it would be possible for these sheets to be and to remain *canonical*; and I shall add to their number, if God grants me life, without changing my style; for the latter comes from my very intimate and permanent Catholic sentiment. [65]

65. Letter to Olga von Meyendorff, Villa d'Este, October 1, 1879.

1880

The two parts of *Faust* were given three times this season. The public flowed in with such numbers that the box office couldn't answer the demands for tickets; a rare embarrassment for Weimar! [66]

66. Letter to Marie zu Sayn-Wittgenstein, Weimar, May 12, 1880.

Pohlig is staying at the Villa d'Este and composes lugubrious and heroic pieces. Friedheim and Reisenauer are hard at work in Rome. I sometimes envy them certain illusions with which I have never been afflicted. What people term my artistic career developed entirely on its own without any pretension on my part. If I pursue it this is solely from a sense of duty. [67]

67. Letter to Olga von Meyendorff, Villa d'Este, October 12, 1880.

1881

This afternoon's concert in my honor was a complete success both as a performance and in terms of the favorable attitude of the large audience. When you used to hear my Dantesque Symphony at the same Sala Dante some fifteen years ago, it seemed to the great majority of the audience a tissue of extravagance. People assure me that this is no longer the case. [68]

68. Letter to Olga von Meyendorff, Rome, December 6, 1881.

You intimate the friendly desire that I should revisit Paris. Traveling at my age becomes burdensome, and I greatly fear that I should be found out of place in capitals like Paris or London, where no immediate obligation calls me. This fear does not make me less grateful towards the public, and especially towards my Parisian friends, to whom I acknowledge myself to be so greatly indebted. Besides, I should not like completely to give up the thought of ever seeing them again, although the deplorable performance of the *Gran Mass* in 1866 left a painful impression upon me. This is easily explained on both sides. Nevertheless, it would be too much for me in future to expose myself to such misapprehensions. Without false modesty or foolish vanity I cannot allow myself to be classed among the celebrated pianists who have gone astray in composing failures. [69]

69. Letter to Camille Saint-Saëns, Rome, December 12, 1881.

1882

At the time when Berlioz was attacking the *Messe de Gran* and condemning it as 'the negation of art,'my two old friends, he and d'Ortigue, were disowning me at their leisure in Paris (in the winter of '66), concluding with 99 percent of the public that I was very wrong to concern myself with composition, since I had no talent and should limit myself to my success as a pianist. Not to follow this peremptory advice amounts, in the religion of art, to final impertinence. My sincere Catholicism does not prescribe that I should seek the absolution of people who dislike my music, such as it is. Opinions and sensations are free and I make no claim whatever to imposing mine on anyone. To go on working is enough for me. [70]

70. Letter to Olga von Meyendorff, Budapest, February 27, 1882.

1883

Palm Sunday, I shall be at Pressburg. They are giving *Elizabeth* there. I no longer have any interest in it, since its success has already been sufficiently established in various countries. [71]

71. Letter to Marie zu Sayn-Wittgenstein, Budapest, March 6, 1883.

1886

On the 20th of March I shall be in Paris, where the *Gran Mass*, too much criticized, and even hissed by some low fellows (in 1866), is to makes its reappearance. This time I am assured that it will be *better understood* now. [72]

72. Letter to Countess Mercy-Argenteau, Budapest, February 17, 1886.

Yesterday, after the second performance of the *Messe de Gran* at Saint-Eustache, attended by thousands of people, the emotion was lively and deep. [73]

73. Letter to Olga von Meyendorff, Paris, April 3, 1886.

In comparison with the poor reception and pitiful performance of the *Gran Mass* in 1866, this time it made a good impression—even twice in one week—something almost without antecedents for a piece of Church music. [74]

74. Letter to Marie zu Sayn-Wittgenstein, Paris, April 3, 1886.

I hardly expected such successes in Paris and London; but since they came to me spontaneously I cannot grumble. This would be boorish of me. [75]

75. Letter to Olga von Meyendorff, Antwerp, April 21, 1886.

Bibliography

Ellis, W. Ashton (ed.). *Correspondence of Wagner and Liszt*. [1897] New York: Haskell House, 1969.

Gazette Musicale. (May-October, 1835; January, 1837; February 12, 1837; November 12, 1837; February 11, 1838; May 27, 1838; August 23, 1840.

Hugo, Howard E. (ed). *The Letters of Franz Liszt to Marie zu Sayn-Wittgenstein*. Cambridge: Harvard University Press, 1953.

La Mara, *Letters of Franz Liszt*. New York: Scribners, 1894.

Briefwechsel zwischen Franz Liszt und Carl Alexander. Leipzig: Breitkopf & Härtel, 1909.

Le Monde (December 11, 1836)

Liszt, Franz. *Frederic Chopin*. [Paris: Escudier, 1852]. Translated by Edward N. Waters. London: Collier-Macmillan Ltd., 1963

The Gipsy in Music. [1859] London: William Reeves, 1960.

Marix-Spire, Thérèse. Les Romantiques et la musique le cas George Sand. Paris, 1954.

Neue Zeitschrift für Musik (1855) XLIII

Ollivier (ed.) *Correspondance de Liszt et de La Comtesse d'Agoult*. Paris, 1933.

Ramann, (ed.). 'Marx and his book, The Music of the 19th Century [1855],' in *Gesammelte Schriften*. Leipzig, 1880–1883, V. [Paris: Escudier, 1852].

Tyler, William R. (trans.) *The Letters of Franz Liszt to Olga von Mayendorff* 1871–1886. Washington: Dumbarton Oaks, 1979.

Revue des Deux Mondes. (December, 15, 1935).

About the author

David Whitwell is a graduate ('with distinction') of the University of Michigan and the Catholic University of America, Washington D.C. (Ph.D., Musicology, Distinguished Alumni Award, 2000) and has studied conducting with Eugene Ormandy and at the Akademie für Musik, Vienna. Prior to coming to Northridge, Dr. Whitwell participated in concerts throughout the United States and Asia as Associate First Horn in the USAF Band and Orchestra in Washington, D.C., and in recitals throughout South America in cooperation with the United States State Department.

At the California State University, Northridge, which is in Los Angeles, Dr. Whitwell developed the CSUN Wind Ensemble into an ensemble of international reputation, with international tours to Europe in 1981 and 1989 and to Japan in 1984. The CSUN Wind Ensemble has made professional studio recordings for BBC (London), the Köln Westdeutscher Rundfunk (Germany), NOS National Radio (The Netherlands), Zürich Radio (Switzerland), the Television Broadcasting System (Japan) as well as for the United States State Department for broadcast on its 'Voice of America' program. The CSUN Wind Ensemble's recording with the Mirecourt Trio in 1982 was named the 'Record of the Year' by The Village Voice. Composers who have guest conducted Whitwell's ensembles include Aaron Copland, Ernest Krenek, Alan Hovhaness, Morton Gould, Karel Husa, Frank Erickson and Vaclav Nelhybel.

Dr. Whitwell has been a guest professor in 100 different universities and conservatories throughout the United States and in 23 foreign countries (most recently in China, in an elite school housed in the Forbidden City). Guest conducting experiences have included the Philadelphia Orchestra, Seattle Symphony Orchestra, the Czech Radio Orchestras of Brno and Bratislava, The National Youth Orchestra of Israel, as well as resident wind ensembles in Russia, Israel, Austria, Switzerland, Germany, England, Wales, The Netherlands, Portugal, Peru, Korea, Japan, Taiwan, Canada and the United States.

He is a past president of the College Band Directors National Association, a member of the Prasidium of the International Society for the Promotion of Band Music, and was a member of the founding board of directors of the World Association for Symphonic Bands and Ensembles (WASBE). In 1964 he was made an honorary life member of Kappa Kappa Psi, a national professional music fraternity. In September, 2001, he was a delegate to the UNESCO Conference on Global Music in Tokyo. He has been knighted by sovereign organizations in France, Portugal and Scotland and has been awarded the gold medal of Kerkrade, The Netherlands, and the silver medal of Wangen, Germany, the highest honor given wind conductors in the United States, the medal of the Academy of Wind and Percussion Arts (National Band Association) and the highest honor given wind conductors in Austria, the gold medal of the Austrian Band Association. He is a member of the Hall of Fame of the California Music Educators Association.

Dr. Whitwell's publications include more than 127 articles on wind literature including publications in Music and Letters (London), the London Musical Times, the Mozart-Jahrbuch (Salzburg), and 39 books, among which is his 13-volume History and Literature of the Wind Band Ensemble and an 8-volume series on Aesthetics in Music. In addition to numerous modern editions of early wind band music his original compositions include 5 symphonies.

David Whitwell was named as one of six men who have determined the course of American bands during the second half of the 20th century, in the definitive history, The Twentieth Century American Wind Band (Meredith Music).

A doctoral dissertation by German Gonzales (2007, Arizona State University) is dedicated to the life and conducting career of David Whitwell through the year 1977. David Whitwell is one of nine men described by Paula A. Crider in The Conductor's Legacy (Chicago: GIA, 2010) as 'the legendary conductors' of the 20th century.

'I can't imagine the 2nd half of the 20th century—without David Whitwell and what he has given to all of the rest of us.' Frederick Fennell (1993)

www.ingramcontent.com/pod-product-compliance
Lightning Source LLC
LaVergne TN
LVHW080309110826
845155LV00023B/100